THE BASICS

Modernism: The Basics provides an accessible overview of the study of modernism in its global dimensions. Examining the key concepts, history and varied forms of the field, it guides the reader through the major approaches, outlining key debates, to answer such questions as:

- What is modernism?
- How did modernism begin?
- Has modernism developed differently in different media?
- How is it related to postmodernism and postcolonialism?
- How have politics, urbanization and new technologies affected modernism?

With engaging examples from art, literature and historical documents, each chapter provides suggestions for further reading, histories of relevant movements and clear definitions of key terminology, making this an essential guide for anyone approaching the study of modernism for the first time.

Laura Winkiel is Associate Professor of English at the University of Colorado at Boulder, USA.

The Basics

For a full list of titles in this series, please visit www.routledge.com/
The-Basics/book-series/B

MODERNISM

THE BASICS

Laura Winkiel

Routledge
Taylor & Francis Group

LONDON AND NEW YORK

First published 2017
by Routledge
2 Park Square, Milton Park, Abingdon, Oxon OX14 4RN

and by Routledge
711 Third Avenue, New York, NY 10017

Routledge is an imprint of the Taylor & Francis Group, an informa business

British Library Cataloguing-in-Publication Data
A catalogue record for this book is available from the British Library

Library of Congress Cataloging-in-Publication Data
A catalog record for this book has been requested

ISBN: 978-0-415-71369-6 (hbk)
ISBN: 978-0-415-71370-2 (pbk)
ISBN: 978-1-315-72676-2 (ebk)

Typeset in Bembo and Scala Sans
by Apex CoVantage, LLC

CONTENTS

ILLUSTRATIONS

ACKNOWLEDGMENTS

The author and publisher would like to thank the following for granting permission to reproduce material in this work:

Musée d'Orsay, Paris, for the image of *Count Robert de Montesquiou* (1897) by Giovanni Boldini; Pablo Picasso *Les Demoiselles d'Avignon* © 2016 Estate of Pablo Picasso/Artists Rights Society (ARS), New York; Wilfredo Lam *La Jungla* © 2016 Artists Rights Society (ARS), New York/ADAGP, Paris. Permission to reprint lines #1–5 of the translation of Yosano Akiko's "Morning After" by Janine Beichman, *Embracing the Firebird: Yosano Akiko and the Birth of the Female Voice in Modern Japanese Poetry* University of Hawaii Press, 2002, pg. 200, granted by the University of Hawaii Press. © 2002 University of Hawaii Press. Permission to use materials of Dr., The Honorable Louise Bennett Coverley, has been granted by the Co-Executors of the LBC, Estate, Judge Pamela Appelt, and Fabian Coverley, B.TH, emails appelt@cogeco.ca, and fcoverley@gmail.com. Excerpts from "The Waste Land" from *The Complete Poems & Plays, 1909–1950* reprinted by permission of Faber & Faber, Ltd. Excerpts from "The Waste Land" from COLLECTED POEMS 1909–1962 by T. S. Eliot. Copyright 1936 by Houghton Mifflin Harcourt Publishing Company. Copyright © renewed 1964 by Thomas Sternes Eliot. Reprinted by permission of Houghton Mifflin Harcourt Publishing Company. All rights reserved. "In a Station of the Metro" by Ezra Pound from *Personae* © 1926 by Ezra Pound. Reprinted by permission of New Directions Publishing and Faber & Faber, Ltd. Permission to reprint an excerpt from W. C. Williams' "The Red Wheelbarrow" has been granted by Carcanet Press Ltd, UK; and by W. C. Williams, from THE COLLECTED POEMS: Volume I, 1909–1939, © 1938 by New Directions Publishing Corp. Reprinted by permission of New Directions Publishing Corp., USA. Excerpt from W. B. Yeats' "The Second Coming" and "Lapis Lazuli" reprinted with the permission of Scribner, a division of Simon & Schuster, Inc. from THE COLLECTED WORKS OF W. B. YEATS, edited by Richard J. Finneran. "The Second Coming" © 1924 by The Macmillan Company, renewed 1952 by Bertha Georgie Yeats. All rights reserved. "Lapis Lazuli" © 1940 by Georgie Yeats, renewed 1968 by Bertha Georgie Yeats, Michael Butler Yeats, and Anne Yeats. All rights reserved.

Every effort has been made to contact copyright holders for their permission to reprint material in this book. The publishers would be grateful to hear from any copyright holder who is not here acknowledged and will undertake to rectify any errors or omissions in future editions of this book.

I would also like to thank the graduate students in my "Global Modernisms" and "Global Literature and Culture: James Joyce" seminars for enthusiastically exploring the pitfalls and promises of an expanded notion of modernism. Much appreciation also goes to Kevin Dettmar and Paul Saint-Amour for organizing the NEH Seminar "Ulysses: Texts and Contexts" in Dublin, Ireland. They, and the wonderful seminar participants, created a community of Joyce scholars who have impacted this work in ways scholarly and more. I thank the members of the University of Colorado English faculty writing group for reading a portion of the manuscript: Emily Harrington, Cheryl Higashida, Janice Ho, Jason Gladstone, Ben Robertson, Maria Windell and Mark Winokur. Special thanks to Janice Ho for help at the outset of this project. Much gratitude goes to Ali Hasan for reading the manuscript with a poet's eye and to Gayle Rogers for reading it with an editor's eye. Atiya kept me smiling, and Allison Shelton was an invaluable and dedicated research assistant. Namasté to Joy, Meghan, Sophie, Tunde, and Janelle for lifting my spirits and showing me what was possible. Special thanks are due to the anonymous readers at Routledge who challenged me to make this book a much better one. And, finally, I thank the editorial staff at Routledge, especially Andy Humphries for commissioning this book, Polly Dodson for overseeing it, and Ruth Hilsdon, Zoe Meyer and Katherine Wetzel for shepherding it through to publication.

USER'S GUIDE

This book can be read in a linear fashion, chapter by chapter. However, the reader is invited to read different sections of chapters, or chapters in a different order. If a discussion is building upon points made in another part of the book, that reference is noted.

- Each chapter ends with a summary of the topics discussed.
- The author presumes that the reader has no prior knowledge of texts used as examples.
- References listed at the end of each chapter are kept to a minimum: only texts that are quoted directly are listed.
- Each chapter is followed by suggestions for further reading. These are listed under their corresponding topics covered in the chapter. The reader can regard these suggestions as a next stage of reading.
- Terms in **bold** are listed and defined in the glossary at the end of this book.
- The reader is encouraged to study the time line in the back of the book for a snapshot of modernism that this book presents at length.

1

WHAT IS MODERNISM?

"DIE in the Past/Live in the Future."

Mina Loy, *Aphorisms on Futurism* (1914)

"One must be absolutely modern!"

Arthur Rimbaud, *A Season in Hell* (1873)

"Literature is news that STAYS news."

Ezra Pound, *ABC of Reading* (1934)

"Colonial idiocy will be purified in the welder's blue flame."

Suzanne Césaire, "Surrealism and Us" (1943)

This book introduces readers to the basics of modernism. It is addressed to students located throughout the English-speaking world. You, the reader, may be coming to modernism with no prior knowledge of it, studying for an exam in secondary school or university, teaching it for the first time, or seeking to update your seasoned understanding of it. The aim of this book is to provide you with two key tools essential to the study of modernism:

- how to closely read modernist texts and paintings;
- how to contextualize those close readings in the histories, locations and intercultural exchanges that inform modernist works.

How a work of modernist literature or art registers its social, political, intercultural and historical surroundings is subject to much scholarly debate. Accordingly, this book will also inform you about the history and current developments in the study of modernism. In the end, it hopes to persuade you that understanding modernism is a valuable endeavor – despite its sometimes off-putting first encounter – because it will give you a sense of and appreciation for the tectonic shift in social and political relations, philosophy and artistic representation that occurred in the early to mid part of the twentieth century, the reverberations of which are still felt today.

The basic story about modernism goes like this: something extraordinary happened in the arts around the beginning of the twentieth century. This new art was chaotic and fragmented in its form, and allusive and indirect in what it meant. It was often difficult to understand *because* it was so fragmented, allusive and indirect in what it meant. Though only a small group of artists and writers practiced this groundbreaking art, it gradually became central to the study of the literature and painting during this time period. It came to be called "modernism" – meaning "the new and the now." Helping to popularize the study of these difficult modernist texts after World War II in the Anglophone (English-speaking) university system, a group of professors and scholars crafted a special kind of expertise – a set of **close reading** skills and formal analyses that came to be known as New Criticism – and successfully made this method predominate in the teaching of literature. Generations of readers came to see these difficult texts – such as T. S. Eliot's *The Waste Land*, James Joyce's *Ulysses*, Ezra Pound's *The Cantos* and Virginia Woolf's *Mrs. Dalloway* – as monuments of art and works of modernist genius. And while these works are certainly worth studying, as we will see, we will also discuss how this emphasis on difficult literature obscures from view other kinds of modernist writing underway during this same period of time, the study of which we will be calling "the new modernisms."

Traditionally, modernist scholars consider the period 1890–1910 as the prehistory of modernism, when only a few artists and writers, mostly in France, experimented with new forms. (In recent decades, this period has been stretched back to 1850 to include poet Charles Baudelaire and novelist Gustave Flaubert.) The period between 1910–30 is called "high" modernism and denotes the time when the most recognizably modernist works, such as *Ulysses* and *The Waste Land*, were created. Finally, "late" modernism, 1930–55, supposes modernism's gradual extinction in favor of postmodernism. Even under this traditional periodizing rubric of modernism, certain disciplines – modernist architecture, for example – have always challenged this time frame. International-style modernist architecture arguably held sway until around 1972, when Robert Venturi published *Learning from Las Vegas: The Forgotten Symbolism of Architectural Form*, a book that embraced *post*-modernist styles (for a discussion of postmodernism, see the Afterword).

Given this story, it is likely that if you have any previous conception at all regarding what modernism is, you probably assume that modernism is difficult and that we need to study the important "high" modernist texts and paintings carefully in order to decipher their meanings. To give you a sense of modernism as it is understood this way, we will begin this chapter with a close reading of portions of the canonical masterpiece of modernist poetry, *The Waste Land* by T. S. Eliot (1922), followed by an examination of the visual abstractions of cubism, as demonstrated in *Les Demoiselles d'Avignon* (1907), the breakthrough painting by Pablo Picasso. While the emphasis in this book is on modernist literature, we will occasionally use painting as a visual teaching tool. For instance, we turn to Picasso's painting in order to understand important formal qualities of modernist literature and painting, especially in terms of how they differ from realist representation. **Realism** is a mode of literary and artistic representation that aims to convey its subject matter in a faithful or true-to-life manner. (Although we are here distinguishing realism from modernism in order to define modernist formal qualities, the two terms, "modernism" and "realism," are not mutually exclusive, as we will discuss in Chapter 4.)

Then we will consider our second point: why it is no longer sufficient to think of modernism as strictly the domain of experimental art by white European men, with perhaps a sprinkling of experimental women artists, such as Virginia Woolf or Gertrude Stein, thrown into the mix. For those readers whose interest lies primarily with the canon of modernist authors, you are invited to consult the "further reading" section at the end of this chapter for introductions to modernism that concentrate on difficult "high modernist" texts and paintings. A strict emphasis on the canon, however, curtails a fuller understanding of how modernism took place in many locations and in many forms. It misses the forest for a few difficult trees. *Modernism: The Basics* is different from other introductions to modernism because it includes the most recent developments in the study of modernism, what are often called "the new modernisms." In short, our emphasis on "the new modernisms" reflects the growing awareness that modernism arose around much of the world, often through social movements (such as women's, labor and national independence movements), and during an ongoing period of great technological, economic and political change. New media – print, sound, visual and communication technologies – also transformed how artists and writers saw the possibilities of their art. This dynamic version of modernism will show the reader that there are many kinds of modernism, sometimes at odds with one another, but often sharing similar concerns and formal inventions.

The word **modernism** derives from the Latin *modernus* (modo, "just now"); it relates to "mode," or fashionable novelty, as well as to a break from tradition, the orthodox or inherited way of doing things (Latham and Rogers 19). How did modernists "make it new," as the poet Ezra Pound termed it? To understand the formal techniques and content of the "newness" of modernism, we need to extend our understanding of the *contexts* in which modernism arose. By **contexts**, we mean the various conditions in which a text is produced: how, when, where, why and by whom was it written or painted? In exploring the many historical, conceptual and locational contexts of modernism, the reader will learn that modernism:

- arose through intercultural borrowings;
- travels around the world and takes different forms in different locations;
- expresses forces "from below," whether new media, popular culture, or social movements.

Of course, it is impossible to cover fully these developments or to discuss modernism as if it were a single "thing." Modernism, a notoriously vague and slippery term, can denote many different things. It has been used to designate a historical period (usually 1890–1940), an experimental form of artistic production, and a rethinking of all aspects of life, from industrialization to religion and from sexuality to interior design. To manage this complexity, this book introduces the reader to one possible way of mapping the vast terrain of modernism: with an attention to the "histories," "forms" and "concepts" of modernism. In addition, this particular map refers the reader to other sources so that you can choose to focus on one point, widen your gaze or find a different map, depending on your interests.

CLOSE READING: *THE WASTE LAND* AND *LES DEMOISELLES D'AVIGNON*

Close reading refers to the activity of carefully analyzing a text or painting in strictly its own terms: content, language, style and form. This critical practice began after World War I in Anglo-American literary institutions in order to assess how a work of art creates meaning in ways that go beyond "mere" words. Let's see how this activity works by closely reading a section of *The Waste Land*, a long poem that served as a preeminent cultural resource for the development of close reading techniques and for the initial Anglo-American definition of modernism. We take the following quotation from Section Two, "A Game of Chess." In this scene, the narrator describes a painting hung above a fireplace in a sitting room in early twentieth-century London (when poetry describes a painting, it is often called *ekphrasis*):

> Above the antique mantel was displayed
> As though a window gave upon the sylvan scene
> The change of Philomel, by the barbarous king
> So rudely forced; yet there the nightingale
> Filled all the desert with inviolable voice
> And still she cried, and still the world pursues,
> "Jug Jug" to dirty ears.

(8, #97–103)

At a first read, this quotation seems almost illegible, so densely packed are its literary allusions to other poems, sparked by the narrator's reflections as he/she gazes at the painting. The allusions, once we understand them, will allow us to perceive the underlying conceptual and formal structures, or what Eliot calls the "mythical method" (178). Eliot explained this method while reviewing James Joyce's experimental novel *Ulysses*, but critics have often pointed out that this method equally applies to Eliot's *The Waste Land*. Let's begin: above the old-fashioned fireplace, the narrator sees a picture of Philomela changed into a nightingale, a story told by the Latin poet Ovid (43 BCE–17 CE) in *The Metamorphosis*, an allusion that Eliot makes explicit for the reader in a footnote. "As though a window gave" suggests a sudden, unexpected glimpse of paradise that brings a moment of relief to the narrator. But "sylvan scene," an allusion to Milton's *Paradise Lost*, Book 4, darkens the mood because it describes Satan's approach to Eden and prefigures the fall of humankind from paradise. It also describes the narrator's disillusioned state in present-day Europe, just after the First World War, and his/her own sexual sterility and paralysis. The narrator's despair is mirrored by Philomela's song. Though she was changed into a nightingale after her rape and mutilation (her tongue was cut off) by the barbarous King Tereus, she nevertheless sings of her woes: her voice is inviolable; it won't be silenced. The desolation and sterility of her song is suggested by the use of "desert" rather than paradise and "cried" rather than "sang." With the use of the adverb "still" twice in the last two lines, the poem flashes forward from the myths of antiquity to the present moment. The world, like the barbarous king, still pursues – and violently destroys – beauty and nature. "Jug Jug," though a conventional Elizabethan poetic reference to the nightingale's song, hardly sounds like a beautiful, if mournful, song. It suggests a vaguely sexual, threatening and vulgar sensibility, especially because "dirty ears" are hearing her song in this way. The courage and beauty of Philomela's song is negated by its sordid reception by the current state of civilization. (See also Wilson 92–93.)

There is much more that we can closely read and analyze in this quotation. We could pay attention to line breaks, noting where a statement seems to hang in the balance and how the breaks leave the reader to imagine what the poem does not say, such as the actual violation of Philomela. We could note that the diction, or the way in which the poem says what it says, is generally commonplace. Outside of classical and Renaissance allusions, the language is neither frilly nor archaic. The meter is in iambic pentameter, a traditional poetic form, something that much of the rest of the poem rejects. The last line, beginning with "Jug Jug," is shorter, jarring the reader awake with its opening spondaic (long, long) foot, suggesting in formal terms what the words also convey: that the unlettered masses who now dominate Western European societies disregard high culture. Their conversations, rendered in **free verse** (vers libre), which is unmetered and uses colloquial or ordinary speech, in the next part of the poem, also testify to this fact. Now, let's take these raw analytic materials and make some observations about what seems particularly *modernist* about this poem.

The first thing we might note is the extraordinary compression in these lines. An early (1931) explicator of modernist poetry, Edmund Wilson, quantifies this compression:

> In a poem of only four hundred and three lines (to which are added, however, seven pages of notes), [Eliot] manages to include quotations from, allusions to, or imitations of, at least thirty-five different writers (some of them, such as Shakespeare and Dante, laid under contribution several times) – as well as several popular songs; and to introduce passages in six foreign languages, including Sanskrit.

> (93–94)

Why such dense allusiveness, and what makes this **technique** modernist? In a 1932 essay, F. R. Leavis argues that "the seeming disjointedness" related to Eliot's allusions and abrupt jumps in time, place and reference "reflect the present state of civilization" (173–74). In this, he is echoing Eliot's own words in "The Metaphysical Poets" (1921) where Eliot states that the "variety and complexity" of the contemporary world necessitates that the poet be "more comprehensive" by referencing other works of art and culture, and more indirect in order "to force, to dislocate if necessary, language into meaning" (65). This modernist fragmentation is a response to an increasingly chaotic, unknowable world in which the coherence of any one culture and any single narrative is irrevocably lost. (For more on this topic, see Chapter 3, "Histories.") The speaker in Eliot's poem openly admits this state of affairs at the poem's conclusion in a self-conscious statement: "These fragments I have shored against my ruins" (20, #430). The quotation above, then, is modernist in its use of the technique of **displacement** (the breaking of continuous time and space) and **dissonance** (the discordant or jarring juxtaposition of classical and popular references) as the narrator gazes at a picture of a nightingale, relates it to poetry by Milton (1608–74) and Ovid, and jumps to the present time in order to despair at its violent and vulgar state.

Eliot calls this technique the "mythical method," a way of writing that "manipulate[s] a continuous parallel between contemporaneity and antiquity" (177). As he famously put it, the mythical method serves as "a way of controlling, of ordering, of giving a shape and a significance to the immense panorama of futility and anarchy which is contemporary history" (177). We'll explore in Chapter 3 why many modernists felt that the present was anarchic and futile, but for now we'll emphasize the formal, structuring quality of this method. In comparing the present with the classical past, Eliot creates a sense of **simultaneity** that monumentalizes the present by comparing it to – and even reanimating – the classical past to make it live in the present. This method bypasses the logic of cause and effect. In jumping quickly between times and places, Eliot's poetry is fleeting, fragmentary and, as such, evokes a series of dreamlike, indefinite sensations and impressions rather than facts, evidence and narrative causality (first this happened, and then that happened). Facts, evidence and narrative causality are hallmarks of **realism**, a literary and painterly technique, as mentioned earlier, that attempts to imitate a rational, empirically experienced and knowable social world: what you see is what there is, true to life. In contrast, Eliot says that the mythical method "is a step toward making the modern world possible for art" (178). For him, as for many modernists, the real world is too fragmented, irrational and chaotic to be mirrored by realism. Myth provides form, a way of shaping the complexity, scale and diversity of the modern world into something recognizable. In the example above, mythic form – the rape of Philomela, the fall from Eden and the desecration of art – says something poetic about post-World War I Europe.

In order to visualize modernist conceptual and formal structures, we will turn next to another difficult modernist work, Pablo Picasso's *Les Demoiselles d'Avignon* (see Figure 1.1). This painting is remarkable because of its shocking content – a group portrait of five nude prostitutes – and its striking formal innovation – Picasso Africanized the women's faces, painting them as masks arrayed in

Figure 1.1 Pablo Picasso, *Les Demoiselles d'Avignon*, 1907 (Museum of Modern Art)

geometrical, dehumanized shapes. We also see the front and side of the women's faces at once, a technique that suggests the **simultaneity** of multiple perspectives. Also note the flatness of the pictorial surface. The radical foreshortening of the background refuses a vanishing point by which to orient the viewer. The vanishing point, also called Renaissance perspective, gives the illusion of pictorial depth, a **realist** technique that mirrors the three-dimensionality (depth, height and width) in which we inhabit the world. Picasso instead emphasizes the flat two-dimensionality of the actual canvas.

He reduces the women's bodies and their bordello to a linear grid, fracturing and abstracting the bodies and surrounding space into multiple, angular "cubes." The colors in the painting (that we cannot see in our black and white version) likewise do not reflect a realistic portrayal of the subject matter. Vivid green and blues suggest an emotion or sensation on the part of the painter, conveyed only indirectly to the viewer. Guillaume Apollinaire (1880–1918), an early spokesperson for cubism (the name for the style of painting exemplified by *Les Demoiselles*), explains,

> Verisimilitude [life-likeness] no longer has any importance, for the artist sacrifices everything to the composition of his picture. The subject no longer counts, or if it counts, it counts for very little. [. . .] The new painters provide their admirers with artistic sensations due exclusively to the harmony of lights and shades and independent of the subject depicted in the picture.
>
> (186–87)

Cubist painting, as Apollinaire describes it, is autonomous, free from slavishly representing reality. Instead, the viewer, much as he/she reads the compressed play of allusions in *The Waste Land*, perceives various shapes and colors on the canvas and experiences sensations of beauty, repulsion, desire, fear or sadness. The artistic or textual object is the focus, not what it represents.

Picasso's superimposition of African masks onto the prostitutes who stand and squat in aggressive, sexualized poses suggests a correlation with Eliot's mythical method. The geometric, dark, hard masks contrast with the soft, pink flesh of the women and the white folds of drapery. We experience **dissonance,** a lack of harmony and continuity, in this contrast. We also feel compression as continuous time and space are fragmented and displaced. The African masks and prostitutes conjoin without rational explanation or causation for the strange mixture. Early twentieth-century European women are juxtaposed with what was then believed to be "primitive" tribal objects. **Primitivism** describes the way in which Europeans exoticized Africans and other non-Western peoples. Because Africans were believed to be less civilized than Europeans, they were thought to act mainly from instinctual impulses, and, not having an Enlightenment or scientific worldview, acted from a belief in magic.

Picasso later recounted the genesis of *Les Demoiselles* as a desire for the supernatural:

> The Negro pieces were intercesseurs [intercessors between humans and the supernatural], mediators. [. . .] They were against everything – against the unknown, threatening spirits. I always looked at fetishes. I understood; I too am against everything. I too believe that everything is unknown, that everything is an enemy!
>
> (qtd. in Seckel 219)

He understood painting to be a form of magic that both confronts and wards off humanity's deepest fears. It is, he says, "a way of seizing the power by giving form to our terrors as well as our desires" (qtd. in Seckel 220). Analogous to how Eliot used classical myths to ward off the "futility and anarchy that is contemporary history," Picasso used African masks to protect from the terror of reality (Eliot, 177). But more than allowing Picasso to exorcise his fears (including his fears of female sexuality) as the myth of primitivism suggests, the masks interrupt realistic representation. They stand between the artist and the world and provide a form that is geometrical, abstract, and seemingly outside the flux of history. African art was a singular transformative influence on Picasso because it possesses what art critic Clive Bell called "significant form": "a combination of lines and colours [. . .] that moves [the viewer] aesthetically" (20). Non-European art profoundly shaped modernism.

SUMMARY

Close reading involves: (1) analyzing *how* a text or painting makes meaning (for example, we discussed Eliot's and Picasso's juxtapositions, displacement, allusions, color, geometrical form); and (2) thinking about *why* the text or painting does what it does. What is its meaning?

WHAT IS MODERNISM, THEN AND NOW?

There are two questions for determining what modernism is:

- What are the specific objects (paintings, poems, novels, plays) that critics consider to be modernist?
- What are the criteria for judging those objects to be modernist?

The prevailing definition of modernism that held sway at least until the 1980s focused on the criterion of **difficulty**. The canon consisted of experimental forms of poetry, prose and painting chosen for their difficulty. They are densely allusive, fragmented and abstract, as we have seen in reading *The Waste Land* and *Les Demoiselles d'Avignon*. The early creators of close reading techniques would probably chide me for telling you, in step two of the summary above, that you need to consider *why* a text or painting does what it does. An early proponent of close reading, Cleanth Brooks, might have accused me of "the heresy of paraphrase" by which he meant that a modernist painting or poem cannot be summarized in a prosaic statement of what it means. Instead, according to him, the reader must attend strictly to how the poem's parts render a unified aesthetic experience, a sensation of beauty or experience of emotion that cannot be adequately described by words. Reading difficult poems or prose, therefore, became something like having a religious experience, only instead of encountering the Divine, the reader is suffused with beauty or with a specific emotion. The same inventors of close reading techniques, not coincidentally, were also the critics most responsible for inventing what initially passed as modernism.

In the past few decades, prevailing understandings of modernism have expanded to include many other kinds of writing and painting besides ones deemed difficult. The newly expanded understanding of modernism falls under the rubric of the "new modernisms." In fact, two critics have recently put it thus: "There's no such thing as modernism – no singular definition capable of bringing order to the diverse, multitude of creators, manifestos, practices, and politics that have been variously constellated around this enigmatic term" (Latham and Rogers 1). Modernism has meant, and continues to mean, many different things to many different people, depending on the *criteria* they use and the *objects* they select. We will next take a look at how the definition of modernism has changed over the past century so that you, the reader, can better understand why this book is giving you the basics of modernism in terms besides that of *difficulty*.

The artistic term *modernism* was first deployed in reference to experimental French visual art circles, the bohemian subcultures of the 1850s and 1860s, and its use soon spread to French avant-garde poets and prose writers. In 1873, the French poet Arthur Rimbaud declared that one must be "absolutely modern!" The term traveled across the English Channel, most notably in 1908 when poet and critic T. E. Hulme, in his "Lecture on Modern Poetry," announced that he had "no reverence for tradition," and spoke "from [a] standpoint of extreme modernism" (260, 67). He was, as Latham and Rogers put it, "the first poet-critic to begin sketching what modernism might mean as a formal concept or movement in English-language literature" (25). Prefiguring what Eliot was to do in *The Waste Land*, Hulme advocated a poetics of geometrical art: impersonal and "virile" in its hard-nosed juxtaposition of past and present and utilizing dissonant, antagonistic materials. Modernist poetry, as Hulme envisioned it, should emulate sculpture in its static, formal properties. Young, aspiring poets and writers, especially Ezra Pound, T. S. Eliot and Wyndham Lewis, soon began producing this kind of modernist writing.

It was this formal quality that, over the course of the 1930s, 1940s and 1950s, would be emphasized as modernist to the exclusion of many other kinds of aesthetic expression. Already in 1927, poets Laura Riding and Robert Graves singled out the new formal poetry for special consideration as "modernist" in *A Survey of Modernist Poetry*. They explained that modernist poetry is difficult because their authors were reacting against "rules made by the reading public" of the late nineteenth century (83). They believed that modernist poets were rebelling against a profit-driven literary marketplace by creating poems that were art objects, free from worldly concerns, including money, morality and politics. (For more on the autonomy of art, see Chapter 2.) In 1938, Cleanth Brooks and Robert Penn Warren published *Understanding Poetry* in which they enshrined the "great" works of modernist poetry – works by Pound, Eliot, H. D. (Hilda Doolittle) and E. E. Cummings – when they included them with poetry by Shakespeare, Pope and Keats in order to study poetic technique. Though many kinds of written expression were unfolding in this historical period, these writers were singled out from the wider field, and modernism was "officially" limited to formally experimental and difficult writers (Latham and Rogers 50).

With its emphasis on closely reading formal innovations, bracketed from historical and other *contexts*, the modernist movement, by 1960, had become moribund, a victim of its own success, and it took its place as yet another part of literary and artistic tradition.

Harry Levin's retrospective essay, "What was Modernism?" (1960), comments on a new apartment complex in New York City called The Picasso. Rather than repelling its prospective tenants by invoking images of "collapsible staircases" and "neighbors with double faces and blue-green complexions," "Picasso" now provides a "warrant of domestic respectability" (609). Modernism, as the New Critics (such as Brooks and Warren) had mapped it, had definitely lost its edge.

During the 1980s, 1990s and into the twenty-first century, teachers and scholars of modernism rebelled against the narrow confines of experimental form and insisted on putting those forms (and others) into widened *contexts*: popular culture (film, music, fashion and new entertainments), new technologies, literary and artistic salons, little magazines, anthologies and exhibitions. This expanded understanding of modernist innovation has extended into interdisciplinary studies that conjoin fields such as dance, architecture, design, philosophy, linguistics, science, anthropology, psychology, everyday life and others. They also began discussing modernist *content* that reflected other groups of people (women, workers, colonized people and people of color) who wrote about their lives during the modernist period. As a result, even difficult writers like T. S. Eliot became more enlivened as critics began discussing his "high" modernism in relation to popular culture: jazz, vaudeville, pornography, black vernacular speech, among other popular sources.

Beginning in the 1990s, critics also became attentive to the ways in which modernism has always been a *worldwide* phenomenon. Not only was modernism influenced by other cultures (as we saw above with Picasso's African masks), it was also profoundly shaped by the massive imperial expansion of the late nineteenth and early twentieth centuries. *The Waste Land*, for instance, in an early draft, began with an epigram − "the horror, the horror" − from Joseph Conrad's *Heart of Darkness*, a novella that declared the colonization of Africa a misguided and fantastic "idea." Its narrator, Marlow, says of his experience in colonial Africa, "I've never seen anything so unreal in my life" (27). Eliot, too, at the end of his poem, calls imperial civilizations (the centers of empire) "unreal" and doomed to fall: "Jerusalem Athens Alexandria/Vienna London/Unreal" (17–18, #374–76). The poem looks to the East, specifically to the Upanishads of Hinduism, for relief. Its final words are "Shantih, shantih, shantih" (glossed by Eliot as "the Peace which passeth understanding"; 20, #433 and 26). In ending this poem with a sacred text of India, is Eliot participating in the imperial project that Conrad decries? A lively debate continues today concerning the relation of modernism to a worldwide modernity and whether the spread of modernism is itself an aspect of Westernization. Does modernism blot out other cultures, histories, languages and other ways of living? In order to begin to answer this question, we will give careful consideration to *context* as we map how modernism travels in this book.

Though what counts as modernism has grown, we can still define a central preoccupation among all its practitioners, no matter to what group or location they may belong. This shared concern comprises the first part of our working definition of modernism that I borrow from Pericles Lewis (xviii).

> Definition, part one: **modernism** is "a crisis in the ability of the arts to represent reality"

We will be using this definition – a crisis in representation – as a means to map modernism. This crisis was both a crisis in what could be represented (content) and in how it could be represented (form). We will examine in detail the change in content in Chapter 3, "Histories," and the change in form in Chapter 4, "Forms." But it's also important to know that modernists adapted both the content and form of art in varying combinations to keep up with the pace of change. The importance of this fact lies in the modernists' self-conscious break with the past. As mentioned earlier, the term **modern** means "now" as opposed to the past of tradition. It is a narrative category, a story one tells about a way of life: we used to do things in a traditional manner; now we do them differently. Because this narrative can be filled with different content depending on its location and history, modernism can be identified according to flexible formal and historical rubrics. This narrative coherence (then versus now) presents modernism in all of its richness and complexity, even as the break itself – how is *now* different from *then*? – comes to mean many different things (Ross and Lindgren 2).

One key question for students who are exploring how modernism spans the globe is *how* to talk about modernism when it takes so many different forms. Even the term "modernism" is not always the preferred term for crises in the ability of the arts to represent reality across different geographic and linguistic traditions. For instance, in the Spanish language, Nicaraguan poet Rubén Dario first coined the term *modernismo* in 1888 in reference to Latin American symbolist poetry and as a declaration of cultural autonomy from Europe. The French prefer the term *avant-garde*, the Germans *Expressionismus*, the Italians *decadentismo* to refer to what we call *modernism* in the English language (P. Lewis viii). And when the term moves outside the Western context, "modernism" becomes even trickier to use, given that it carries with it the history and prestige of the term as a European phenomenon. In Asia, as Eric Hayot explains, the "terms for 'modernism' and 'modernist' appear in Asia initially as *transcriptions* rather than as translations: *modeng* in 1930s China, *modanizumu* in Japan" (152). Rather than translate "modernism" into an already existing Asian tradition, the lack of translation signals its trendy foreignness, similar to how the French term *chic* registers in predominantly English-speaking countries as French style and sophistication that has no equivalent in Anglophone countries. The prestige of modernism, he argues, is inseparable from the prestige and power of Western Europe at this time. This imitative absorption of a European trend will be discussed in the Afterword, but, for now, it is enough to say that the term "modernism" carries with it the history of uneven power dynamics between the West and other regions of the world, and that history can make the term tricky to use in non-Western contexts.

As the variations in the term "modernism" indicate, the story of how modernism arose in each particular location differs greatly, too. The crisis in representation by which we map modernism did not simply occur in Europe first and then travel outward to other locations. Rather, the crisis in representation occurred as global inter-actions among cultures brought the crisis into being in different ways around the world. Japanese watercolor painting and calligraphy, for instance, shaped European modernism almost as greatly as Western modernism influenced that of Japan. Japanese Noh plays influenced Irish poet and dramatist W. B. Yeats; classical Chinese poetry inspired Ezra Pound's *Cantos*; and Native American mythologies underwrote D. H. Lawrence's later novels, to take some other well-known European examples. When we consider what modernism means in each location, it is necessary to understand the very different historical and cultural **contexts,** or circumstances, that influence the creation of innovative art.

In sum, the study of modernism has expanded considerably in terms of its historical reach, laterally in terms of its geographic compass, and vertically in terms of its embrace of modernists who were less experimental in *how* they wrote or painted and more controversial in terms of *what* they wrote or painted (Mao and Walkowitz). Our map of modernism (a historical period of intensive innovation in the arts in response to a crisis in representation) needs to be accompanied by a discussion of the term "modernity" so that we can better understand the contexts in which modernism occurs.

GLOBAL CONTEXTS

Definition, part two: **modernism** is a form of critical and artistic engagement with modernity

Modernity, as we'll see, is a worldwide historical phenomenon. This added element of our definition of modernism decenters the West so that it becomes just one player in a worldwide system of trade and cultural exchange. (Though, to be sure, it was a dominant, colonizing player.) As we will see in later chapters, modernism was practiced all over the world, often concurrently with European modernism. Nor can we say that women's, antiracist, anticolonial and workers' movements that fermented below "high" modernism were irrelevant or secondary to the crisis in the ability of the arts to represent reality. Indeed, they were central. Modernism, as I hope to demonstrate in this book, arose as a geographically interconnected and vertically integrated phenomena. Essential to understanding modernism as an interconnected cultural phenomenon is the revision of modernity as likewise worldwide, multidirectional and formed by competing forces. Modernity, like modernism, is a highly capacious word that means many different things to many people. For our purposes, the word "modern," as mentioned above, means "now" as opposed to the past. To fully embrace the newness of the present moment is to break from the past that includes inherited beliefs, social conventions and a resigned acceptance of the status quo because it appears to have always been that way. Different modernists negotiate the "new" in different ways, some even self-consciously recasting *tradition* itself as a buffer against the sweeping changes that they disliked, especially imperialist incursions into their lands.

While intercultural and economic exchange have been going on all over the world for millennia, we will be examining the intensification of this process that arose via technological and historical developments beginning in the late nineteenth century. These include the economically viable passenger steamship, wireless telegraph, telephone, bicycle, automobile and airplane, as well as the rise of imperialism through the entire world, resulting in the spread of money economies, global trade, wage labor, urbanization, industrialization and massive migrations. These technologies and the social, political and economic transformations that they enabled accelerated the experience of modernity to become a "mode of vital experience," according to Marshall Berman. To be modern, Berman says, is "to find ourselves in an environment that promises us adventure, power, joy, growth, transformation of ourselves and the world – and, at the same time, threatens to destroy everything we have, everything we know, everything we are" (15). **Modernity** is the social, cultural, political, economic and philosophical conditions that allow one to be modern. **Modernization** is the process of becoming modern. As the quotation suggests, however, modernity is a double-edged sword. On the one hand, it is exciting and allows endless possibility for growth and transformation of ourselves and our surroundings. But, on the other hand, modernity has a very dark side that threatens to wipe out all the achievements made in its name.

I turn next to Marx and Engels' famous declaration of the problems and opportunities of modernity in "The Communist Manifesto" (1848) in order to underscore how modernist writing expresses both sides of modernity: excited optimism in the possibilities of the modern and woeful critique of its problems. Marx and Engels describe modernity as both a positive and negative force that spreads around the world. In the following stirring passage, they describe how the "bourgeoisie," or ruling class, creates massive means of production:

> Subjection of nature's forces to man, machinery, application of chemistry to agriculture and industry, steam navigation, railways, electric telegraphs, clearing of whole continents for cultivation, canalization of rivers, whole populations conjured out of the ground – what earlier century had even an intimation that such productive power slept in the womb of social labor?

(477)

While this catalogue of activity and innovation is indeed exciting and transformative, Marx and Engels cast a dark shadow over their description of the tremendous power of modernity with the phrase "whole populations conjured out of the ground." "Conjured" evokes the magical power of a sorcerer, a demonic and terrifying force that, in its blindness to conquer the world, demands that "whole populations" enter into its system. Marx and Engels explicitly argue that

> [t]he discovery of America, the rounding of the Cape, opened up fresh ground for the rising bourgeoisie. The East-Indian and Chinese markets, the colonisation of America, trade with the colonies . . . gave to commerce, to navigation, to industry, . . . a rapid development.

(474)

This description includes the colonization of the New World, Africa and large parts of Asia, and the forcible removal of indigenous populations from their land. Even when existing societies such as the Chinese were not explicitly colonized, they were made to trade with the West at the end of the gun during the Anglo-Chinese Opium Wars (1839–42, 1856–60). The phrase "clearing of whole continents for cultivation" suggests the environmental devastation that industrialization and industrial agriculture have wreaked on the natural world. As the geographical expanse of the conquered world grew, so too did its historical dimension widen, as scientists and explorers looked to themselves and their abilities to encounter and transform the physical world, rather than looking to God in the heavens to fulfill their destiny.

This new way of life and expanded geographical horizon crucially contributed to the crisis in literary and artistic representation. One defining example, which we will discuss further in Chapter 3, is the way in which the competition of imperial powers for overseas markets and resources (including England, France, Germany, Belgium) ignited into World War I, a cataclysmic event that directly influenced many works of literature and art. In addition, in the early twentieth century, cultures, peoples and languages were on the move: new communication technologies, including telegraph, transatlantic cables, film and enhanced print technologies, coupled with faster travel times via steamship, trains, airplanes and cars, meant that cultural interaction – and reaction – was inevitable. Though much of this travel was involuntary – the period was characterized by massive troop mobilization and enforced migrations – the effect of this tremendous increase in intercultural connections was that many people were brought face-to-face with the limits of their world. This fact ushered in a felt uncertainty regarding what the result of modernity might actually be. Writers from around the world, including Jean Rhys, Futabatei Shimei, Oswald de Andrade, André Gide, Tayeb Salih, Chinua Achebe, Yosano Akiko, Ralph Ellison and Nella Larsen, probed their social settings for the conflicts, contradictions and possibilities of modern life.

Furthermore, this worldwide conception of modernity challenges the historical parameters concerning when modernism began and when, or whether, it ended. The periodization of modernism, under this critical debate, is stretched backward and forwards in time. For example, many colonized territories in the Global South (Africa, the Caribbean and large parts of Asia) gained their independence and began to build their nations in the post-1945 period. In our examination of modernism, we begin in the mid-nineteenth century and end, depending on the location, anywhere from 1940 to 1973 and beyond. In the Afterword, we will discuss the afterlives of modernism as a literary technique that continues in the present time. What is important to note is that different fields of modernism demand different historical parameters. (See also the modernist time line.)

If we consider the implications of the second element of our map of modernism – a critical and artistic engagement with modernity – we then can understand *modernism as a worldwide phenomenon*, an innovative form of artistic production that varies dramatically from place to place. Whereas the first element of modernism named a crisis in representation, this second element places attention on modernism as a response to modernity that functions differently in various locations around the world.

We turn next to the second painting in this chapter, Wifredo Lam's *La Jungla* (1943), in order to show the reader how the worldwide **contexts** in which modernism is produced matters greatly to us in the twenty-first century. Traditional accounts of modernism ignored Lam. But because the field of modernism is a shifting one, it has become – as two critics in 1976 put it – "what it could hardly have expected ever to be: a usable past, leading into the present and the future" (Bradbury and McFarlane 12). Because our world is so interconnected and compressed, we look to modernism for a pre-history of our present and future. In addition, present-day feminist, ethnic and postcolonial struggles have generated new looks back at modernism. The term **postcolonial** refers to the historical condi-tion of having been colonized and the ongoing need to revise all the structures (linguistic, representation, economic, social, etc.) that the colonizer has brought to that society because it situates the post-colonial nation as second class. Accordingly, we can now value Lam's painting as articulating a postcolonial modernism. He dem-onstrates how Africa, Europe and the Americas challenge each other, antagonistically revising and influencing one another. In discussing Lam's painting, we will be triangulating the modernist network of influence between Africa, France/Spain and Cuba.

The Cuban painter Wifredo Lam, whose father was an inden-tured Chinese laborer and whose mother was African and Spanish, traveled to Spain in 1923 to study art in Madrid. In 1938, after a dra-matic departure from Barcelona, Spain, as it was being overtaken by Nationalist forces during the Spanish Civil War, he arrived in Paris, where he met the painter Pablo Picasso and studied Picasso's use of African sculpture in his painting (as we saw above in *Les Demoiselles*). Lam, however, did not imitate Picasso. In fact, he described his own artistic strategy as "being that of the reappropriationist, the 'Tro-jan horse' that would infiltrate the art establishment and 'disturb the dreams of the exploiters'" (Sims 222). That is, rather than being per-ceived as an Afro-Cuban who travels from the uncivilized Caribbean to the center of the civilized world to study the European masters of art and imitate them, Lam interrupted the one-way process of vio-lently appropriating art from Africa to create European modernism. Just as Europeans seized the right to borrow from Africa in their own art, they also assumed that people from Africa were not capable of producing great modern art. Lam fought against his exclusion from this art world. In 1943, he painted *La Jungla* (*The Jungle*), a reworking of Picasso's *Les Demoiselles*, with the aim of overcoming the civilizational divide between Europe and Africa (see Figure 1.2). To begin, the painting is not set in a jungle but instead incorporates Cuban sugar and tobacco plantations as its background. Rather than offering five static figures set against a blank background as Picasso's *Les Demoiselles* does, *La Jungla* conveys a "reciprocal flow from fig-ure to figure, figure to nature, form to counterform" (Krempel 88).

Figure 1.2 Wifredo Lam, *La Jungla*, 1943 (Museum of Modern Art)

The figures mingle with the background; deities appear on skulls, legs and torsos; and human shapes grow out of the overabundant vegetation. "No figure, no object is frozen into a fixed stage of existence; every earthly organism belongs at the same time to the plant family and every plant to the animal or human form" (Krempel 88–90). The sexuality is fecund, blurring male and female parts with nature in proximate, intimate contact. The painting simultaneously refers both to Orishas (West African nature deities) and to the large group portraiture of Picasso's *Les Demoiselles* and to Paul Cézanne's *Les Baigneurs* (*The Bathers*, 1892–94). But instead of juxtaposing the

African mask with the body of the European prostitute, Lam visually integrates these discrete elements into what seems to be an endless, and continuous, body.

Lam combines European modernism with Afro-Cuban culture in order to transform both, offering a dynamic, mutable force of life in a state of freedom. In his painting, references to Africa are no longer made via exotic inert objects like the African masks in Picasso's painting. Instead, references to Africa are made via Afro-Cuban culture, where they are incorporated into new syncretic religious and cultural practices that combine European (Spanish Catholic) and African cultures. Neither African nor European cultures predominate; they are transmuted into something new. In fact, Lam said that the figure brandishing scissors in the upper right-hand corner of the painting was "necessary to sever all ties with the colonial culture" (qtd. in Sims 223). These ties include the sense of inferiority and mimicry of European culture. Even further, Lam's painting transforms the subject/object dichotomy that characterizes how Europeans represent modernity. The painting blurs subject and object distinctions as well as the spatial representations of foreground (figure) and background (vehicle). The configuration of persons interpenetrated with nature and plantation life resonates with the fact that slaves and indentured laborers were not viewed as subjects but, rather, were owned by their masters. They were objects of property and therefore part of the means of plantation production. They worked the fields just as the oxen might. (Lam notably descended from European masters, African slaves and Chinese indentured laborers. His heritage evolved from both the subjects and objects of plantation life.) As in our earlier discussion of modernist form in Eliot and Picasso, we still see **dissonance** and **displacement** in the juxtapositions of so many contradictory figures; **simultaneity** of the natural, divine and human worlds; as well as nonlocal color and geometrical shapes that do not reflect reality but rather give rise to particular aesthetic sensations and affect in the viewer.

This example of a geographically expanded understanding of modernist art should give the reader a sense of how modernism reflects diverse experiences of modernity. So far, we've only concerned ourselves with two locations: the metropolitan capitals of France and England filled with nuance and sophistication, and the grueling outpost of Cuban plantation life where subject and object distinctions blur. But we will explore other locations in the pages to follow.

NETWORKS OF MODERNISM

My account of modernism so far has been of heroic male poets and painters whose work demonstrates an awareness of other cultures in their art. So, too, my account of modernity has been one of development, exploration and travel. We have seen women in modernism thus far as objects: prostitutes (Picasso), victims of male violence (Philomela in Eliot) and as human intermingled with nature (Lam). In the mid-1990s, however, an important correction to this story appeared that refused to accept the male-dominated nature of modernity in which women were simply the passive objects of that story. If we highlight instead how modernity concerns a sense of newness in everyday life (the habitual, repetitive ordinary features of living), then the story of modernism changes. In the epigrams to this chapter, feminist writer and artist Mina Loy declares, "LIVE in the future," (149) and Afro-Caribbean writer Suzanne Césaire, writing in the former French colony of Martinique, prophesized that "Colonial idiocy will be purified by the welder's blue flame" (492). Women, whatever race, were reinventing themselves through cultural and political organizations, changes in domestic and working life, and as writers and artists. They transformed the heroic, individual narrative of modern development and transformation (as in Marx and Engels' account above) into multidimensional, affiliative and often uneven and contradictory accounts of modern life.

Even when we account for modernity being a double-edged sword, offering both positive and negative elements in its sweeping transformations of social and economic organizations, we still reduce the experience of modernity to a single narrative of cataclysmic change. Rita Felski summarizes the problem of this reduction as follows:

> Women have experienced these changes [of modernity] in gender-specific ways that have been further fractured, not only by the oft-cited hierarchies of class, race, and sexuality but by their various and overlapping identities and practices as consumers, mothers, workers, artists, lovers, activists, readers, and so on.

(21)

To be sure, male experiences of modernity should also be broken down further to account for the uneven and multiple effects and experiences of modernity for them. But women, because of their reproductive role and their general subordination to men in the modernist era and beyond, experienced more strongly the uneven effects of modernity. One response to this gendered need to consider modernism in its multifaceted dimensionality has been to emphasize the *networks* of modernism, particularly as they contributed to the material production of modernist literature and art.

While we have thus far introduced modernism by means of some of its most spectacular works of art and literature, it is important to recognize that modernism as a recognizable *movement* in the arts was achieved through the work of countless others: publishers, especially of independent presses, and translators, bookstore owners, editors, patrons, hostesses, critics and curators, actors, stage designers, directors, musicians, fashion and interior designers, among others. In her study of the modernist literary scene in Paris between the wars and the role that women played in promoting modernist writing, Shari Benstock asks,

How crucial was it to the Modernist movement – as a movement – that Nancy Cunard or Caresse Crosby published and printed books that were sold by Adrienne Monnier and Sylvia Beach (themselves the publishers in English and French of James Joyce's *Ulysses*); or that Maria Jolas worked steadily, as did Margaret Anderson, Winifred Ellerman, Jane Heap, Amy Lowell, and Harriet Weaver, to publish in little magazines work so radically experimental that it could have no other outlet; or that Janet Flanner, in her "Letter from Paris" in the *New Yorker*, announced each of these publishing events to an American public eager for news of the Paris literary scene?

(21)

The answer is, of course, highly important. It is conceivable that without these women publishers, editors and patrons, much of what is most experimental and famous about modernism would not have been published at all. When we widen the geographical purview of these modernist little magazines and independent publishers, we can envision these small press publications offering a public, print forum in which writers, readers, critics and translators could imagine themselves taking part in a worldwide modernist movement. Consider the publication of the following little magazines: *Shirakaba* (Japan) 1910; *Ma* (Hungary) 1916; *Kallol* (India) 1923; *Martín Fierro* (Argentina) 1924–27; *La Revue Indigène* (Haiti) 1927; *Voorslag* (South Africa) 1926; *The Beacon* (Trinidad) 1931; *Tropiques* (Martinique) 1941; *Kyk-over-al* (Guyana) 1945; *Bim* (Barbardos) 1942; *Focus* (Jamaica) 1943; *Black Orpheus* (Nigeria) 1957; *Transition* (Uganda) 1961; and *Okyeame* (Ghana) 1961 (Bulson 272–73). While not all of these journals concerned themselves with experimental literature, they uniformly sought to engage in debate concerning how their local, national or regional cultures should become modern. Meanwhile, small independent presses, such as Virginia and Leonard Woolf's Hogarth Press, offered publishing platforms for writers from Africa, the Caribbean and Asia to find an international audience. In addition, important journals featuring the political liberation of British women, African-Americans, Irish and US workers (to name just a few groups) emerged during the first decades of the twentieth century. These journals often combined politics with articles on modern life, art and literature. Some of the most famous in the Anglophone West include *The Freewoman*, *The Woman's Dreadnought*, *The Irish Citizen*, *The Crisis* and *The Masses*.

Bringing our critical gaze back to the European capitals where we began, we come full circle around to the difficult "high" modernists. Scholars working on mass culture and the networks of modernism have overturned the notion that great modernist authors and painters were uniformly hostile to mass culture. Our initial reading of T. S. Eliot's *The Waste Land* noted the narrator's hostility toward mass culture in the line "Jug Jug" to dirty ears (8, #103). The subsequent New Critical enshrinement of "difficult" modernist literature as the sole modernist work worthy of study further enacted "the great divide," as Andreas Huyssen calls it, between high art and mass culture. In fact, modernists were very much alive to the potential of mass culture, especially commercial advertising and mass-market publications. Picasso and other Cubist painters collaged newspaper headlines into their art; *The Waste Land* sings, "O O O O that Shakespeherian Rag/It's so elegant/So intelligent" (9, #128–30). Rags originated in African-American communities (notably in St. Louis, where Eliot was born). They feature syncopated rhythm and were a precursor to jazz. Other "high" modernists, such as Wyndham Lewis, Ezra

Pound and Virginia Woolf, embraced commercial advertising and self-promotion through the culture of celebrity, as Aaron Jaffe, Jane Garrity and others have shown. Meanwhile, Caribbean fiction writer Jean Rhys explored the poses, cosmetics and fashion of single women who try to make a life for themselves in the cities of Western Europe, and James Joyce explicitly drew on women's mass-culture magazines in the "Nausicaa" episode in *Ulysses*, while the main protagonist of that novel, Leopold Bloom, canvasses for newspaper ads.

At the same time, mass culture was growing exponentially. Higher literacy rates, greater leisure hours, and lower print-production costs (including the ability to reproduce images more cheaply) fueled this culture and raised the ability to market to niche sectors. As mentioned above, marketing to women in little magazines, for instance, not only sold goods but advanced the women's suffrage movement as well as modernism. Suffrage periodicals were interspersed with short stories, journalism and manifestos that promoted modernist art and thought. The short-lived *Blast*, edited by Ezra Pound and Wyndham Lewis, offered catchy slogans – "Recognize no taboos" – and circulated flyers to promote the modernist art and literature published between its covers. Scholars working on mass culture and modernism have showed how modernism vividly asserted a public function, especially in terms of remaking and renewing society, and it did so by means of mass-market practices (Morrisson 6).

Some scholars draw on book history and archival research to recover a sense of how a modernist work initially appeared to readers prior to its canonization. George Bornstein argues that the "semantic features of [a text's] material instantiations" be considered in understanding a text's meaning (6). By this, he means that a book's cover design, page layout or spacing, preface, dedication and the periodical or press in which it appears all contribute to the reception and interpretation of the work. In addition, he draws attention to how subsequent versions of a work can erase from memory how modernism first appeared to the public. For instance, the "Hades" episode of Joyce's *Ulysses* takes place in a graveyard in Dublin in 1904 and has long been interpreted as being primarily concerned with Ireland's leaders from the nineteenth century. However, when we consider that this episode was first published as a stand-alone piece of writing in a 1918 issue of the *Little Review* just as World War I was drawing to a close, its meaning changes. This issue "was surrounded by stories, poems, and letters about death, mourning and memory" concerning the victims of the global conflict (Latham and Rogers 180). "Hades" then reflects as much on a contemporary worldwide conflict as it does on Ireland's past.

SUMMARY

We see from the examples above that modernism can vary a lot, not only between the various locations in which it is practiced, but also between different kinds of media (poetry vs. painting, magazine vs. book, etc.). But we have also introduced certain characteristics in modernism; namely, that modernism:

- is a crisis in the ability of the arts to represent reality;
- can take many forms;
- occurred during an historical period of sweeping political, technological, economic and social transformations, mainly between 1890–1940, but modernist techniques have been used before and after this time period;
- is a critical and artistic engagement with modernity, showing both the promises and dangers of modernity;
- was promoted by means of a worldwide network of noncommercial publishers, little magazines, reviews, bookstores, salons, cabarets, editors and anthologies;
- is a term that often carries with it the history of imperialism and Western dominance.

A GUIDE TO SUBSEQUENT CHAPTERS

This book is organized according to various contexts for understanding modernism. Chapter 2, "Concepts," investigates in more detail the philosophical and underlying conceptual aspects of modernism touched on here. It begins by looking at the crisis of representation and the concept of artistic autonomy. It covers several nineteenth-century literary movements – symbolism, aestheticism and decadence – that directly influenced the major modernist avant-garde groups. It discusses the revolution in language and the crisis of reason, including the discovery of the unconscious, as well as the impact of new technologies and media on modernist artistic production.

Chapter 3, "Histories," surveys the historical and political contexts that prevailed in the first half of the twentieth century. These include imperialism, colonialism, the world wars, and the rise of mass political movements, including fascism, communism, women's and sexuality movements. In addition, it outlines various modernisms from around the world, including those from Harlem, Ireland, Japan and South Asia. Chapter 4, "Forms," explores modernist fiction, poetry and drama from around the world in terms of their aesthetic and critical engagement with modernity. It hopes to convey that modernist art and literature can be compelling – even enjoyable – once the basic premises are understood.

Finally, the Afterword addresses the question of whether modernism is a viable aesthetic category today. It discusses this debate through reference to the relation of modernism to postmodernism and to postcolonial literature. In sum, the aim of this book is to introduce modernism as a series of mutually informing European and non-Western aesthetic innovations. We hope that it will convey the rich and complex diversity of artistic achievement that continues to influence the present.

FURTHER READING

On the experience of modernity, see Marshall Berman *All that's Solid Melts into Air: The Experience of Modernity* (New York: Penguin, 1988); and Rita Felski *The Gender of Modernity* (Cambridge: Harvard University Press, 1995).

For overviews of modernism that have changed over time, see Malcolm Bradbury and James McFarlane, ed. *Modernism: A Guide to European Literature, 1890–1930* (New York: Penguin, 1976); Bonnie Kime Scott, ed. *The Gender of Modernism: A Critical Anthology* (Bloomington: Indiana University Press, 1990); Sandra Gilbert and Susan Gubar *No Man's Land: The Place of the Woman Writer in the Twentieth Century* 3 Vols. (New Haven: Yale University Press, 1987–94); Peter Nicholls *Modernisms: A Literary Guide* (Berkeley: University of California Press, 1995); Christopher Butler *Modernism: A Very Short Introduction* (New York: Oxford University Press, 2010); Peter Brooker, Andrzej Gasiorek, Deborah Longworth and Andrew Thacker *The Oxford Handbook of Modernisms* (New York: Oxford University Press, 2010); Pericles Lewis *The Cambridge Introduction to Modernism* (New

York: Cambridge University Press, 2007); and Mark Wollaeger and Matt Eatough *The Oxford Handbook of Global Modernisms* (New York: Oxford University Press, 2012). For work on modernist periodicals and print culture, see Ann Ardis and Patrick Collier, eds. *Transatlantic Print Culture, 1880–1940: Emerging Media, Emerging Modernism* (New York: Palgrave, 2008); Shari Benstock *Women of the Left Bank: Paris, 1900–1940* (Austin, TX: University of Texas Press, 1986); and Mark S. Morrisson *The Public Face of Modernism: Little Magazines, Audiences, and Reception 1905–1920* (Madison, WI: University of Wisconsin Press, 2001).

PERTINENT WEBSITES

Journal of Modern Periodical Studies. http://muse.jhu.edu/journals/journal_of_modern_periodical_studies/

The Modernism Lab at Yale University. http://modernism.research.yale.edu/index.php

Modernism/Modernity (the official journal of the Modernist Studies Association). www.press.jhu.edu/journals/modernism_modernity/

Modernist Commons. http://modernistcommons.ca

Modernist Cultures. www.euppublishing.com/journal/mod

Modernist Journals Project. http://modjourn.org

Routledge Encyclopedia of Modernism. www.rem.routledge.com

WORKS CITED

Apollinaire, Guillaume. "On the Subject of Modern Painting." In *Art in Theory: 1900–2000: An Anthology of Changing Ideas.* Eds. Charles Harrison and Paul Wood. Malden, MA: Blackwell, 2003. 186–7. Print.

Bell, Clive. *Art.* New York: Putnam, 1981. Print.

Benstock, Shari. *Women of the Left Bank: Paris, 1900–1940.* Austin, TX: University of Texas Press, 1986. Print.

Berman, Marshall. *All That's Solid Melts into Air: The Experience of Modernity.* New York: Penguin, 1988. Print.

Bornstein, George. *Material Modernism: The Politics of the Page.* New York: Cambridge University Press, 2001. Print.

Bradbury, Malcolm and James McFarlane, eds. *Modernism: A Guide to European Literature, 1890–1930.* New York: Penguin, 1991. [A reissue of 1976 edition] Print.

Brooks, Cleanth. *The Well Wrought Urn: Studies in the Structure of Poetry.* New York: Harcourt Brace, 1947. Print.

Brooks, Cleanth and Robert Penn Warren. *Understanding Poetry*. New York: H. Holt & Co., 1938. Print.

Bulson, Eric. "Little Magazine, World Form." In *The Oxford Handbook of Global Modernisms*. Eds. Mark Wollaeger and Matthew Eatough. New York: Oxford University Press, 2012. 267–87. Print.

Césaire, Suzanne. "Surrealism and Us." In *Manifesto: A Century of Isms*. Ed. Mary Ann Caws. Lincoln, NE: University of Nebraska Press, 2001. Print.

Conrad, Joseph. *Heart of Darkness*. New York: Modern Library, 1999. Print.

Eliot, T. S. "The Metaphysical Poets." In *Selected Prose of T. S. Eliot*. Ed. Frank Kermode. New York: Harcourt, Brace, 1975. 59–67. Print.

———. "Tradition and the Individual Talent." In *Selected Prose of T. S. Eliot*. Ed. Frank Kermode. New York: Harcourt, Brace, 1975. 37–44. Print.

———. "Ulysses, Order, and Myth." In *Selected Prose of T. S. Eliot*. Ed. Frank Kermode. New York: Harcourt, Brace, 1975. 175–78. Print.

———. *The Waste Land*. Ed. Michael North. *Norton Critical Edition*. New York: Norton & Co., 2001. 5–26. Print.

Engels, Friedrich and Karl Marx. "The Communist Manifesto." In *The Marx-Engels Reader*. Ed. Robert C. Tucker. New York: W. W. Norton, 1972. 469–500. Print.

Felski, Rita. *The Gender of Modernity*. Cambridge, MA: Harvard University Press, 1995. Print.

Hayot, Eric. "Chinese Modernism, Mimetic Desire, and European Time." In *The Oxford Handbook of Global Modernisms*. Ed. Mark Wollaeger and Matt Eatough. New York: Oxford University Press, 2012. 149–70. Print.

Hulme, T. E. "Lecture on Modern Poetry." www.uni-due.de/lyriktheorie/texte/1908_hulme.html (accessed 01/08/16).

Huyssen, Andreas. *After the Great Divide: Modernism, Mass Culture, Postmodernism*. Bloomington, IN: Indiana University Press, 1986. Print.

Latham, Sean and Gayle Rogers. *Modernism: Evolution of an Idea*. New York: Bloomsbury, 2015. Print.

Leavis, F. R. "The Significance of the Modern Waste Land." In *The Waste Land: A Norton Critical Edition*. Ed. Michael North. New York: Norton, 2001. 173–85. Print.

Levin, Harry. "When Was Modernism?" *Massachusetts Review*. 1.4 (Summer 1960): 609–30. Print.

Lewis, Pericles. *The Cambridge Introduction to Modernism*. New York: Cambridge University Press, 2007. Print.

Loy, Mina. "Aphorisms on Futurism." In *The Lost Lunar Baedeker*. Ed. Roger L. Conover. New York: Farrar, Straus and Giroux, 1996. Print.

Mao, Douglas and Rebecca L. Walkowitz. "The New Modernist Studies." *PMLA*. 123.3 (May 2008): 737–48. Print.

Morrisson, Mark S. *The Public Face of Modernism: Little Magazines, Audiences, and Reception 1905–1920*. Madison, WI: University of Wisconsin Press, 2001.

Ross, Stephen and Allana C. Lindgren. "Introduction." In *The Modernist World*. Eds. Stephen Ross and Allana C. Lindgren. New York: Routledge, 2015. 1–13. Print.

Seckel, Hélène. "Anthology of Early Commentary on *Les Demoiselles d'Avignon*." In *Studies in Modern Art Vol. 3*. Eds. William Rubin, Hélène Seckel and Judith Cousins. New York: The Museum of Modern Art, 1994. 213–56. Print.

Sims, Lowery Stokes. *Wilfredo Lam and the International Avant-Garde, 1923–1982*. Austin, TX: University of Texas Press, 2002. Print.

Wilson, Edmund. *Axel's Castle*. New York: Charles Scribner, 1931. Print.

2

CONCEPTS

"I have transformed myself *in the zero of form* and have fished myself out of the *rubbishy slough of academic art*."

Kasimir Malevich, *From Cubism and Futurism to
Suprematism: The New Painterly Realism* (1915)

This chapter looks at the ideas behind modernism and asks: how did crises in philosophy, science, politics and society lead to this thing we call modernism? Let us remember from Chapter 1 that modernism designates a crisis in the ability of the arts to represent reality. This crisis will be further broken down into three particular issues. This chapter, "Concepts," discusses two crises that fundamentally shaped modernism: the crisis of representation (in art, philosophy and linguistics); and the crisis of reason (in philosophy and science). In Chapter 3, "Histories," we will examine the crisis of empire (politics and economics) that also affected modernism (see also Lewis). Understanding these crises will help us to achieve the second of our aims delineated in Chapter 1: namely, to contextualize, or situate, close readings of modern art and literature within their underlying concepts that gave them shape.

The focus of this chapter will be on European and North American modernism, because the West exported its literary and visual art, science and technology, and economic and political ideologies across the globe through elite university education and cultural and economic prestige in ways that strongly affected non-Western modernisms. While we will show in later chapters that modernism circulated widely, sometimes bypassing the West altogether, these particular European crises are essential to understanding what modernism is, as it has been historically understood.

CRISIS OF REPRESENTATION

This section on the crisis of representation has two parts: first, we will examine why it was that modern artists wanted their art to be autonomous or free from traditional expectations about what art should do and how it should look and sound. To do this, we will begin in the mid-nineteenth century, several decades before the modernist period. Understanding the later nineteenth century is important because the conditions under which art was being produced in Europe were already changing profoundly. Our chief example of this early form of artistic autonomy will be the poetry of Charles Baudelaire. Second, we will discuss a philosophical and linguistic "revolution in language." This revolution emphasized a static, spatial form of language that we will consider via the Imagist school of poetry. Finally, we'll consider the role of the avant-garde in modernism, especially with its oppositional stance toward the public, including significant nineteenth-century avant-garde precursors (aestheticism and decadence) and twentieth-century radical versions (futurism, vorticism, dada and surrealism). At times, we will also examine a few literary techniques in order to illustrate the concepts.

THE AUTONOMY OF ART

We begin with the concept of **artistic autonomy** to show how and why modernist artists retreated from the commercial market. Rejecting base considerations of profit, they sought a realm of independence for their artistic practice. The commercial market depends upon telling an entertaining and easy-to-grasp story in order to sell thousands, even millions, of copies to a wide audience. Therefore, the refusal to write for this market entailed a crisis of representation: to represent differently was to disobey the commercial demands of publishing.

When and where did this hostile stance begin? The German–Jewish critic and philosopher Walter Benjamin (1892–1940) provides one useful story of how modernism came to be. He analyzed the architecture and artworks of nineteenth-century Paris as a form of wish fulfillment. He argued that any kind of creative work (buildings, decorative arts, literature, painting, music), because it contained imaginary elements, revealed a society's collective desire for a better life. He says, "Every epoch not only dreams the next, but also, in dreaming, strives toward the moment of waking" (1978: 162). In the first half of the nineteenth century, in the aftermath of the French Revolution, the wish carved into the buildings and streets of Paris was for a classless, utopian society of leisure, beauty, equality and freedom, and one that was at home and at peace with the wider world. Thus, the shopping arcades, the novels, and the great paintings of the French Empire were made to herald a democratic society in the making. "The arcades," Benjamin writes, "are a center of trade in luxury goods. In their fittings art is brought in to the service of commerce" (1978: 146). Art dreams of a better world in which machines help to produce – rather than to undermine – a beautiful life. As part of his critical and historical reconstruction of nineteenth-century Paris, Benjamin references an illustrated guide to Paris of 1852 that describes the arcades as

> a recent invention of industrial luxury. [They] are glass-roofed, marble-paneled corridors extending through whole blocks of buildings. Lining both sides of these corridors, which get their light from above, are the most elegant shops, so that the *passage* is a city, a world in miniature.
>
> (2003: 19)

In a Parisian arcade, a precursor to the shopping mall, pedestrians strolled through the halls, at once looking at the merchandise on display, looking at others, and, in turn, being seen, as they became part of the spectacle while other shoppers gazed at them to determine their fashion sense and attractiveness (see Figure 2.1).

Despite the utopian allure and spectacle of the arcades, a series of failed revolutions across Europe in 1848 dashed the hope that capitalist societies could become fully democratic. It became clear in France and elsewhere that the middle class, what they called the bourgeoisie, would not relinquish their power to the masses of workers, the

Figure 2.1 Nineteenth-century Paris arcade (public domain)

unemployed, and the peasants who worked the land. This fact was carved into the face of Paris by Baron Haussmann's "urban renewal" project of the 1860s. Haussmann tore down working-class neighborhoods and cut large avenues through the city so that the military could move easily to quell uprisings and to discourage revolutionary barricades. As a result of their growing disillusionment with the class-bound society and its accompanying social injustices, some writers and artists began to express a more critical, less optimistic role of the arts. It is here that European modernism is often said to begin, with the poetry of Charles Baudelaire.

Baudelaire (1821–67), the main source of inspiration for Benjamin's work on the arcades, walked the streets and arcades of Paris and wrote poetry that conveyed the simultaneously luxurious and sordid visual spectacle of the new, modern city, a city that displayed conspicuous consumption, popular entertainment and the sufferings of the working classes in equal measures. Remember from Chapter 1 that we defined modernity as exhibiting growth and social transformation as well as the displacement and destruction of whole populations and environments. Rather than hoping that the first element of modernity – positive social transformation – would take hold completely, by the mid-nineteenth century, it became obvious that the second element of modernity – displacement and destruction – was also a permanent feature. In the face of a general disillusionment with modernity, Baudelaire created the poetic persona of the *flâneur*, an anonymous stroller of the streets of Paris, who records the sufferings of the people whom he passes and aestheticizes (i.e., makes into art) in the scenes he beholds. Note that the persona of the flâneur is not Baudelaire himself. The poet assumes the mask of the flâneur. The persona allows for an **ironic** stance, a form of self-criticism, of the poet towards the flâneur. The **irony** here is sometimes called "romantic irony," a subtle form of dissimulation in which what appears on the surface to be the case, often is not actually the case. We are never sure whether Baudelaire agrees with the persona's attitudes or not. Though the flâneur is not the poet himself, he resembles him. They both occupy the margins of society. Benjamin says of the flâneur that he "is still on the threshold, of the city as of the bourgeois class. Neither has yet engulfed him; in neither is he at home" (1978: 156). Baudelaire's threshold or borderline position is crucial for understanding his poetry as modernist. The flâneur is marginal to the city and to the middle class, meaning that he (or she) is both a part of them and outside of them as a detached, critical observer. Think here of standing in a doorway on the threshold: you are neither in the room nor fully outside of it. This position allows you to see the whole of a room, or, in this case, the whole of a society of which you are also a part.

By being marginal, Baudelaire's flâneur adopts a tone of critical detachment, a blasé, nothing-can-ruffle-my-feathers tone. Rather than conveying a passionate engagement with social wrongs as a romantic poet might have done, Baudelaire writes dispassionately, directing his critique at his social surroundings, the idea of poetic language, and himself. In fact, Baudelaire, with his rebellious drug taking, downwardly mobile lifestyle and sexual experimentation, is often said to have begun the bohemian – later called the hippie – counterculture. While the earlier romantic artist was often a rebel too, we might distinguish modernism from romanticism by noting that modernism offers a "much more wholesale challenge [. . .] to such systems of representation as pictorial perspective and to the ideal of transparent or mimetic language" (Lewis 8). For example, in one of Baudelaire's poems about a prostitute, he connects her troubles to his own in order to reflect upon the predicament of poetry and artistic representation in the modern age:

> In order to have shoes, she has sold her soul;
> But the Good Lord would laugh if, in the presence of that vile woman,
> I played the hypocrite and acted lofty –
> I who sell my thought and wish to be an author.
>
> (qtd. in Benjamin 2003: 17)

In this poem, the flâneur and Baudelaire appear to be almost identical. Though the flâneur goes to the marketplace to look at the wares on sale, in reality, as Benjamin says of this poem, he is looking for a buyer for his own commodity: his poetry. Like the prostitute, art is degraded by its sale in the marketplace, except that the poet can also write about this problem, thereby momentarily surmounting his sordid surroundings through self-conscious awareness. He is both a detached observer and an object himself: a poet whose poems are for sale. By contrast, according to Baudelaire, the prostitute must sell her entire being on the market – body and soul – without critical detachment. He cruelly looks upon the prostitute, without attempting to rescue her, as if she were a laboratory rat. Peter Nicholls says that Baudelaire's confrontation with an "absolute other" – here, the prostitute – produces an ironic mask that "obscur[es] the social location of the writer's voice" (4). On the one hand, Baudelaire compares himself equally with the prostitute; on the other hand, he differentiates himself from her by self-consciously criticizing this position. As a poet, his position is different, more disinterested or autonomous, from those who sell goods that have immediate use value: bodies to have sex with, food to eat, tools to make things, clothes to wear. The net effect is to emphasize the speaker's shifting positions and multiple perspectives. He is both a seller of his wares and above it all.

The gendering of this pairing – the masculine poet strolls the city and creates eternal works of art while the woman sells her body while she can – is, to some extent, ameliorated by the frequent posing of the flâneur as a **dandy**. Still strolling through the city, the dandy went a step further than the flâneur and actively sought to startle the crowds around him with outlandish behavior and dress. Note that the dandy was almost always in the mid- to late-nineteenth century a man. The dandy was an eccentric figure, sporting carnations in his jacket lapel and wearing foppish, or frivolous, feminine outfits (see Figure 2.2). Through his dress, the dandy undermined middle-class gender norms. His feminine outlook "became a provocative emblem of the contemporary crisis of values and the much-proclaimed decadence of modern life. Masculinity, it seemed, could no longer be taken for granted as a stable, unitary, and self-evident reality" (Felski 92). The dandy challenged the dominance of the bourgeois world by refusing to accept their normative gender identities for men and women. The dandy figure would, by the later nineteenth century, become "symbolic of border crossings in terms of class lines, gender roles, sexualities, and (later) racial identities" (Miller 183).

Dandies, in Baudelaire's words, stood for

> opposition and revolt; they are all representatives of what is finest in human pride, of that compelling need, alas only too rare today, of combating and destroying triviality. It is from this that the dandies obtain that haughty exclusiveness, provocative in its very coldness.
>
> (1964: 28)

This statement that "the dandy is powerful in style and art" seems to be a contradiction, because art, as we've seen, is marginal to modern society. But art can be, paradoxically, politically powerful in its criticism. This is so for two reasons:

Reason one: art endures. It becomes "timeless" in museums or becomes part of the canon of "great" literature or music. By becoming "great," it transcends the marketplace and everyday life. Baudelaire famously pronounced modern art to be "the ephemeral, the fugitive, the contingent, the half of art whose other half is the eternal and the immutable" (13). Modernist art mimics the marketplace where the commodity comes and goes, always outdone by the next new thing, even as it goes beyond, or transcends, market ephemerality by conveying

Figure 2.2 Giovanni Boldini, *Count Robert de Montesquiou*, 1897 (public domain)

something "eternal" and "immutable" about modernity, something that cannot be pinned down into a simple thing-like meaning or fact. Baudelaire's poet or artist "extract[s] from fashion whatever element it may contain of poetry within history, [and] distill[s] the eternal from the transitory" (12). Modern life may be ugly, with its urbanization, poverty, social conflict and industrialism, but beauty may be distilled from it when the poet or artist seizes it in a flash of recognition and preserves it as art. Of course, a present-day critic, going a step further than Baudelaire, would say that beauty, too, is commodified. By this, our present-day critic means that even artistic beauty, which appears to transcend modern life, is turned into an object to be bought and sold on the market. Art, therefore, is neither eternal nor immutable, but is caught up in the same market forces as any commodity. It only momentarily appears to transcend the market.

Reason two: art can intervene in the "naturalness" of the bourgeoisie. Modernist art and literature, as pioneered by Baudelaire and others, aim to get their audience to think critically about the social status quo and to become *self-conscious* about how we support it on a daily basis. Think about the calculated coldness of the dandy's stance. While this impervious stance detaches from the surrounding social turmoil on the city streets – much like the bourgeoisie's detachment from the social struggles around it, for example, as it traverses the city through carriages, set apart from and above the commoners walking the streets – the dandy is also a spectacle. He is just as much the object of others' (including the working classes) amused stare as he is the one who gazes with pleasure at others, often called a voyeur. As a threshold figure, both critical of others and attracting criticism, he mocks the bourgeoisie even as he, to some extent, is part of them. This form of resistant art has its drawbacks. Baudelaire concludes his remarks on the dandy by calling him "the last spark of heroism amid decadence" (28). The modernist artist is the marginalized, overlooked and even despised hero in a society dedicated to pleasure in the here and now, even if that heedless pursuit of pleasure brings about catastrophe (such as World Wars I and II). Because the dandy is so marginal, it is unlikely that his critical stance will bring large-scale, long-term change. But he, or sometimes she, keeps that hope alive.

We've discussed Baudelaire's poetry in some depth in order to demonstrate one of modernism's most fundamental critical concepts: **autonomy**. Modernism, as a critical and artistic engagement with modernity, begins in the mid-nineteenth century to take form in Baudelaire's refusal to accept the commercialization of art. Baudelaire conceptualized the role of the autonomous artist who no longer could claim to represent the wider public, standing as he/she did on the critical margins of society. This is our first crisis of representation.

Autonomous art generates its own rules and refuses to obey market-driven or conventional demands.

SYMBOLISM

We have already seen in Chapter 1 aspects of the autonomy of art in Eliot's *The Waste Land* and paintings by Picasso and Lam. But given our discussion of Baudelaire, it is evident that the autonomy of art has a history that developed before Eliot wrote or Picasso painted. In particular, symbolist poetry of the 1860s, 1870s and 1880s emphasizes the autonomous artistic expression that Baudelaire pioneered. French symbolist poet Stéphane Mallarmé's "Crisis in Poetry" explains symbolist poetry's turn away from **mimesis**, or the representation of the real world in art and literature: "It is not *description* which can unveil the efficacy and beauty of monuments, or the human face in all their maturity and native state, but rather evocation, *allusion, suggestion*" (Kolocotroni 125, italics in original). Rather than imitate as closely as possible a monument or human face (mimesis), Mallarmé opts for suggestion and indirection to *evoke* a state of being a particular object. For instance, instead of describing in exact terms "the actual and palpable wood of trees," Mallarmé says that the poet should gesture to "the forest's shuddering or the silent scattering of thunder through the foliage" (125). While "shuddering" and "silent scattering of thunder" are quite arbitrary and inaccurate accounts of a forest (how can thunder be silent?), nonetheless, they suggest a state of being or the "spirit" of the forest. Mallarmé says that these tendencies in poetry to use arbitrary phrases both limits poetry and "sets it free" (125).

And, according to the followers of **symbolism**, poetry no longer needed to follow strict metrical and rhyme schemes. Instead, they advocated *vers libre* or **free verse** so that "words may fly, upon subtler wings" (Kolocotroni 135), according to the English critic and poet Arthur Symons (1865–1945), who introduced symbolism to English-speaking audiences. Symbolist poets, including Baudelaire, Mallarmé, Paul Verlaine, Arthur Rimbaud and the Irish poet W. B. Yeats, broke the rules of conventional poetry in order to gesture to the ineffable truths of the soul and to achieve a freedom of expression unbound from everyday life and moral duty. First, they confused the senses (one could taste colors and see perfumes, for example) in order to render their poems dreamlike and irrational. Yeats, for instance, became interested in other worldly realms beyond the senses (especially the enchanted world of Irish faeries or Sidhe) as a symbol for the imagination itself (Wilson 31). Second, symbolism followed music insofar as it sought to intimate or suggest meanings – think of how we listen to music for how it indirectly suggests moods, events or situations. The goal was, in the words of Jean Moréas, "to house the Idea in a meaningful form" (Caws 50). The idea symbolized is abstract: a rose might symbolize love, for example. Thus, we see how the autonomy of ideas and art took precedence over straightforward mimetic communication.

THE REVOLUTION IN LANGUAGE

While the symbolists sought ideal states of being beyond language, other artists and writers engaged more directly with language itself, responding to a philosophical and linguistic **crisis of representation** that first emerged during the Romantic Era (roughly from the late eighteenth to the early nineteenth centuries). The late-eighteenth-century German philosopher Immanuel Kant argued that we never really know the object world because our concepts and conventions of language interfere in grasping the "thing in-itself," objects as they exist independently of the human senses. Kant said that our representations never capture the thing in-itself, but that our transcendental ideals (that come *before* our experience of the world) can direct our actions toward an adequate meaning in the world. According to Kant, we can create a good, ordered society on the basis of our ideas about what that means, even though we are prevented by language from ever having direct access to the objective world. As we'll explore below, by the late nineteenth century, Kant's transcendental ideals (the universality of space, time and European humanism more generally) were coming under fire by scientists, anthropologists, psychologists and philosophers. As a result, modernist writers tended to abandon the belief in transcendental ideals and focused instead on the subjective or particular world of meaning and appearances.

In the literary arts, this turn towards the subjective took the form of an attention to *how* language signifies, rather than *what* language referred to in the world. The attention to the *how* of language is a crisis of representation. For example, when we say "cup," we pronounce the conventional Anglophone sound and word (**signifier**) that alludes to the referential object or **signified** (a real coffee cup sitting on the counter, for instance). If we can never know the cup in-itself, and our word "cup" is purely conventional, then, according to modernist writers, let's stop concerning ourselves with the cup in-itself. Instead, let's focus on altering representational and generic conventions in order to convey the only reality we *can* grasp: our subjective perceptions of the world.

This is not to categorize all modernists as turning inward; however, it's pretty fair to say that they all experimented with representational form and content to more adequately convey modern life, including the *experience* of language and form. They did this by paying attention to the medium: *how* art is conveyed. In general, modernists rejected the assumption that representation and form could entirely capture the real world. Though nineteenth-century writers and artists were never so naïve as to believe their art *could* adequately reflect reality, they didn't alter the codes and conventions of art to the extent that modernism did. Modernists created versions of what Stephen Dedalus in James Joyce's novel *Ulysses* refers to as "a symbol of Irish art. The cracked lookingglass of a servant" (I.147). While many modernists did not identify with servants and enjoyed wealth, often derived from colonies such as Ireland, they nonetheless cracked the looking glass of art to draw our attention to *how* art represents rather than merely *what* it represents. Even Joyce's word "lookingglass" breaks conventions by joining together two separate words. Further, we only see this effect on the written page. We cannot *hear* the space between "looking" and "glass," so we don't hear when it is removed. We can only read it. By breaking the code for writing words properly in the *medium* or the material object of the book, Joyce draws attention to *how* we make meaning through writing. This is a signature gesture of modernism. It is often what makes us feel baffled by modernism because it insists on breaking the rules for art. When a painting, novel or poem presents something counter to our expectations, we easily become frustrated (or, in the early years of modernism, outraged). But it makes us think about what it is we do when we look at art or read a book.

Joyce's wordplay goes a step further in his 1922 novel *Ulysses* – for instance, he coins the term "pornosophical" (15.109) – to create a **portmanteau** word that evokes multiple meanings. "Pornosophical" suggests simultaneously pornography and philosophy, and wields an underhanded dig at philosophy, especially as undertaken by Stephen Dedalus in the Dublin Red Light District. Portmanteau is the French word for "suitcase," and both words, "portmanteau" and "suitcase," are compound nouns that join two words into one meaning (in French, the term means "carry overcoat," and in English, "a case for a suit"), whereas a portmanteau word takes a small portion of each word to create multiple meanings: "brunch" means a bit of breakfast *and* a bit of lunch, at any time between late morning and mid afternoon.

To sum up, in literary modernism the referential function of language – the *what* that is signified – often became less important than *how* a work of literature signifies. Mallarmé put it well when he wrote, "Languages are imperfect because multiple; the supreme language is missing" (Kolocotroni 124). There is no language that signifies the world in perfect correspondence – word to thing – so writers should stop trying to get language *right* and instead embrace their newly found freedom. As we've seen, symbolist poets abandoned conventional meter, rhyme and diction; indeed, Mallarmé says "any poet with an individual technique and ear can build his own instrument" (Kolocotroni 124). Henceforth, language becomes a medium – an instrument – to shape according to the formal requirements, or the technique, and the locational content of the individual poet.

This break from convention in poetic signification corresponded to a transformation in the study of language itself. Linguists Ferdinand de Saussure (1857–1913) and philosopher Ludwig Wittgenstein (1889–1951) rejected, albeit in very different ways, the nineteenth-century philological emphasis in linguistics that compared different languages to see how each has evolved over the centuries. Postulating an ur-language (as in the biblical story of Babel) from which each language family descended, nineteenth-century philologists traced the development of languages in terms of how each language family signifies the world. Instead, Saussure and Wittgenstein avoided the referent, or "real" world, as an object of study. Rather than focus on how languages represent things in the world and change over time, they examined snapshots of language system – static structures of how words signify through their difference from other words within the same language. Saussure, for instance, asserted that, "the linguistic sign unites, not a thing and a name, but a concept and a sound-image" (66). He defined the sound-image as "sensory," or material, what we "recite mentally" without necessarily moving our lips, whereas the concept is more abstract, the idea of a cup rather than the sound-image "cup" (66). Importantly, Saussure stated that this relation of concept and sound-image is arbitrary. That is, there's no real reason we call a cup, a "cup." Indeed, if we were French, we would call that object "tasse"; if Spanish, "taza"; if Japanese, "kappu"; and if Zulu, "inkomishi." Each language system creates meaning by each sign's difference from other signs within that same system. We know that a "cup" is not a "saucer," and a "table" is not a "chair." Instead of comparing languages to one another and showing how some evolved (became more complex) while others (supposedly) did not, this revolution in the study of language argues for the *relativity* of all languages. Saussure refused to place Indo-European languages at the top of the evolutionary tree and study their development over time: "If [the linguist] takes the diachronic [historical] perspective, he no longer observes language but rather a series of events that modify it" (90). For Saussure, a language system should be studied in terms of how it functions within its own parameters in the present time. This view of language sets the stage for analyzing how literary and pictorial language within a single poem, painting, drama or novel is an autonomous system of signification.

In a related vein, Wittgenstein called this static system of signification, "a **language game**." Rather than defining this term, Wittgenstein shows *how* it works in communicating meaning in specific language situations. The term "situation" suggests the spatial and self-contained nature of signification. A language game does not reflect the "real" world outside of language. In fact, Wittgenstein stated, "*The limits of my language* means the limits of my world" (1922, #5.6, italics in original). Permanently in exile in Cambridge, England, the Austrian–Jewish Wittgenstein experienced the limits of meaning imposed by linguistic exile. For Wittgenstein, meaning is not derived from universal or transcendent categories (as Kant argued); rather, it is culturally constructed through language games, such as a child learns when first acquiring language. He writes, "*What belongs to a language* *game is a whole culture*" (qtd. in Perloff 1996: 61, italics in original). The meaning of what lies outside a language game is inaccessible to us. The radical relativism of this conception of meaning entails refraining from judging other cultures as inferior or superior to one's own and by making one's ordinary language strange. Wittgenstein explores the latter by comparing language to a "tool-box": "there is a hammer, pliers, a saw, a screw-driver, a rule, a glue-pot, glue, nails and screws" (1958, #11); and to "an ancient city: a maze of little streets and squares, of old and new houses, and of houses with additions from various periods; and this surrounded by a multitude of new boroughs with straight regular streets and uniform houses" (1958, #18). (See also Perloff 1996: 68.) One can use the tools of language to assemble a new combination of materials, an altered way of seeing the world. In the second example, one can probe the old city center for forgotten angles, meanings and uses of language that can render the newer boroughs more complexly layered and diverse. Each example emphasizes the spatial, static quality of language. One can point to the words on a page as a construction, a deliberate choice to assemble words *just so* in order to highlight new relations among words and ideas. Even silence or empty space plays a role, as we'll see below in the Imagism section.

Wittgenstein emphasizes the crucial role of literary writers in rendering ordinary objects and words unfamiliar. He writes, "language is a labyrinth of paths. You approach from *one* side and know your way about; you approach the same place from another side and no longer know your way about" (1958, #203, italics in original). Every system of signification becomes conventional and over-used unless imaginative practices provide new perspectives on the same terrain. One doesn't need to conquer new territory because there's plenty to make strange right where one already is. Other theorists of art and literature concurred with Wittgenstein's view. In the 1920s, Viktor Shklovsky, a member of the heterogeneous group of critics and linguists commonly called the Russian Formalist School, also wrote that the function of art was to defamiliarize [*ostranenie*] objects and to renew perception. (See Kolocotroni 217–21.)

IMAGISM AND SPATIAL FORM

Wittgenstein's emphasis on language as a "labyrinth of paths" suggests what, in 1945, an early modernist critic, Joseph Frank, called modernism's "**spatial form**." Both writers highlighted *how* language signifies in relation to other words in a spatial, static, nondevelopmental fashion, and this new method drew attention to the crisis of representation: not *what* is being said but *how* it is said mattered most. Drawing on the Romantic philosopher Gotthold Lessing, Frank argued that we should understand modern literature "spatially, in a moment of time, rather than as a sequence" (10). His touchstone for this spatial conception of modernism is imagism, an Anglophone poetic movement that began just before World War I (1914–18). Its chief spokesperson, Ezra Pound, states: "An 'Image' is that which presents an intellectual and emotional complex in an instant of time"; it is this instantaneous complex, Pound says, that provides a "sudden sense of freedom from time limits and space limits" (Caws 356). We see the poem as an image – all at once – in a manner that transcends space and time constraints. Another imagist, F. S. Flint, maintained that a cardinal rule of imagism is "Direct treatment of the 'thing,' whether subjective or objective" (Caws 352). The imagists rejected narrative that conveys change over time in order to attempt to present the immediacy of the poetic image to the reader. Let's examine Pound's famous two-line imagist poem:

"In a Station of the Metro" (1913)

The apparition   of these faces   in the crowd;
Petals   on a wet, black   bough.

(35)

In this poem, the reader's attention is given to the "interplay of relationships within the immobilized time-area" (Frank 17). We see two images superimposed: the first is a ghostly image of a group of faces in the underground Paris subway; the second is an image of flower petals on a dark branch of wood. It is highly significant that Pound adopts the Japanese Haiku form for his Euro-modernist invention. Urban subway transportation melds into nature; the terror of the masses swarming the underground station is overlaid by the serenity of beauty; technology mingles with nature; European mobility freezes into Asiatic stasis. The silent spaces in the second line reinforce the serenity of nature and Japanese aesthetics. The interplay of these two images, according to Frank, is one of "reflexive relations among the units of meaning" that are "juxtaposed independently of the progress of narrative" (17). That is, we see the poem as a total unit of meaning. Within this unity, we shift between the images and see them simultaneously. We look at language from two poetic perspectives, East and West, to make European culture new again.

Some modernist writers became highly adept at building their own signifying systems – or labyrinths – within their works. Joyce's *Ulysses*, for instance, teaches its readers to look for recurrent motifs, characters, locations and objects, within the system of the novel itself, and through intertextual reference to Joyce's previous works: *Dubliners* and *A Portrait of the Artist as a Young Man*. Stephen Dedalus's story begins at age three in the unpublished draft of *Stephen Hero* (published posthumously in 1944) and then in finished form in *A Portrait* (1916). (The fact that the name "Daedalus" refers to the architect in Greek mythology who was hired by King Minos to build a labyrinth in which to confine his wife's son, the Minotaur, a human-bull hybrid, only serves to underscore the use of intertextuality, in this case external to Joyce's oeuvre.) At the conclusion of *A Portrait*, Stephen is a university student who intends to quit school in order to pursue literature in Paris. His story resumes a few years later in *Ulysses* after he returns to Ireland to attend his mother's funeral. We learn that he has not yet become a successful writer. This **intertextuality** (in which Stephen's story begins in one novel and continues in another) gives characters an effect of lifelike continuity, as Stephen's story seems to go on even when Joyce isn't writing about him. Conversely, the system of signifying motifs in *Ulysses* turns the novel inward towards its own autonomous construction, or "spatial form." For example, an anonymous man wearing a Macintosh coat appears in the novel many times, but we never know who he is and he has no plot function; he seems to haunt the novel. When a reporter named Hynes asks Leopold Bloom the name of that man, he mistakenly thinks Macintosh *is* the man's last name and later publishes "M'Intosh" in the list of attendees at Paddy Dignam's funeral that morning (Joyce 16.1261). The effect of this defamiliarizing transformation (whereby a coat becomes a man) is to draw attention to the artifice of language and literature. As Joyce's novel demonstrates, language and literature produce their own rules of signification that are contingent (i.e., they are randomly assigned meaning in relation to other words in the same system) rather than reflective of a nonlinguistic reality. (Though *Ulysses* also refers, in a realistic vein, to actual Dublin street names, people and buildings.) In a wider sense, literature creates imaginary worlds – systems of representation – that do not exist in the "real" world, but that have real-world effects, such as teaching us about modern life and its random occurrences. Frank says of *Ulysses'* spatial form that

> the reader is forced to read *Ulysses* in exactly the same manner as he [sic] reads modern poetry, that is, by continually fitting fragments together and keeping allusions in mind, until, by reflexive reference, he [sic] can link them to their complements.
>
> (20)

These texts are puzzles, in the sense that they require spatial participation on the part of the readers; we have to hold the entire novel in our mind, spatially, in order to fit the pieces together.

While some literary modernists, such as Samuel Beckett, Gertrude Stein and Joyce in his last work, *Finnegans Wake* (1939), focus on autonomous language systems and try to reflect the real world as little as possible, oftentimes modernists transgress the rules of art by representing new content. In this, they enact the crisis of representation in terms of *what* can be said. This new content concerns aspects of everyday life: the overlooked minutiae of the domestic sphere; the newly visible world of advertising (billboards, handbills, storefront windows and street scenes); intimate physical realities (hygiene, sexuality, defecation and other bodily by-products); uncensored thoughts (including mental illness and socially prohibited actions); new kinds of affect (boredom, anxiety, numbness, disassociation); newly visible subjects (manual laborers, bar maids, prostitutes, criminals, drunkards and revolutionaries) and illicit desires (details of adultery, same-sex relations and promiscuity). We will turn next to consider how modernism altered the content of literature. We begin by discussing several highly publicized trials as well as several iconoclastic schools of art and literature that cropped up during the latter half of the nineteenth century. These developments broke the implied agreement between artists and their audiences as to the proper content for art. This was a crisis in the kinds of *content* that could be represented.

THE ARTIST VERSUS THE PUBLIC

The modernist crisis of *what* can be represented in literature began, in part, when two highly publicized obscenity trials took place in

France in 1857. The trial involving Gustave Flaubert's novel of adultery, *Madame Bovary*, was eventually overturned. The court found that

[Flaubert] has committed only the fault of sometimes losing sight of the rules that no self-respecting writer should ever infringe and of forgetting that literature, like art, if it is to achieve the good that it is called upon to produce, must be chaste and pure not only in its form but in its expression.

(qtd. in LaCapra 52)

By contrast, the trial concerning Charles Baudelaire's poetry collection, *Les Fleurs du mal* (*The Flowers of Evil*), succeeded in banning six poems with controversial erotic themes: lesbian desire and heterosexual sadomasochism (Lewis 37). The significance of these trials, Lewis writes, were that they

mark a new form of tension between the arts and the established social order that helped to define the oppositional spirit of modernism. [. . .] Their trials bespoke the broader trials, such as industrial revolution, changing attitudes to sex, and social transformation, through which French society was passing in the process of modernization.

(37)

Baudelaire and Flaubert rejected the moral and didactic *content* of literature that were intended to solidify society by advancing the notion of social duty. Instead, their pursuit of truth in literature set them at odds with middle-class values and conformity. Flaubert's use of irony and ambiguity, for instance, refused to deliver an objective, moral judgment of his character, Emma Bovary, who engages in two extramarital affairs. It was primarily this refusal to obey the conventions of morality in art that most enraged the prosecutor and the public.

One way that the scandalous content of Flaubert's novel escaped censorship was through Flaubert's **realist** style that presents wide-ranging social scenes from an impersonal, impartial, objective point of view. Flaubert's extreme realist style contrasts with the use of a third-person **omniscient narrator** who can convey characters' inner thoughts and who presents the normative viewpoint of society. Nineteenth-century novelists such as Charles Dickens, George Eliot,

Honoré de Balzac and Leo Tolstoy often used this omniscient technique. In contrast, Flaubert in *Madame Bovary* advanced the narrative technique of **free indirect discourse.** When a writer employs this technique, the narrator refrains from presenting the characters from a socially normative point of view; in fact, the line between the narrator and the character blurs. Instead of a direct presentation of the character's thoughts in quotations – Madame Bovary said, "I am in love with Léon" – free indirect discourse involves the narrator paraphrasing a character's thoughts:

> The smooth folds of her dress concealed a tumultuous heart, and her modest lips told nothing of her torment. She was in love with Léon, and she sought solitude because it allowed her to revel in thoughts of him at leisure.

(93)

Is this tumult one that the narrator (or for that matter, the author) shares with Emma? It's impossible to tell. We cannot discern between the narrator's and the character's points of view. Flaubert did not invent the technique of free indirect discourse; novelist Jane Austen (1775–1817) and German poet, novelist and essayist Johann Wolfgang von Goethe (1749–1832) had used it before him. But modernists used the technique in a deliberate – and new – attempt to avoid moralizing about characters' actions. They could now claim that they were merely *representing* details about a sordid character, not condoning their thoughts or actions, and, therefore, they could present new intimate, or scandalous, material. In addition, the blurred line between narrator and character highlights the artificiality of representation and challenges the division between a hypocritical public morality and private thoughts and desires. (See also Lewis 41–42.)

The realist school of the nineteenth century culminated in **naturalism**, a school of realist drama and novels by such authors as Theodore Dreiser, Émile Zola, George Gissing and Henrik Ibsen. Taking objectivity to an extreme, these novels conveyed in great detail the dark side of society, especially the underworld of crime, addiction and prostitution. As if in a scientific laboratory, these novelists recorded social details without flinching from their brutality. Sometimes their writing sparked social reform. For example, though not a strictly naturalist novel, Joseph Conrad's *Heart of Darkness* (1899) exposed the atrocities of King Leopold II of Belgium's rule in the Congo, in which Africans who refused to work on rubber plantations had their hands hacked off. His novel aided in reforming this particularly brutal colonial regime.

The reformist and scandal-mongering zeal of naturalism led to further battles between public morality and modernist writers over the content of their works. These trials included the prosecution of French novelist Émile Zola for libel. Zola's open letter, "J'accuse," published on January 13, 1898, in the newspaper *L'Aurore*, defended the cause of Alfred Dreyfus, a Jewish captain in the French Army who had been falsely convicted of treason. "L'affair Dreyfus" split the country between defenders and opponents of Dreyfus's innocence. It also brought into the spotlight of public debate the anti-Semitism pervading the military, clergy, and other powerful factions in the country. In 1898, Zola was convicted of libel for his criticism of the state and military justice system. He was exiled to London for a year, after which his case was reopened and the charges dropped. Zola's courage in taking a public stand against state authorities secured the image of the artist as a rebel against the state and a defender of the rights of minorities and other marginal persons.

In England, many sensational trials against late-Victorian-era and modernist authors, and their controversial literature, took place. The most notorious of these was the "Wilde Trial" in which the essayist, novelist and playwright Oscar Wilde (1854–1900), the flamboyant Irishman and dandy who had conquered literary and high society in London, was successfully tried for sodomy (a crime in England and Wales until 1967) and sentenced to two years of hard labor in prison. The trial and prison sentence effectively killed him; he died three years after his release from jail, in exile in Paris, stripped of his reputation, wealth and family.

While the trials of Émile Zola and Oscar Wilde were not strictly literary or modernist, they set the stage for many acts of literary censorship in England, the US, South Africa and elsewhere that occurred in the early part of the twentieth century. Joyce's *Dubliners* and *Ulysses* were banned in England, the US and Ireland. *Dubliners* eventually saw publication in England, after a delay of nine years. *Ulysses*, however, could only be legally purchased in Paris when it was first published in 1922. Pirated copies of the novel were smuggled into the Anglophone world until a 1933 trial in the US lifted the ban.

The UK followed suit in 1936, and Ireland in 1960. Radclyffe Hall's *The Well of Loneliness* (1928) was censored because it portrayed Stephen Gordon as an "invert" (a sexological term for a man trapped in a woman's body) who falls in love with another woman. D. H. Lawrence's *Lady Chatterley's Lover* (1928) was banned in England until 1960. This novel portrayed in graphic, orgasmic terms an extramarital love affair between the upper-class Lady Chatterley and her groundskeeper, Mellors, while her husband, rendered paralytic and impotent by World War I, languishes in a wheelchair. Called by one reviewer "A Landmark in Evil," Lawrence's novel was condemned for "prostituting art to pornography" (Lawrence, xxi). On stage, censorship was even stricter, and the plays by Norwegian Henrik Ibsen (1828–1906) were either rewritten to smooth over the portrayal of the war between the sexes or banned outright. The Lord Chamberlain's Office in London censored Ibsen's *Ghosts* (1891), forbidding it to be performed before the public because of its portrayal of syphilis and incestuous desire. In South Africa, William Plomer, Laurens Van der Post and Roy Campbell fled their country after beginning a modernist magazine *Voorslag* (Afrikaans for "whiplash") in 1927 that pilloried South Africa's provincial and racist society. In sum, censorship was common wherever controversial modernist literature circulated.

THE AVANT-GARDE

The **avant-garde** took the attack on artistic institutions and conventions (both *how* and *what* are represented) to extreme proportions. We still refer to modernism when we use the term "avant-garde," but avant-gardism is modernism carried to a highly oppositional and often populist extreme. Peter Bürger has influentially argued that, above all, the avant-garde sought to integrate art with life by attacking the institution of art itself (art schools and salons, publishers and publics). These attacks on museums and salons by the avant-garde failed because they are now part of the history of the same institutions they attacked. For example, Duchamp's urinal ("Fountain," 1917) scandalized the art world because it is not art at all, only a "found object" associated with bodily waste. To add to the insult, Duchamp signed the so-called sculpture "R. Mutt." Now, replicas of "Fountain" (the original, if one can call it that, was lost) are proudly displayed in the San Francisco Museum of Modern Art and the British Tate Modern as representing a vital episode in the history of art. Despite its failure to demolish the institution of art, the avant-garde succeeded in transforming how art is made. Rather than relying on conventional arbiters of cultural value, the avant-garde took art directly to the populace in the streets, cafés, cinemas and theaters.

Rooted in French military language, the term "avant-garde" was first used by radical groups during the French Revolution to describe a revolutionary political stance intended to reach past military circles towards a broader audience of "patriots" (Calinescu 1987: 100–11). After the aborted European revolutions in 1848, the term came to refer to artists and writers who sought to change society and politics through art rather than through direct political channels. The term itself evokes the image of small, elite shock troupes sent ahead of the larger body of soldiers to attack the enemy, a metaphor that suggests that avant-garde artists and writers rejected dominant middle-class conventions and sensibility, and allied themselves with the margins instead. Not that this was always the case. The avant-garde notoriously defied almost every expectation and every definition.

In an early example of this oppositional spirit, painter Gustave Courbet (1819–77) was excluded from official art exhibitions because of his preference for painting everyday life in the present moment, as opposed to classical subjects from ancient Greece and Rome and mythological Romantic subjects. He rejected the label of "realism," but he also used the term, stating in the "Realist **Manifesto**" that "Labels have never, in any age, given a very accurate idea of things; if it were otherwise, the works would be superfluous" (Kolocotroni 169). Hence, we need to approach the notion of avant-garde "schools" of art and literature with a note of caution. The actual works of art are usually much more complex and aren't neatly slotted into any one category, realist or otherwise. For instance, T. J. Clark notes that "flatness" in avant-garde art, a concern with the two dimensions of the canvas and not with the three dimensions of representation, which traditional Renaissance perspective allowed, carried "complex and compatible values [. . .] which necessarily derived from elsewhere than art" (13). The meaning of "flatness" could include an affiliation of the artist with the working class in which painting became

> plain, workmanlike, and emphatic [. . .] painting was henceforth honest manual labour. [. . .] Or flatness could signify modernity with the surface

meant to conjure up the two dimensions of posters, labels, fashion
prints, and photographs.

(13)

Or the flatness could be borrowed as part of *Japonisme*, a craze
for Japanese art and aesthetics, especially the flat simplicity of *ukiyo-e*
woodblock prints. Finally, Clark reminds us, the flatness might
"represent the simple fact of Art, from which other meanings
were excluded" (13). In sum, avant-garde art could represent many
things – the seedy working-class and down-and-outs, the exotic, the
mass-produced object, or autonomy – though it usually defined itself
against conventional content conveyed in a traditional manner. The
irony of avant-garde art is that rather than changing the institution
of art, its iconoclasm eventually ensured its welcome within those
same institutions.

Let us next examine a few more precursors to modernist avant-
gardes. The purpose of doing so is to explain some of the prevailing
concepts underlying modernist art movements. An understanding
of these concepts will allow you to contextualize and therefore
better understand the often strange and baffling modernist artworks and literary texts. Symbolism, which we've already discussed,
altered poetic convention and set the stage for new kinds of literary experimentation. In the last decades of the nineteenth century,
a school of art known as **aestheticism** refused the idealism of
symbolist practices and held that art had no moral values whatso-
ever, taking Flaubert's strategy a step further. For example, Oscar
Wilde's preface to his novel *The Picture of Dorian Gray* (1891) pro-
vocatively states that, "No artist has ethical sympathies" and that
"all art is useless" (18). The novel details Dorian's gradual demise as
he becomes corrupt, debauched by sex and drugs and even murder,
while in appearance, he remains a beautiful and innocent-looking
youth. His portrait, meanwhile, stashed away in a locked attic room,
reflects the gradual degradation of his moral character: in the end,
it pictures a Dorian who is "cunning," "wrinkled," "loathsome"
and with blood on his hands (232). When Dorian puts a knife
through the picture, the images switch and Dorian, the beautiful
aesthete, becomes a hideous, aged monster lying dead on the floor.
This shocking story (one that was also threatened with censorship)
demonstrates indifference to social mores and even to transcendent

artistic values. Instead, it embraces ugliness and degeneration as part of art.

The concern with degeneration and decline was rampant in Europe around the turn of the twentieth century, a period often referred to as the *fin-de-siècle*. Many thinkers who were influenced by Charles Darwin's *On the Origin of Species* (1859) believed that humanity's ordered progress depended upon hard work, discipline and moral duty. In this way, humanity might discover the natural laws that determine its survival as a species. The sense that European artists, writers and the pleasure-seeking urban crowds were turning away from these values led some alarmists to warn of decline and degeneration. For many, modernization raised fears of anarchy and chaos as increased mobility, leisure time and individuality tore apart the social fabric. These fears were also due to the closing of the colonial frontier: without the dangers and hardships of conquering new lands and peoples, Europeans, it was believed, were becoming lax, effeminate and diseased. While racial science (the bogus study of how the European "race" was the pinnacle of civilization) justified colonization, it also brought its classifying rubrics to bear on Europe itself. Racial science linked moral traits to physical attributes and graphed them along an evolutionary scale of development. Racial scientists believed that they could determine a person's moral character and evolutionary development on the basis of how he/she looked: the shape of the skull (phrenology), the expression on the face, posture, etc., determined one's place on the scale of evolution. For instance, altruism was one of the most civilized traits, signaled by one's classical (i.e., beautiful) features; and criminality was a degenerate trait, signaled by one's ape-like or primitive features.

The Hungarian-Jewish journalist and writer Max Nordau's 1892 polemic *Degeneration* was aimed at diagnosing the moral ills of society, a diagnosis that included modernist artists. Nordau's diatribe against modernist artists runs as follows:

> They fritter away their life in solitary, unprofitable, [ae]sthetic debauch, and all that their organs, which are in full regression, are still good for is enervating enjoyment. Like bats in old towers, they are niched in the proud monument of civilization, which they have found ready-made, but they themselves can construct nothing more, nor prevent any deterioration. They live, like parasites, on labour which past generations have

accumulated for them; and when the heritage is once consumed, they
are condemned to die of hunger.

(540)

Nordau's description of modern artists prefigures Bram Stoker's classic horror story *Dracula* (1897), in which Count Dracula drinks the
lifeblood of healthy, morally upright English men and women. By
manipulating signs and perceptions rather than producing anything
"useful," artists underscored how consumer capitalism and growing
urbanization disrupted local communities and traditional meanings.
Money, markets, faster transportation, consumer-driven commodities
and new writing technologies intervened in direct relations between
people. Artists and writers, in particular, seemingly made passive
consumption the center of their lives. This stereotype was confirmed
in Joris-Karl Huysmans's novel *À Rebours* [Against Nature, 1884],
in which the main character Duc Jean Floressas des Esseintes, the
degenerate last of his aristocratic line, enjoys an extreme refinement
of sensibility that eventually results in his demise. Living alone, away
from society, surrounded by exotic and esoteric *objets d'art*, including
a living tortoise whose shell is encrusted with jewels, des Esseintes
discusses (in free indirect discourse) his choice of colors for his artificial interior:

> leaving out of account the majority of men, whose coarse retinas perceive
> neither the cadences peculiar to different colours nor the mysterious
> charm of their gradation; leaving out also those bourgeois optics that
> are insensible to the pomp and glory of the clear, bright colours; and
> considering only those people with delicate eyes that have undergone the
> education of libraries and art-galleries, it seemed to him an undeniable
> fact that anyone who dreams of the ideal, prefers illusion to reality, and
> calls for veils to clothe the naked truth, is almost certain to appreciate
> the soothing caress of blue and its cognates, such as mauve, lilac, and
> pearl grey, always provided they retain their delicacy and do not pass the
> point where they change their personalities and turn into pure violets
> and stark greys.

(29)

This passage, all one sentence, meanders through a patina of colors,
playing with hues and enjoying the impressions of color upon the

refined senses (as in impressionist painting, a precursor to the modernist school of post-impressionism, of which cubism is part). What is important is *how* one perceives colors and their effect on one's sensibility, because it marks one's cultural distinction. In drawing attention to effete young men, like Des Esseintes, who was modeled after a real person, Robert, Comte de Montesquiou-Fezensac (see Figure 2.2), Nordau's text provoked anxieties about the strength of European nation-states. If the intelligentsia of a nation were this debauched, how could the nation successfully defend itself? This anxiety was, in some ways, well placed. As we'll discuss in Chapter 3, the closing of the colonial frontier signaled an impending crisis in which European nations would fight to the finish (in World Wars I and II) over the world's finite resources.

Just prior to World War I, modernist artists and writers switched tactics. While the avant-garde writers and artists of the 1890s had posed as aesthetes and decadents, ensconced in claustrophobic over-decorated interiors, by 1909, the avant-garde began actively to intervene in public debates about the future of their nations. (As was the case with Italian futurism and English vorticism, though in fact these avant-garde groups were thoroughly cosmopolitan or multinational. Their members spoke several languages and came from nations across Europe and North America, though rhetorically – to gain the public's attention – they called for a strong single nation, either Italy or England.) The action-oriented manifestos of the Italian futurists, for example, advocated "scorn for women" and "the love of danger." Shockingly, they propounded violence to produce a new society of supermen by social cleansing of the "unfit": we "glorify war – the world's only hygiene" (Kolocotroni 251). They used mass-movement propaganda techniques – such as dropping leaflets from bell towers and automobiles – to deliver their message to large crowds. In advocating aggressive masculinity, heroism, and Italy's imperialist invasion of Libya and involvement in World War I, they turned the tables on decadent artists and entered the fray of history.

Marjorie Perloff calls this pre-war, or avant-guerre, period of the avant-garde "the futurist moment," a remarkable "arena of agitation" that brought together innovative aesthetic practices, radical politics and popular culture (1986: xvii). We can see the effects of such boundary-breaking transformation of an entire way of life in Mikhail Larionov and Natalya Goncharova's "Rayonist Manifesto"

(1913): "We exclaim: the whole brilliant style of modern times – our trousers, jackets, shoes, trolleys, cars, airplanes, railways, grandiose steamships – is fascinating, is a great epoch" (qtd. in Perloff 1986: xvii; see also Caws 242). The pre-war avant-garde typically sought to synthesize multiple aspects of modern experience, including fashion and interior design. Combining poetry, painting, train travel and publicity event, Blaise Cendrars and painter Sonia Delaunay collaborated to produce *La Prose du Trans-sibérien* (1913), subtitled "poems, simultaneous colors in an edition attaining the height of the Eiffel Tower: 150 copies numbered and signed" (Perloff 1986: 3). Each copy was seven feet long, divided into two columns; the left column was a painting, featuring semi-abstract forms in bright primary colors, and the right column was Cendrars' poem, in various typefaces and broken by odd-shaped planes of mainly pastel colors, prefaced with a Michelin railway map of the trans-Siberian journey from Moscow to the Sea of Japan (Perloff 1986: 3). Attached from end to end, the 150 copies were as tall as the Eiffel Tower. The circulation of such an outsize, multimedia production drew attention to the concept of **simultaneity** and **spatial form** that we've discussed above and in Chapter 1. Perloff describes the effect of Cendrars and Delauney's project:

> During the fall of 1913, the Cendrars-Delaunay *Prose du Transsibérien* was exhibited in Paris (the annual Salon D'Automne), Berlin (the Herbst Salon), London, New York, Moscow, and St. Petersburg. It became not only a poem but an event, a happening. In St. Petersburg, the poet-painter Victor Smirnoff gave an accompanying lecture called "Simultaneous Contrasts and Plastic Poetry." At the *Montjoie!* exposition in Paris on 24 February 1914, Mme Lucy Wilhelm stood on a chair so as to recite the gigantic poem, which was hung on the wall. Beginning at ceiling level, she gradually bent her knees and finally sat down on the chair to read the conclusion.
>
> (1986: 11)

Art, in this avant-garde setting, became a live event. It was collective and performed. No longer frozen in a museum setting, or reproduced over generations in order to emulate classical and Renaissance masters, art was alive and changed each time it was performed before a live audience. Experimental music, theater, film and dance became the order of the day. In pre-war Paris, Igor Stravinsky's *Le Sacré du Printemps* (*The Rite of Spring*) featured avant-garde music and choreography by Sergei Diaghilev and the *Ballets Russes* (*Russian Ballet*). The dancing and music attempted to portray an ancient pagan ritual and featured rhythmic repetition, uneven meter and tonal dissonance. The ballet climaxes when a young girl is chosen as a sacrificial victim and dances herself to death. The performance was highly controversial when first staged. Other dancers, such as Loïe Fuller (1862–1928) and Isadora Duncan (1877–1927), revolutionized this art by abandoning the corset and tight-fitting costumes and performing, instead, "natural" flowing dance. Another performer, Josephine Baker (1906–75), rose from an African-American ghetto in St. Louis to the vaudeville stage (a popular form of comic variety acts) and then to worldwide fame for her "danse sauvage" (wild dance) in Paris. Wearing a risqué costume largely composed of bananas, Baker gyrated to a primitivist fantasy of African female sexuality for white theater-going audiences. Most other times, however, she stylized racial difference as preeminently modern.

The avant-garde gesture of breaking boundaries continued during and after World War I. As we've seen above, in 1917, Marcel Duchamp, associated for a time with the dada movement, an anarchic and nihilist post-war avant-garde, placed an upside-down urinal in an art museum, signed it "R. Mutt," and called the piece "Fountain." By placing a "ready-made," mass-produced object in an art museum, Duchamp turned the entire event into a joke on everyone: spectators, artists, the museum, and the institution of art that produces what counts as "high" art. Why is great art only that which hangs in museums? In essence, avant-garde modernism is iconoclastic: it breaks the conventions of the institutions of art, genres and media. Poetry becomes more like prose; novels like poetry; painters collage newspaper headlines and found materials into their works; and new media – film (1895), phonograph, which could record and play sounds (1877), and typewriter (1873) – transfer to literature greater autonomy.

Lastly, surrealism arose from the ashes of dada despair in 1919. Eager to break out of a stifling tradition of French culture and literature that many believed had led to the folly of the First World War, André Breton and Philippe Soupault began the movement by promoting automatic writing in *Les champs magnétiques* (the magnetic fields). Automatic writing was, according to Breton, "born of the discovery of the productive power of the phrases that come to mind as one is falling asleep" (Chénieux-Gendron 33). Integrating the psychoanalytic "discovery" of the unconscious (see below), surrealism sought to free the creative imagination from the repressive confines of bourgeois propriety by exploring the uncensored unconscious that spoke to artists while dreaming or in other kinds of hypnotic trance states. They brought the erotic, the mystical and the irrational to their painting, sculpture and writing, and they were influenced by symbolist poetry in its indirection of meaning. The political affiliations of surrealism were constantly shifting: first aligning with communism, then breaking from organized politics. Wayward members were excommunicated. In addition, the movement was internationally focused and drew upon non-Western alternatives to European culture. Inspired by cubism, including Picasso's *Les Demoiselles*, they were drawn to ethnographic investigations and, as James Clifford puts it, used "disturbing syncretisms" (131) to question European values and prejudices. Juxtaposing, as surrealist Marcel Griaule puts in the journal *Documents*, "the *beautiful* and the *ugly*, in the European sense of these absurd words," the surrealists "provided a *style* of scientifically validated cultural leveling" (Clifford 131). These fragments of cultures from around the world contested notions of historical continuity and organic structure (that grows up over centuries). These two beliefs help to justify racial hierarchies because they argue that differences between groups have evolved over millennia and cannot change.

Because surrealism was interested in non-European cultures and belief systems, many writers and artists from non-Western parts of the world found a way to join with it. Its affiliates included painter Frida Kahlo (Mexico), Aimé and Suzanne Césaire (Martinique), Léopold Sédar Senghor (Senegal) and Salvador Dalí (Catalonia). Sur-realism (beyond realism) was adapted to express the indigenous marvelous, a kind of writing that, through the novel form, was popularized as "magic realism" in the later twentieth century. Magic realist writers include Alejo Carpentier (Cuba), an early proponent of *real maravilloso* or "real marvelous," Gabriel García Márquez (Colombia), Salman Rushdie (India/Pakistan), Arundhati Roy (India), Dambudzo Marechera (Zimbabwe) and Ben Okri (Nigeria).

NEW MEDIA

The new media developments at the turn of the twentieth century revolutionized the production, dissemination and reception of artistic production in society, and fundamentally transformed both *what* and *how* artistic representation occurred. These developments include cheaper print and image reproduction technologies, the commercial typewriter (invented in 1873), the telephone (1876), the phonograph and microphone (1877, 1878), film (1895) and the radio or wireless (1896), among others (Goody 2). It is very likely, for instance, that the new media played a role in the surrealist discovery of automatic writing, because these new technologies drew attention to *how*, rather than *what*, we write and read. Friedrich Kittler shows how the new media isolated each of the senses: "The historical synchronicity of cinema, phonography, and typewriting separated optical, acoustic, and written data flows, thereby rendering them autonomous" (14). In effect, human sensory capacities were separated from one another and replaced by machines. Scientists could now study via machines the separate human senses of sight and hearing. The camera could capture only the visual, while the tape recorder reproduced only sounds. In the same vein, writing is depersonalized. While before the typewriter, writing had flowed from one's hand in a cursive stream, now each letter on the typewriter was a material block that could be rearranged. Gertrude Stein, in "Composition as Explanation" (1926), put it thus: "No one thinks these things when they are making when they are creating what is the composition, naturally no one thinks, that is no one formulates until what is to be formulated has been made" (Kolocotroni 424). To paraphrase Stein, the writing writes the author. We know what we think after we have written, not before. Nietzsche, one of the first philosophers to use a typewriter, also said as much: "Our writing tools are also working our thoughts" (qtd. in Kittler xxix). Of course, the recursive effect of writing and other media do not entirely determine what a person thinks. The particular location and history from which one writes, along with one's creative and intellectual abilities, determine the rest. But the net result – that modernist literature became just one of many sensory media and just one kind of memory – had a decentering effect on human subjectivity. We are part of a network of media rather than the fount from which all truth flows.

These networks were becoming global: telegraph cables spanned the Atlantic and beyond, and photography (later film and radio) as well as ethnographic studies and collections ensured that people did not even need to travel to encounter other cultures. Modernists, as a result of new media, conveyed in their art this new ability to store and transmit information across vast geographical distances. What the New Critics perceived to be the difficulty, simultaneity and dense allusiveness of modernist writing can be understood as an influence of radio and telegraphy on literary form. For instance, in Eliot's *The Waste Land*, many voices drift into and out of the poem, without context. It is as though we are hearing a radio receiver that picks up many broadcasts at once (Kalliney 122). The gramophone, too, plays an important part in the proliferation of disembodied voices in the poem.

Conversely, Ezra Pound's imagist poem, "In a Station of the Metro," discussed above, uses new media to reduce complexity. It removes a busy scene in a Paris subway station from the flux of time through reference to visual technology. The brevity of the poem has long been likened to a photograph, a single image at an instant of time. The photographic image of faces, frozen in time, for Daniel Tiffany, "is an apparition, a phantom, because it represents the return of a lost or dead object, a moment when the poet is *haunted* by reality. The spectral image presents life imaged as death, a living death" (qtd. in Kalliney 136). Photography mummifies the living, presenting them as a *memento mori*, a remembrance of the dead. The faces in the metro station, however, are superimposed onto another image: that of flower petals on a dark, wet tree branch. The second image, as Christopher Bush suggests, conveys an affinity between photography and Pound's fascination with the Chinese "ideograph," a kind of writing that signifies by means of a visual likeness: the ideograph, or sign, for the setting sun looks like a sun setting. To put this in Saussure's terms, the ideograph's signifier and signified are not arbitrary. Because the reader does not need to speak the Chinese language to see the meaning, Pound hoped that it might form a universal language (Pound was wrong about this). For Pound, China is the scene of "universal visuality" (Bush 69), a way in which to "somehow write the world" (Kalliney 137). Other modernists sought a universal language in Esperanto (a simplified language one could learn easily that was largely composed of European words), silent film, dance and other media to bring the world into a single field of communication, without the distortion and difference that translation brings.

While the new media often inspired innovation in the arts, some artists felt threatened by the new technologies. These media devices, they said, could make art itself redundant. The exponential growth of information and the irrelevant details and ambient noise that the new media recorded and stored without discernment short-circuited human reason and expression by flooding the perceptual field with senseless noise and visual and verbal overload (North 9–11; see also Kalliney 123). In part, the mechanization of society and cultural expression – an expression governed by machines and generating immediate, unreasoned pleasure in its audience – influenced the crisis of reason.

CRISIS OF REASON

The emphasis on irrationality – blind impulses rather than enlightened reason – was referred to more broadly as the **crisis of reason**. Four thinkers, in particular, shaped this crisis and profoundly influenced the concepts behind modernist thought and its representational practices: Charles Darwin, Karl Marx, Sigmund Freud and Friedrich Nietzsche. They offered a *surface-depth* model of human subjectivity: these thinkers, in very different ways, held that civilized behavior is a recently acquired surface that masks a much deeper set of physiological impulses that propelled humans to engage in violence, irrationality and other forms of antisocial behavior. They also rejected the notion of Divine Order: the belief that a Supreme Being is in charge of the universe, and the teleological belief that humanity is becoming ever more civilized. First, Darwin's theory of evolution held that variations among species occurred through random chance, and that human reason was merely a tool for survival. This theory of biological transformation divorced science from religion (as it disproved creationism, the belief that the world was created by God in seven days) and from teleology (the belief that humanity was progressively becoming more civilized and rational). Evolution suggested that humans could be extremely brutal and destructive as they fought for survival over limited resources.

Second, Karl Marx formulated a concept of mediation between man and nature that he called a "metabolic interaction" (Marx 283).

As humans work to change nature into something that they can use, they act on nature and nature acts on them. Alfred Schmidt glosses this metabolic process as follows: "men incorporate their own essential forces into natural objects [and] natural things gain a new social quality as use-values. . . . [Hence] nature is humanized while men are naturalized" (qtd. in Smith 34). Marx refused philosophical duality, whereby humans objectify nature and merely consume it or shape it according to their will. Instead, he argued that the production process – the circulation of forces and things including raw material, capital, money and labor – controls human actions rather than vice versa (Marx 167–68). His emphasis on the shared material conditions of human society and nature led him to adapt language in which human ideas and social facades hide a deeper materialist meaning. Marx's language frequently relies on a surface/depth model that promises to reveal "the mysterious character of the commodity-form," that is, how the money-form "conceals the social character of private labour" (164, 168), which is located in the "hidden abode of production" (279). This model, whereby latent or hidden meanings (the exploitative reality of wage labor) are masked by surface phenomenon, like the purchase of an item by means of money, links him to the last two thinkers who strongly influenced the crisis of reason: Sigmund Freud (1856–1939) and Friedrich Nietzsche (1844–1900).

Sigmund Freud, the inventor of psychoanalysis, postulated that humans are driven less by reason (what he called the "superego") than by unconscious, instinctual drives (the "id"). Moreover, we have no access to our unconscious. It speaks to us indirectly through dream images, slips of the tongues, hysterical symptoms (such as aphasia or loss of speech), phobias (such as the irrational fear of water, germs, snakes, crowds, flying, etc.) and neurosis (such as compulsive cleaning or eating, addictions, insomnia, etc.). The unconscious contains latent or hidden meanings that a psychoanalyst tries, through therapeutic sessions, to make manifest or conscious by interpreting these symptoms for the patient. Importantly for the development of modernism, Freud argued that the language of the unconscious is both condensed and displaced. **Condensation** refers to the multiple meanings of dream language: riddles, puns and borrowings from other languages. Condensation points to the unstable and polysemantic nature of language – how it contains multiple meanings that elude intentionality. That is, we might say one thing and mean another, or we might be interpreted by an interlocutor in a manner we don't intend. Freud warns that a dream always has more meanings than we know, so that the work of interpretation never ends. **Displacement** in dream language refers to the notion that dreams are imaginary, external to rational systems, empty of history or logical connection; its images are arbitrarily juxtaposed. In addition to the rebus (visual puzzle) form of dream-language, the waking consciousness censors or distorts its recollection of the dream from its latent to its manifest content. The conflict between unconscious dream-thoughts and censoring dream-work (recollecting one's dreams) creates an almost unreadable communication. Freud says, "the whole mass of these dream-thoughts are broken into fragments and jammed together" (1965: 347). Narrative or temporal sequence is lost, and we get the effect of **simultaneity** and **spatial form**. In essence, dream-language disregards logical subordination (causality) and continuous time and space. Instead, it stands outside history and social forms, offering what Freud saw as a mythic glimpse at humankind's bestial, atavistic core.

Finally, the German philosopher Nietzsche, in a posthumously published fragment called "On Truth and Lie in an Extra-Moral Sense," does not say that truth is hidden so much as he says that we forget that Truth is an illusion. The real truth for Nietzsche is that from the perspective of the vast, uncaring universe: humanity is no more important or permanent than a mosquito. Like the buzzing mosquito, all we can do is speak. And for Nietzsche, language is merely "the image of a nerve stimulus in sounds" (45). Words are a biological phenomenon, untethered to a metaphysical Truth, "the thing in itself," or reality beyond appearances. Anticipating the revolutionary linguistic work of Saussure, Nietzsche argues that language is not a reflection of the external world, but instead is a closed system of signs that only indicate their difference from one another. For Nietzsche, words are simply metaphors, a translation of one unlike thing or idea into another unlike thing or idea. We never get to Truth. He sums up: "truths are illusions about which one has forgotten that this is what they are; metaphors which are worn out and without sensuous power; coins which have lost their pictures and now matter only as metal, no longer as coins" (47). Permanent, metaphysical truth is a myth; all we can do is create new illusions. Modernist writers accepted Nietzsche's challenge to enliven language – to make us aware of the illusion, and indeed the impossibility that language conveys Truth – by creating new metaphors and images and by drawing attention to the materiality of language (language as a material *thing* like a coin that can be dulled through frequent use, especially as it is exchanged for money on the market, or brightened by means of new metaphors). By treating language and pictorial images as an autonomous system (a thing or a *what*, something that cannot communicate Truth), modernism underscores how representation is only an illusion of reality. Here is an example from Joseph Conrad's *Heart of Darkness* (1899): "They were called criminals, and the outraged law, like the bursting shells, had come to them, an insoluble mystery from the sea" (18). The term "criminals," replete with the full backing of the European state and legal system behind it, is foisted upon West Africans, like "bursting shells," violent but evanescent and ineffectual. The law is "an insoluble mystery" to Africans unfamiliar with European customs and beliefs; hence, in Africa, the law is only an *illusion* of reality perpetuated by the European minority, and it is therefore meaningless (except for the horrific violence it occasions) to the West Africans.

MODERN TIMES

The crisis of reason is important because it facilitated ways in which modernist artists and writers could rebel against the standardization of time-space enabled by advances in technology. Chief among these were Kantian ideas of universal time and space that were actively being imposed upon the world. In 1884, the Prime Meridian Conference in Washington, DC gathered together representatives of twenty-five countries in order to establish the Observatory in Greenwich, England, as the zero meridian. They decided upon the exact length of day, divided the globe into twenty-four time zones precisely one hour apart, and determined the beginning of the universal day (Kern 12). The prime reason for establishing a uniform time zone upon the world's surface was to coordinate telegraph transmission and railway travel. France, resistant to the idea of a zero meridian located on English soil, took a belated lead in universal standardization by hosting the International Conference on Time in 1912 in order to establish a "uniform method of determining and maintaining accurate time signals and transmitting them around the world" (Kern 13). The procedure was as follows:

> The observatory at Paris would take astronomical readings and send them to the Eiffel Tower, which would relay them to eight stations spaced over the globe. [. . .] The independence of local times began to collapse once the framework of a global electronic network was established.
>
> (Kern 14)

While the English could claim "ground zero" of global time zones at the Greenwich Observatory, the French could now proudly say that official time, "minute zero," was in France.

This electronic temporal grid, along with the mapping of the globe along coordinates of latitude and longitude, functioned to highlight the authoritarian pressures of modernization. Industrialization and the rise of wage labor demanded that all persons obey the rule of time. Silent films by Fritz Lang [*Metropolis* (1927)] and Charlie Chaplin [*Modern Times* (1936)] feature parodies of workers literally swallowed by cogs in machines and nailed to the hands of giant clocks (see Figure 2.3). They portrayed the subjection of human

Figure 2.3 Film still, *Metropolis*, 1927 (public domain)

affective and biological rhythms to the tyranny of ten-hour work-days in which repetitive assembly-line production was carried out under unforgiving electric lighting. It was highly appropriate, then, that in Joseph Conrad's *The Secret Agent* (1907), a Russian anarchist's assignment is to blow up the Greenwich Observatory. In fact, many modernists reacted against the abstract temporal grid by exploring the internal rhythms of personal time and especially the fact that, for human consciousness, time doesn't simply move forward.

One famous example of subjective or internal time occurs in Marcel Proust's *À la Recherche du Temps Perdue* (*In Search of Lost Time*) (1913–27). This multivolume novel began when Proust's semi-autobiographical narrator, Marcel, bites into a petite madeleine (a French cookie) and its taste suddenly awakens a childhood memory involving a similar cookie. Proust called this trigger **mémoire involuntaire** (involuntary memory), the belief that the past is stored in the body – in this case, in sensory data of taste and smell – and can be triggered by a similar prompt in the present. The philosopher Henri Bergson (1859–1941) calls this interpenetration of past and present "duration." He writes,

> My memory is there [in the present], which conveys something of the past into the present. My mental state, as it advances on the road of time, is continually swelling with the duration which it accumulates: it goes on increasing – rolling upon itself, as a snowball on the snow.
>
> (4)

Human time, for Bergson, combines past with present and always grows. We never lose our past experiences; they are lodged somewhere in our bodies and move with us into the future. If one accepts Bergson's philosophy, he promises, one "will see the material world melt back into a simple flux, a continuity of flowing, a becoming" (401).

Psychologist and philosopher William James (1842–1910) also saw human consciousness as a fluid interface between past and present, though James, unlike Bergson, distinguished between recent memories that are part of the present and distant memories that are recollected as separate from the present moment. In 1890, James made popular his term **stream of consciousness** to describe the interconnection of mental events:

> Consciousness, then, does not appear to itself chopped up in bits. Such words as "chain" or "train" do not describe it fitly. . . . It is nothing

jointed; it flows. A "river" or a "stream" are the metaphors by which it is most naturally described. *In talking of it hereafter, let us call it the stream of thought, of consciousness, or of subjective life.*

(239, italics in original)

Consciousness, or awareness, in both Bergson's and James's treatment, can never be divided up into past and present. Rather, past and present are synthesized (as one makes use of past experience to understand the present) and ever changing. Human interior time cannot be quantified like geographical time zones and official clocks.

James's "stream of consciousness" became widely used by modernist writers as a technique that could be modified for presenting **interior monologue** (for full-on stream of consciousness narration, see Chapter 4). Unlike free indirect discourse, the narrator appears to be completely absent in this form. We seem to be inside a character's mind as he/she freely associates whatever memories, ideas or perceptions flow through their consciousness. In Virginia Woolf's *Mrs. Dalloway* (1925), for example, Clarissa Dalloway's interior monologue shifts dramatically between the middle-aged Clarissa in London in 1923 to her memories of a youthful summer holiday at Bourton in 1890. To a first-time reader of modernist literature, this style of narration can be disorienting. Here's how the novel begins:

Mrs. Dalloway said she would buy the flowers herself.

For Lucy had her work cut out for her. The doors would be taken off their hinges; Rumplemayer's men were coming. And then, thought Clarissa Dalloway, what a morning – fresh as if issued to children on a beach.

What a lark! What a plunge! For so it had always seemed to her, when, with a little squeak of the hinges, which she could hear now, she had burst open the French windows and plunged at Bourton into the open air.

(3)

Thirty-three years and two locations span this train of thought. Clarissa "plunges" into the depths of her memories, triggered by the fresh air and the remembered squeak of the hinges, as indicated by the repetition of these terms in the passage. As we follow the "duration" of Clarissa's and other character's thoughts in the course of the novel,

Big Ben periodically sounds the hour, suggesting that interior or personal time is radically at odds with public standard time. However, even Big Ben's "leaden circles dissolved in the air" (Woolf 47), implying that even standard time cannot stand still and be properly quantified, at least not in art.

Modernists were also concerned with reaching further back into the past, beyond individual memories. In Chapter 1, we discussed Eliot's "mythical method" as a way of animating the classical literary past. Some writers reached back even further into the archeological past as a way of making familiar modernist technological innovation. In an 1888 essay, "The Perfected Phonograph," the inventor of the phonograph, Thomas Edison, states that ancient Assyrian and Babylonian baked clay cylinders are similar to his own cylinders that recorded the vibrations of a voice. An early film critic, Abel Gance, wrote of cinema, "By a remarkable regression, we are transported back to the expressive level of the Egyptian" (qtd in Bush 22). In making these comparisons to ancient civilizations, both statements indicated that the new technologies reveal the non-rational or primitive in the heart of the modern. The moving image and the recording device captured all manner of noise, happenings, movement and tone, and this lack of discernment reflected the "primitive" nature of modern mass culture. Any major city in the early twentieth century daily saw thousands of ordinary people traveling through city streets, whether protesting, marching, traveling, commuting to work or enjoying the new mass forms of leisure (fairs, movies, shopping, exhibits, etc.). The postulation of a "primitive," non-rational impulse in crowds and their popular entertainments revealed a distrust of mass culture.

This dark view of humanity led many modernist thinkers to argue that people would only behave in a civilized manner if repressive forces (a severe father, a police state) held their base instincts in check. The modernist fascination with instinctual drives, often displaced onto European women, the working classes and non-European peoples is called **primitivism**. Primitivism was the belief that less "civilized" peoples, women and the working classes had weaker superegos and, therefore, expressed their instinctual impulses more openly. (Recall Picasso's shocking painting *Les Demoiselles* in Chapter 1 in which prostitutes wear African masks in a manner that conflates female sexuality with African primitivism, a connection also leveraged by Josephine Baker in the *danse sauvage*.) And while primitivism maintained a problematic hierarchy between "advanced" Western cultures and "less civilized, primitive" cultures, classes and gender, it influenced writers and artists around the world to probe their desires and drives for more authentic ways of living, whether that be embracing and acknowledging homosexuality, female sexuality, non-European cultures and religions. These artists and writers revalued "primitivism" as healthier than the over-civilized, repressed European cultures. But because this term also justified racial, colonial and gender oppression, we put "scare quotes" around the term to suggest that we no longer accept the meanings it conveys.

Some writers projected their fear of "uncivilized," irrational behavior onto the modern-day crowds. Gustave Le Bon and Sigmund Freud believed that the crowd "thinks in images," which "call one another up by association" (Le Bon 17; Freud 1957: 172). By "association," Freud suggests that there are no logical connections between these images; they merely appeal to the senses and imagination. (See also "stream of consciousness" in Chapter 4.) The crowd is emotional, more attuned to its bodily passions and impulses than to rational thought, and therefore could be easily transported into "herd" or collective responses. The notion of "herd" mentality also indicates the crowd's bestial nature. In a crowd, individuals regress to their base instincts and lose their rational "checks" on unsocial or unlawful behavior. In a large group, they became sheer energy, available for destructive actions. Freud describes this regression as follows:

Some of [the herd mentality's] features – the weakness of intellectual ability, the lack of emotional restraint, the incapacity for moderation and delay, the inclination to exceed every limit in the form of action – these and similar features . . . [sic] show an unmistakable picture of a regression of mental activity to an earlier stage such as we are not surprised to find among savages or children.

(1957: 194)

Freud's thinking in this passage reveals a common evolutionary assumption held by many modernist thinkers. This assumption is based on Ernst Haeckel's Biogenic Law from the 1890s in which "the young of every species were supposed to recapitulate the evolution of the species" (Everdell 138). In Haeckel's direct terms, "ontogeny recapitulates phylogeny." This now discredited theory of human evolution argues that we begin life as aquatic creatures swimming in our mothers' wombs. Our childhood mirrors that of "primitive" humankind, and, by the time of reaching full adulthood, we successfully arrive at the most advanced stage of rational mastery by repressing our "primitive" impulses.

But this war with our "primitive" selves is only momentarily achieved. We can easily regress back to a "primitive" state in crowds, or when dreams, slips of the tongue, jokes, lapses in memory, and other seemingly innocent behaviors express our repressed instinctual impulses. With the invention of psychoanalysis, the human subject was officially at war with her or his own thoughts:

> The unconscious part of the mind is vast [. . .] and contains multitudes, most of which are silently censored and repressed [. . .] We are of two minds (at least) about everything, and we do not really know what we are doing.

> (Everdell 140)

In this model of subjectivity, humans cannot fully know themselves: they are governed by past traumas, antisocial impulses and preconscious repression that inhibits self-knowledge. Moreover, as we have already seen, the past is never past. It exerts a tremendous influence in one's present thoughts and feelings.

And with the advent of new technologies, so, too, is the past made present again in astonishing new ways. The ability of phonographs, cinema and photography to preserve the past as well as to reveal reality in all its chaotic diversity suggested, above all, that we cannot simply break from the past and herald "the new." In fact, as was suggested by philosophers and psychologists like Le Bon, Freud, as well as Henri Bergson and Joseph Breuer, the past is preserved in the unconscious and even in bodily memory (what we might today call one's DNA). Stephen Kern provides one such example:

> A ghoulish elaboration of the idea of an organic persistence of the past was Bram Stoker's *Dracula* [1897]. The blood of several centuries of victims flowed in the veins of the four-hundred-year-old hero along with the blood of his ancestors – more ancient, the Count boasted, than the Hapsburgs or the Romanovs.

> (41)

The tactics of decadent artists, as we discussed above, then, make sense in this regard: if we are incapable of surmounting the past, we might as well try to dwell in that past through experiments with altered states of consciousness. As we'll see in the next chapter, the crisis of empire and the rise of modernisms from locations around the world accompanied the exhaustion of European high art.

SUMMARY

In this chapter, we focused on the European crises of representation and reason. The crisis of representation was sparked, in part, by the rise of mass culture and new media. Artists and writers created autonomous art that was critical of commercial culture and middle-class conventions. This development influenced modernism's scandalous content and led to trials and censorship. But it also led to modernism's foremost experimental techniques. In addition, the crisis of reason stemmed from philosophical and scientific developments that challenged the notion of a rational subjectivity. It also arose in response to transformations in perception made available through new media like photography, film and phonography.

FURTHER READING

Sanford Schwartz *The Matrix of Modernism: Pound, Eliot and Early Twentieth-Century Thought* shows how modernist poetry was influenced by important developments in philosophy and wider intellectual thought, especially the opposition between conscious "surfaces" and unconscious "depths" and between ordinary experience and a hidden realm of mental life, or the unconscious. Kolocotroni, Vassiliki, Jane Goldman, Olga Taxidou, eds. *Modernism: An Anthology of Sources and Documents* and Mary Ann Caws *Manifesto: A Century of –Isms* are two excellent anthologies of modernist manifestos, essays and prefaces that provide students of modernism with vital archives of key modernist statements. Stephen Kern *The Culture of Time and Space, 1880–1918* explores how the concepts of time and space underwent revolutionary transformations during this time period and how they affected modernist art and culture.

WORKS CITED

Baudelaire, Charles. *The Painter of Modern Life and Other Essays*. New York: Da Capo Press, 1964. Print.

Benjamin, Walter. *Reflections: Essays, Aphorisms, Autobiographical Writings*. New York: Harcourt, Brace, 1978. Print.

———. *Walter Benjamin: Selected Writings: Vol. 4. 1938–1940*. Cambridge, MA: Harvard University Press, 2003. Print.

Bergson, Henri. *Creative Evolution*. New York: Random House, 1944. Print.

Burger, Peter. *The Theory of the Avant-Garde*. Minneapolis: Minnesota University Press, 1984. Print.

Bush, Christopher. *Ideographic Modernism: China, Writing, Media*. New York: Oxford University Press, 2010. Print.

Calinescu, Matei. *Five Faces of Modernity: Modernism, Avant-Garde, Decadence, Kitsch, Postmodernism*. Durham, NC: Duke University Press, 1987. Print.

Caws, Mary Ann, ed. *Manifesto: A Century of Isms*. Lincoln, NE: University of Nebraska Press, 2001. Print.

Chénieux-Gendron, Jacqueline. *Surrealism*. New York: Columbia University Press, 1990.

Clark, T. J. *The Painting of Modern Life: Paris in the Art of Manet and His Followers*. Princeton, NJ: Princeton University Press, 1984. Print.

Clifford, James. *The Predicament of Culture: Twentieth-Century Ethnography, Literature, and Art*. Cambridge, MA: Harvard University Press, 1988. Print.

Conrad, Joseph. *Heart of Darkness*. New York: Modern Library, 1999. Print.

Everdell, William R. *The First Moderns: Profiles in the Origins of Twentieth-Century Thought*. Chicago: University of Chicago Press, 1997. Print.

Felski, Rita. *The Gender of Modernity*. Cambridge, MA: Harvard University Press, 1995. Print.

Flaubert, Gustave. *Madame Bovary*. New York: Bantam Books, 1989. Print.

Frank, Joseph. *The Idea of Spatial Form*. New Brunswick: Rutgers University Press, 1991. A reprint from *Sewanee Review*. 53 (Spring, Summer, Autumn, 1945). Print.

Freud, Sigmund. "Group Psychology and the Analysis of the Ego." In *A General Selection from the Works of Sigmund Freud*. Ed. John Rickman. New York: Doubleday, 1957. 169–209. Print.

———. *The Interpretation of Dreams*. New York: Basic Books, 1965. Print.

Goody, Alex. *Technology, Literature and Culture*. New York: Polity Press, 2011. Print.

Huysman, Joris-Karl. *Against Nature*. NY: Penguin, 1959. Print.

James, William. *The Principles of Psychology*. Vol. 1. New York: Dover, 1950. Print.

Joyce, James. *Ulysses*. New York: Random House, 1986. Print.

Kalliney, Peter. *Modernism in a Global Context*. New York: Bloomsbury, 2016. Print.

Kant, Immanuel. *The Critique of Judgment*. New York: Oxford University Press, 1991. Print.

Kern, Stephen. *The Culture of Time and Space, 1880–1918*. Cambridge, MA: Harvard University Press, 1983. Print.

Kittler, Friedrich A. *Gramophone, Film, Typewriter*. Stanford: Stanford University Press, 1999. Print.

Kolocotroni, Vassiliki, Jane Goldman, and Olga Taxidou, eds. *Modernism: An Anthology of Sources and Documents*. Chicago: Chicago University Press, 1998. Print.

LaCapra, Dominick. *Madame Bovary on Trial*. Ithaca: Cornell University Press, 1982. Print.

Lawrence, D. H. "Introduction." In *Lady Chatterley's Lover*. Ed. Ronald Friedland. New York: Bantam Books, 1968. xiii–xxiv. Print.

Le Bon, Gustave. *The Psychology of Crowds*. Champaign, IL: Project Gutenberg. www.gutenberg.org/ebooks/445 (Accessed 02/16/15). Website.

Lewis, Pericles. *The Cambridge Introduction to Modernism*. New York: Cambridge University Press, 2007. Print.

Marx, Karl. *Capital*. Vol. 1. New York: Vintage, 1977. Print.

Mallarmé, Stéphane. "From 'Crisis in Poetry,' 1886–95." In *Modernism: An Anthology of Sources and Documents*. Eds. Vassiliki Kolocotroni, Jane Goldman, and Olga Taxidou. Chicago: Chicago University Press, 1998. 123–27. Print.

Miller, Monica L. "The Black Dandy as Bad Modernist." In *Bad Modernisms*. Eds. Douglas Mao and Rebecca L. Walkowitz. Durham, NC: Duke University Press, 2006. 179–205. Print.

Nietzsche, Friedrich. *The Portable Nietzsche*. Ed. Walter Kauffmann. New York: Penguin, 1954. Print.

Nordau, Max. *Degeneration*. Lincoln, NE: University of Nebraska Press, 1993. Print.

North, Michael. *Camera Works: Photography and the Twentieth-Century Word*. New York: Oxford University Press, 2007. Print.

Perloff, Marjorie. *The Futurist Moment: Avant-Garde, Avant Guerre, and the Language of Rupture*. Chicago: University of Chicago Press, 1986. Print.

———. *Wittgenstein's Ladder: Poetic Language and the Strangeness of the Ordinary*. Chicago: University of Chicago Press, 1996. Print.

Pound, Ezra. *Selected Poems*. New York: New Directions Books, 1957. Print.

Saussure, Ferdinand de. *Course in General Linguistics*. New York: McGraw-Hill, 1966. Print.

Smith, Neil. *Uneven Development: Nature, Capital and the Production of Space*. Athens, GA: University of Georgia Press, 2008. Print.

Wilde, Oscar. *The Picture of Dorian Gray*. New York: Penguins, 1983. Print.

Wilson, Edmund. *Axel's Castle*. New York: Charles Scribner, 1931.

Wittgenstein, Ludwig. *Philosophical Investigations*. Englewood Cliffs, NJ: Prentice-Hall, 1958. Print.

———. *Tractatus Logico-Philosophicus*. New York: Routledge & Kegan Paul, 1922. Print.

Woolf, Virginia. *Mrs. Dalloway*. New York: Harcourt, 1925. Print.

3

HISTORIES

> "Tranquility to-day is either innate (the philistine) or to be acquired only by a deliberate doping of the personality. It was in the stillness of a seaside suburb that could be heard most clearly and insistently the booming of Franco's heavy artillery, the rattle of Stalin's firing squads and the fierce shrill turmoil of the revolutionary movement striving for clarity and influence. Such is our age . . ."
>
> C. L. R. James, *The Black Jacobins* (1938)

In this chapter, "Histories," you will find a broad overview of significant social, economic and geopolitical movements that impacted modernism around the world. As we mentioned in Chapter 1, modernism was profoundly shaped by massive imperial expansion in the late nineteenth to early twentieth centuries (discussed below). Even when European powers did not directly take control of a territory — as in East Asia, for example — those societies still needed to grapple with modernization. By **modernization**, we mean producing goods for worldwide capitalist markets, wage labor, monetization, commodity production and consumption, industrialization (for some societies, such as Japan), and the transformation of existing social relations and modes of being. Non-Western societies confronted these forces, resisting and transforming them, if possible, to work with their pre-existing social, political and economic structures and modes. Modernist artists and writers from these regions registered these sweeping changes in their art.

Imperialism and the crisis of empire that followed not only shaped non-Western modernism, but also impacted Western modernism. In this chapter, we will discuss how World War I, the Russian Revolution, the women's movement and fascism influenced the art that was produced during this era. And, while these forces did not directly *cause* modernism, they did influence the myriad ways in which modernist artists and writers shaped their works of art and literature.

CRISIS OF EMPIRE

At the mid-twentieth century, critics and scholars identified modernism as a strictly Anglo-American and European phenomenon, as discussed in Chapter 1. One important reason for this identification was that Anglo-American and European modernism arose in conjunction with **imperialism**. Imperialism is the practice in which one state rules over large territories by means of colonization, military force, or some other form of domination. This unequal expansion is usually justified based on ideas of superiority of one people over another, though the (not so ulterior) motive is the generation of wealth for the imperial nation. According to Raymond Williams, European modernism arose from "the magnetic concentration of wealth and power in imperial capitals and simultaneous access to a wide variety of subordinate cultures" (44). As we've seen with Picasso's *Les Demoiselles* and Eliot's *The Waste Land*, Euro-American modernists often appropriated minority voices and non-Western artifacts and writings into their masterworks. And while we can now appreciate the influence that, for instance, the Hindu Upanishads or African sculpture had in the creation of modernism, in the early twentieth century, the extent of European modernism's appropriation *and* emulation of these texts and objects was obscured by imperialist values that viewed the West as the superior and universal (i.e., applicable and desirable to all) beacon of civilization. The same hierarchy of value also disparaged other forms of cultural production – modernisms from below, by women, colonial subjects, non-Western subjects and minorities – as being behind the times and not as sophisticated as "high" modernist literature and art. To understand why non-Western art and literature were, until recently, *not* considered modernist, we need to consider what imperialism was and the ways in which it was resisted around the world.

The European imperialist era was quite short: it began in the 1870s, peaked in 1884 when all of Africa was parceled out amongst the European powers – infamously called "The Scramble for Africa" – and started to decline in 1914 with the onset of the First World War and the rise of national liberation movements. (There are exceptions to this time line. For instance, the liberation of Latin America from the Spanish and Portuguese Empires began in 1810 with Chile's successful revolution, and the Spanish Empire ended in 1898 when it lost the Spanish-American War. Spanish and Portuguese imperialism is slightly older than that of the rest of Europe. The rise of American imperialism began in 1898 and continues today.) In addition to carving up Africa into spheres of European influence, European powers exerted their will more indirectly throughout Asia. Hannah Arendt argues that imperialism arose from the political emancipation of the bourgeoisie (the owners of factories, banks, etc.) who were "the first class in history to achieve economic pre-eminence without aspiring to political rule [though they used the state to achieve their economic goals]" (123–24). Rather than see imperialism, as Russian revolutionary leader Vladimir Lenin did, as the last stage of capitalism, Arendt views it as the first stage of political rule by the bourgeoisie, who imposed capitalist modernity in all of its brutality around the world. In most instances, imperialist incursions stripped indigenous peoples of any rights and protections (124, 138). In this imperialist era, Britain gained 4.5 million square miles and 66 million inhabitants; France gained 3.5 million square miles and 13 million inhabitants; Germany gained a million square miles and 13 million inhabitants; Belgium, through King Leopold II's personal acquisitions, gained 900,000 square miles and 8.5 million persons (Arendt 124). In some cases, this territorial expansion was accompanied by settler **colonialism**, but, on the whole, these vast acquisitions were merely designated "spheres of influence."

Why this tremendous expansion? Mainly, to improve business prospects, including greater trading opportunities, resource extraction and industrial production. Imperialism also provided a release valve for economic downturns and worker agitation at home. Instead of unemployment and dissatisfaction at home, workers could try their luck abroad: prospecting for gold or diamonds, sheep farming, or trading. Furthermore, imperialism, whether one stayed at home or went abroad, provided a sense of national and racial superiority that distracted from lingering economic malaise (Hobsbawm 1989: 70). However, by the time Britain was embroiled in the second Boer War in South Africa (1899–1902), imperialism was attracting criticism for failing to solve problems at home. British economist J. A. Hobson, in 1902, suggested that the chief rationale for imperialism is financial: both debt financing and war making. He argued that imperialist industries benefited only a small, elite portion of the British public because its exports (rails, engines, guns, mining and agricultural equipment), while stimulating important manufacturing sectors, hardly increased levels of consumption, whether in the UK or overseas. Imperialism, then, in Hobson's argument, fails to solve the problem of over-production (too many goods and services chasing too few buyers) and falling rates of profit at the national level. Moreover, these investments are debt-financed: paid for by the British public, but benefiting only foreign-based manufacturing operations (60).

Despite the lack of overall wealth creation, imperialism was enormously beneficial to capitalists. Arendt, in her analysis of totalitarianism (dictatorial regimes such as Hitler's fascist state), points to imperialism as a precursor to this tyrannous form of rule, because under imperialist expansion, "[m]oney could finally beget money because power, with complete disregard for all laws – economic as well as ethical – could appropriate wealth" (137). Imperialism legitimized global land and resource grabs in the name of a "superior" race and civilization with advanced technologies and weapons; its money-hungry leaders had complete contempt for the subject peoples and lands. Arendt adds that, because imperialism is a form of tyrannous rule over foreign people, it cannot succeed. Napoleon's failed attempt to unite Europe under the French flag in 1803–15,

> was a clear indication that conquest by a nation led either to the full awakening of the conquered people's national consciousness and to consequent rebellion against the conqueror or to tyranny. [. . . And tyranny] can stay in power only it if destroys first of all the national institutions of its own people.

(128)

Arendt was right. European imperialism triggered the rise of nationalist consciousness and modernization around the world, as dominated peoples sought to resist Western incursion and to modernize on their own terms. And these modernization movements took different forms from those that occurred in Europe. Rather than imagining modernity looking the same way everywhere (as the universalizing hubris of European hegemony imagines), we need to examine local contexts and specific anticolonial and regional configurations that generated various critiques of modernity *and* imperialism. These critiques and alternative possibilities were often conveyed in literature and painting from these locations in complex, sometimes contradictory, blends of local traditions and European influence. The following sections survey just a few of the most well-known sites and/or movements of anti colonial, non-Western resistance and minority writing conveyed in modernist styles: South Asian, Japanese, Irish and African-American modernisms. Other important modernist sites include the Middle East and Arab world, Eastern Europe, China and Southeast Asia, Australia and Oceania, Sub-Saharan Africa, Latin America, and Canada and the US. Many of these modernisms occurred after World War II, therefore changing how we periodize modernism. For wider explorations of these various modernisms, see *The Modernist World* and *The Routledge Encyclopedia of Modernism*.

SOUTH ASIAN MODERNISM

The first modernist works of literature and painting appeared in South Asia in the early to mid-1880s, a few years before Nicaraguan poet Rubén Darío coined the term *modernismo* to describe a new poetics in Latin America (Dharwadker 129). Building upon the social reforms begun, at least partially, by British **colonialism** (emancipating women through education, ending child marriages, preventing the immolation of widows, improving widows' treatment in society and allowing them to remarry, ending discrimination and violence in the caste system, etc.), Indian modernism begins "as an aesthetic outcome of a quest for social reform and self-modernization under **colonialism**, and not merely as an imitative offshoot of Euro-American *modernismo* or modernism" (Dharwadker 129). The form these aesthetic innovations initially took was that of an idealistic realism, articulating both things as they are and things as they should be (Dharwadker 130). Literary works from this period include Bankim Chandra Chatterjee's *Ananda-matha* (*The Sacred Brotherhood*, 1882) and Rabindranath Tagore's *Ghare-baire* (*Home and the World*, 1916), both written in Bengali. Premchand, writing in both Hindi and Urdu, invented a form of secular social realism that would be foundational to the Progressive Writers Association begun in the 1930s (see Social Realism and the Popular Front below).

The second phase of South Asian modernism began in 1922 and concluded just after the independence of India and Pakistan in 1947. Its twin influences were the first subcontinent-wide *satyagraha* (non-violent moral suasion) protest movement led by Mohandas Gandhi in 1920; and the first European modernist art exhibition in India that featured works by Russian Expressionist painter Wassily Kandinsky, the Swiss-German Expressionist Paul Klee, and included a painting by the English Vorticist Wyndham Lewis, as well as reproductions of paintings by other European modernist artists (Dharwadker 131; Mitter 15). Regarding the latter influence, Benoy Sarkar (1887–1949), writing from Paris, defended the relevance of European modernism for the subcontinent in an article titled "Aesthetics of Young India." This controversial article began a heated debate in India because Sarkar rejected the mythmaking traditionalism in Bengali painting (such as that by Rabindranath Tagore) and advocated instead an avant-garde "aesthetics of autonomy." Sarkar compared artistic self-definition with the "nationalist demand for self rule or autonomy from the Raj [the British system of colonial rule]" (Mitter 16). Experimental modernist forms, like Picasso's geometrical forms, Sarkar argued, are objective – removed from the need to represent the world as it exists in mundane reality – and therefore they are truer than vague stereotypes about the spirituality of Indian culture. These stereotypes, or myths, often functioned in **colonialism** to justify India's colonization. For instance, colonists often believed that Indian peoples were more spiritual than Europeans; therefore, they didn't need material wealth, or much food, for that matter. The spiritualism of India, according to this British argument, coexists with the quiet acceptance of **colonialism**.

Instead, Sarkar opined that aesthetic formalism could rouse the population into demanding self-rule, in a move that dovetailed with Gandhi's *satyagraha* movement in which peasant and urban masses engaged in boycotts, fasts and protest marches. Sarkar's embrace of purely formal expression – the difficult art discussed in Chapter 1 – made European modernism a universal, that is, "a truly international style that overcame all cultural barriers" (Mitter 16). Checking this belief in European universalism, Stella Kramrisch (1896–1993), a specialist in Indian art who taught at the University of Kolkata from 1924–50, contended that Indian artists who used cubist innovations still remained Indian since they drew from the particular cultural experience of India. The geometrical shapes of South Asian cubism, for instance, might be distorted and fragmented in a similar fashion to European cubism, but they drew upon South Asian cultural contexts and histories and are shaped by different artistic agendas (Mitter 27).

In literature, the transitional period of decolonization, from approximately 1936–54, was a remarkably fruitful one and characterized by a modernist break with the recent past and an open-ended future, teeming with social, political and cultural possibilities. Shadowing this optimism was the Partition of (predominately Hindu) India and (predominately Muslim) East and West Pakistan. East Pakistan became Bangladesh in 1971. The Partition occurred on August 15, 1947, and gave violent birth to the independent states of India and Pakistan. Historians estimate that between 200,000 and 500,000 persons were killed in the rioting that ensued in the Partition. Over 14 million Hindus, Sikhs and Muslims were displaced as Hindus and Sikhs moved to India and Muslims to East and West Pakistan in the largest migration in human recorded history. In the midst of these massive changes, many writers across ethnic, religious and gender identities grouped together in what became known as the Progressive Writers Association (PWA) and the Indian People's Theater Association (IPTA). These writers, who included Premchand, Ahmed Ali, Mulk Raj Anand, Sajjad Zaheer, Rashid Jahan, Ismat Chughtai, Saadat Hasan Manto and Khwaja Ahmad Abbas, wrote in both Urdu and English. The forms in which they wrote varied greatly. For instance, Mulk Raj Anand (*Untouchable; Coolie*), and non-PWA writers N. K. Narayan (*Swami and Friends*), Raja Rao (*Kanthapura*) and G. V. Desani (*All About H. Hatterr*), at times explicitly invoked modernist themes, whether of Gandhi, James Joyce or Virginia Woolf; at other times, as with Narayan and Rao, they offered mimetic representations. In all cases, they clearly situate their language, plots, political interventions and descriptive density within South Asian contexts. (See below for discussions of South Asian feminist writers Ismat Chughtai and Rashid Jahan.)

Formal experimentation was less common among artists and writers who sought to create an explicitly Indian or Pakistani national identity. Rejecting the urban, decontextualized forms of European modernism, many painters and writers preferred to explore the rural traditions of Indian villages. For instance, Amrita Sher-Gill's primitive paintings far exceeded merely "indigenous" influences and drew comparisons with her Mexican contemporary Frida Kahlo (Dube 95). This turn away from modern fragmentation, cities and machines accorded with Gandhi's embrace of the peasantry, as formulated in his 1908 pamphlet *Hind Swaraj* (*Indian Home Rule*). In *Hind Swaraj*, Gandhi condemns European civilization (both in Europe and as exported to India through colonization) because it is primarily concerned with bodily well-being and lacks attention to matters of the soul. He characterizes this civilization as destroying authentic being: European civilization demands that people work in dehumanizing factories, rushes them about on trains, and enslaves everyone (including the factory owners and landlords) to the pursuit of money and luxuries. This sped-up, fragmented life, he suggests, destroys the primary elements of human connectivity: love, humility and attention to the soul or one's inner essence. These elements, he writes, are foundational to Indian society. To rediscover and revalue them, Gandhi advocates a return to the rural villages, the restoration of travel by foot or ox cart, the adaptation of local, homespun cotton clothes (made without machines) and the practice of unity among religions by supporting only local, that is, authentic Indian interests (39). In this manner, Gandhi argued, the colonizer will be made to leave India by the non-violent means of Indian non-cooperation with the West. Gandhi drew attention to Indian peasant communities that were untouched by European ways in order to assert India's separate identity from the West. In this regard, primitivism in a South Asian anticolonial context empowered the East to criticize the West and define itself in contradistinction from the West. Rather than imply "uncivilized" and "savage," as it does in Western usage, primitivism in this context means self-supporting and communal.

It is important to note that South Asian modernisms are ongoing today (Dharwadker). In Anglophone Indian literature, for instance,

Arundhati Roy's *The God of Small Things* (1997) intervenes in contemporary India's gender and caste double standards to build a more equitable and secular modern nation. Aligned with nation building, modernization, social issues, migration, diaspora and multiethnic and multilingual realities (South Asia has twenty-six literary languages), modernism's relevance in South Asia extends far past the mid-century mark often taken to serve as the endpoint for European modernism.

JAPANESE MODERNISM

The Western powers never colonized Japan; yet their greater geopolitical strength convinced Japan to emulate the West by modernizing. Emerging from the feudal period of the Tokugawa shogunate (1603–1868), the Meiji period (1868–1912) began absorbing "'Western learning' and break-neck modernization" (Bush 17). The literature in this first period was mainly naturalist, describing some of the grittier realities of urban life in Japan (see below, "Women's Movements") and corresponding to the reformist energies of the time. Futabatei Shimei's *Drifting Clouds* (1887–89) was arguably "the first modern Japanese novel, 'modern' partly for its emulation of [Russian novelist] Turgenev, but also because of its innovative approximation of the contemporary spoken language" (Bush 17–18). (See the discussion of "vernacular" in Chapter 4.) The Taisho era (1912–26) saw a more explicit engagement with European avant-garde movements: futurism briefly flourished, and surrealism had a long-lasting and pervasive influence, but the movement usually credited with launching modernist literature in Japan "was the *shinkankakuha*, usually translated as 'new sensationalism' or 'neo-perceptionism'" (Bush 18). Overall, Japanese literary modernism is characterized by its explicit engagement with popular culture, "including cinema, cabaret, and detective fiction" (Bush 18).

The most significant aspect of Japanese modernity, however, was its military might and successful bid to become an imperial power. The Russo-Japanese War of 1905 over control of Manchuria (in China) and Korea saw Japan victorious over Russia. This victory was interpreted around the world as a darker race prevailing over a major Western empire (Aydin 213). This fact gave the lie to the civilizational and racial theory of Western superiority and proved that an "Oriental" nation could modernize quickly and outpace the "West."

Also significant for Asian and other modernisms, it showed that a non-Western nation could merge its traditional cultural elements with modernity to maintain its distinctive cultural and religious difference from Europe. Japan proved that these native elements were no obstacle to modernization, and that national willpower could close the developmental gap between Europe and Asia (Aydin 224).

CELTIC REVIVAL AND IRISH MODERNISM

Irish culture is neither wholly national (i.e., autonomous or self-defining) nor colonial, but a hybrid of both (Deane 11). British rule on the island began more than 700 years ago and accelerated in 1536 with Henry VIII's decision to conquer Ireland and bring it under crown control (Wikipedia, "History of Ireland"). The Act of Union, 1800–1922, declared Ireland a subordinate but full member of the United Kingdom, while the Anglo-Irish Treaty of 1922 (concluded after four years of war against the British) split the island in half, with the Irish Free State (largely Catholic and nationalist) in the south and Northern Ireland (predominantly Protestant and still in union with Great Britain) capping the island in the north. A year-long civil war that ensued after the Anglo-Irish Treaty between nationalists (Southern) and unionists (Northern) produced a tense cease-fire that reignited in the late 1960s to produce more violence, commonly called "The Troubles," that was concluded in 1998. In addition, many rebellions and agrarian disturbances (between Anglo-Irish landlords and the Irish Catholic peasants who leased small tracts of land from them) occurred over the course of this 700-year period.

Irish modernism began in the late nineteenth century, in part as a response to the Great Famine of 1845–49 in which approximately one million people died of starvation and disease and another one million people emigrated (Wikipedia, "Great Famine Ireland"), causing the population of Ireland to decline between 20–25%. Between 1849 and 1918, when Sinn Fein (which means "ourselves" in Gaelic, or the Irish language, and refers to the home rule nationalist party) triumphed in the general elections, Irish modernism contributed to the efforts by Irish politics and social institutions to **decolonize** or transform Ireland from a British colony into a modern, sovereign (independent) state. The first task of Irish modernism was to reinvent tradition and, in particular, to recover the Gaelic tongue and culture that was gradually being forgotten – a problem that was accelerated by the Great Famine and institutionalized Anglophone schooling that favored English language and culture. This revival impulse had precedents in the early nineteenth century, but became more widespread in the late nineteenth century. In 1884, Michael Cusack formed the Gaelic Athletic Association to promote and preserve Irish games such as hurling, Gaelic football and rounders, as well as Irish music and dance. In 1893, Eoin MacNeill and Douglas Hyde formed the Gaelic League, whose aim was to promote and revive the Irish language. W. B. Yeats wrote poetry featuring Irish folklore and heroes, such as Fergus and Cuchulain. Some Irish writers forged important cultural and political alliances with other colonized territories: Margaret Nobel (1867–1911) met Swami Vivekananda in London and moved to Calcutta (now Kolkata), India, taking the name Sister Nivedita. She was an active participant in the Indian nationalist movement. W. B. Yeats championed Rabindranath Tagore's poetry. Roger Casement (1864–1916) traveled to the Congo and Peru, investigating human rights violations for the British. He became disillusioned with all forms of imperialism and began working for Irish independence. During World War I, Casement sought German military aid for the Dublin Easter Rising, and he was caught and hanged for treason against the British Empire.

Some of Irish modernism's earliest accomplishments to revive Irish culture and language included J. T. Grein's Independent Theater in London that produced George Moore's *Strike at Arlingford*, W. B. Yeats's *Land of Heart's Desire* and Douglas Hyde's *Love Songs of Connacht* (Deane 12). The Celtic Revival also imported elements of modernism from Europe. Joe Cleary notes that many of the most famous Irish modernists spent much of their lives outside of Ireland:

> These earlier figures [of the 1890s: George Moore, George Egerton, Oscar Wilde, and George Bernard Shaw] – who, like Yeats, came of age professionally in fin de siècle England and made their reputations there before World War I – had all been notable enthusiasts of the earliest continental European avant-gardes: Moore championed in turn French impressionism, naturalism, and aestheticism; Egerton [whose given name was Mary Chavelita Dunne, one of the most important "New Woman" writers] was the first writer in English to reference Friedrich Nietzsche and to translate Knut Hamsun [Norwegian modernist writer, 1859–1952]; Wilde was the

most flamboyant English-language practitioner of European decadence; Shaw was a committed advocate of Henrik Ibsen at a time when the Norwegian's work provoked scandal or incomprehension in British theatrical circles.

(2)

Why were Irish modernists so attuned to avant-garde developments in the Continent? If we add to the list above the most famous Irish modernists – poet William Butler Yeats, novelist James Joyce, novelist and dramatist Samuel Beckett, and novelist Flann O'Brien – then Irish modernism can be classified as an exceptionally avant-garde Irish modernist tradition. Cleary argues that the flourishing of an Irish culture of radical experimentation arose due to Ireland's catastrophic colonial history. For most Anglo-American and European writers and painters of the modernist period, World War I (see below) is the defining catastrophe of modernity that impelled them to redefine artistic practices from the ground up. For Irish writers, the Great War and the Irish War of Independence (1919–21) merely confirmed the already cataclysmic times of modern history. So while previous Irish writing was already one of catastrophe (and felt even before the Great Famine in the work of Jonathan Swift, James Clarence Mangan, and in the Anglo-Irish Gothic tradition, among others), Irish modernism goes a step further than its historical predecessors and Continental counterparts. It posits a radical break from a history of oppression and a leap to national self-determination. This proposition is articulated with particular clarity by Joyce's Stephen Dedalus in *Ulysses*, who describes history as "a nightmare from which I am trying to awake" (1986: 28). Stephen, a poet, attempts "to awake" by means of the written word – the modernist literary work – that can counter the *language* of the oppressor. Stephen, and by extension Joyce, interrogate consciousness and everyday life as an antidote to, as Stephen puts it, "those big words which make us so unhappy" (1986: 26). Stephen refers here to words like "history" and "progress" that have spelled disaster for the Irish. Joyce's modernism brushes history against the grain to reveal the spirit and consciousness of the Irish, who are at times portrayed as bowed down by history, and at other times undaunted by their colonization by the British.

Other Irish writers were not so experimental in form, but instead conveyed new types of content: J. M. Synge's play *Playboy of the*

Western World (1907) conveyed the "rich and living" local language of the Irish people living in County Mayo on the western coast of Ireland. The play was first performed in Dublin's Abbey Theater, a central institution of the Celtic Revival, and sparked riots of moral outrage because the play featured an apparent patricide who seduces the innkeeper's daughter. The central character, Christy Mahon, claims to have killed his father (which turns out later not to be true). His position in the adoptive community where he takes refuge shifts by turns from idol to scapegoat. According to one critic in regard to controversial modernist theater in Ireland, "Theatre, unlike bookish literature, is a social art, a discipline of shared imagination and physical display, with a built civic presence and a place of public gathering" (Levitas 111). Modernist theater is reflexive: it draws attention to *how* it enacts social realities. Because of theater's social element, it necessarily participates in the politics of representation, especially in terms of *how* it imagines an independent Ireland and shows the processes for building it. Other more content-driven modernist writers include dramatists Sean O'Casey (1880–1964), Lady Gregory (1852–1932) and Eva Gore-Booth (1870–1926); novelists Elizabeth Bowen (1899–1973), Katherine Cecil Thurston (1875–1911), Alice Milligan (1865–1953), Maeve Brennan (1917–93) and Edna O'Brien (b. 1930).

THE HARLEM RENAISSANCE

The Harlem Renaissance in the US occurred between roughly 1920–35 and was largely the effect of the "great migration" of African-Americans from the rural South to the urban industrial North during the first decades of the twentieth century. These black communities gathered in cities across the US, including Chicago, Detroit, Cleveland, Pittsburgh, Indianapolis, Kansas City, Cincinnati, and especially in the Harlem neighborhood of New York City. During the 1920s, the black population of Harlem jumped from 32% to 70%, a demographic shift that gave rise to African-Americans in leadership positions: schoolteachers, entrepreneurs, landlords, police officers and millionaires. Philosopher, educator and patron of the arts Alain Locke (1885–1954) called Harlem "the greatest Negro community the world has known." As "a race capital," it vibrated with "the spirit of a racial awakening," a palpable sense of solidarity and pride ("Harlem" 629).

This pride, in part, stemmed from African-American participation in the war. Black soldiers, just back from the Great War (see below), had been treated with respect and near-equality while fighting in Europe. Gaining this respect had been an uphill battle since the US military was still a segregated institution. Black soldiers, for instance, trained at a segregated and inferior camp in Iowa. Despite these obstacles, the fifteenth regiment of New York's National Guard, comprised of 1,300 black men and eighteen white officers, was honored by the French and received a hero's welcome when they marched up New York City's Fifth Avenue and home to Harlem (Lewis 3–4). The welcome, however, was short-lived. In the summer of 1919, a spate of race riots broke out around the country and in the UK where African, Afro-Caribbean, Arab, Chinese, South Asian sailors and workers, mobilized by the war, lingered in port towns like Hull, Liverpool, Glasgow, Newport and Salford. Lured to these towns by wartime labor shortages and a steep decline (in the US) of European immigration, blacks and whites fought it out in the streets. In the US, race riots occurred in over two dozen cities, towns and counties. While the police, army, judiciary and citizens were firmly in favor of protecting its white majority population and crushing black rebellions – often through brutal lynchings and Ku Klux Klan terrorism – African-American populations overall were far more militant than before the war. Jamaican poet, novelist and activist Claude McKay (1889–1948), living in Harlem at this time, published his most famous sonnet, "If We Must Die," in the July 1919 issue of the *Liberator*, capturing this spirit of African-American defiance:

> If we must die, let it not be like hogs
> Hunted and penned in an inglorious spot [. . .]
> O kinsmen! We must meet the common foe!
> Though far outnumbered let us show us brave,
> And for their thousand blows deal one deathblow!
> What though before us lies the open grave?
> Like men we'll face the murderous, cowardly pack,
> Pressed to the wall, dying, but fighting back!

(1–2, 9–14)

This sense of strength and resistance among the African-American community fostered the inaugural, modernist rhetoric of the "New

Negro." Black-run newspapers around the country announced the break with traditional, cowering responses to black oppression. The Harlem-based *Crusader* proclaimed: "The Old Negro goes. [. . .] His abject crawling and pleading have availed the Cause nothing." The Kansas City *Call* prophesied, "The NEW NEGRO, unlike the old time Negro 'does not fear the face of day.' [. . .] The time for cringing is over'" (Lewis 24).

Participation in the war effort, better jobs and growing aspirations for social, political and economic freedom led African-Americans to demand integration and equality in mainstream American life and politics. Marcus Garvey, the charismatic West Indian (Jamaican) orator, attracted thousands to his black nationalist "Back to Africa" movement that revalued blackness and promoted Afro-centrism (the belief that people and cultures from Africa are of equal value to those of European origin) as a source of strength and affirmation. W. E. B. Du Bois (1865–1963), the leader of the National Association for the Advancement of Colored Peoples (NAACP, founded in 1909), fought the political and judicial system, demanding equality and radical integration. Interracial conflict simmered down after 1919 and, while anti-lynching and labor organizing movements continued into the 1920s and 1930s, the arts and intellectual communities, as Locke puts it, symbolized "these new aspirations of a people" (630). Locke drew attention to Harlem as a modern "crucible" of diverse elements of Negro life. Unlike the Old World ghetto, "bound by ties of custom and culture," the New Negro was modern (630). Into Harlem, that "laboratory of a great race-welding," the African, the West Indian, the Negro American from North and South, peasants, students, professionals, workers, preachers, artists and social outcasts "mix and react" (630). They combined folk expression with self-determination to create something new. Locke likens the New Negro movement to nationalist movements of dominated peoples elsewhere in the world: "Harlem has the same role to play for the New Negro as Dublin has had for the New Ireland, or Prague for the New Czechoslovakia" (630).

In literature, music, visual arts, theater and dance, the Harlem Renaissance gave birth to black urban, national and international social consciousness. It is important to note that this consciousness was not confined to the US or to Anglophone communities. The African diaspora, or scattering, occurred due to the slave trade, mainly by Europe, and resulted in Afro-diasporic peoples throughout the New World, including the Caribbean and Latin America, and in places like Paris, which gave a warmer welcome to black people in their midst. The disapora was multilingual, that is, expressed in all the European empires' languages. As with most non-European modernisms, these artistic innovations were not traditionally considered to be modernist because they did not slavishly imitate the high experimental forms of T. S. Eliot and James Joyce. In the first work to argue for the modernism of the Harlem Renaissance, Houston A. Baker, Jr. argues that the black arts of the early twentieth century were not artistic *failures* because they did not look or sound Anglo-American or European. Instead, he said, we must follow the distinctive histories (contexts) surrounding each modernist movement. The history of British, Anglo-American and Irish modernisms, he argued, "are radically opposed to any adequate and accurate account of the history of Afro-American modernism" (xvi). This oppositional history is the history of racial discrimination. Because African-American artists and writers emerge from that occluded history, a history that erases or refuses to acknowledge its own racism, they must contort their work and their language. That is, African-American art and literature must configure itself in contradistinction to white America; yet, because white America is dominant, it must still engage in its way of thinking and representing the world. Baker calls this paradoxical aesthetic "'the mastery of form' and 'the deformation of mastery'" (xvi).

Baker finds Alain Locke's inaugural anthology of the Harlem Renaissance, *The New Negro* (1925), an appropriate example of this paradoxical strategy. By this, he means that the anthology tended to reproduce traditional white literary form, such as the sonnet ("the mastery of form"), but blends it with folk forms and discourses like jazz, blues and vernacular speech for a "deformation of mastery," or particularly, the way that African-American modernism yokes together "high" and popular or "low" black culture. The anthology includes poets Claude McKay, Langston Hughes, Countée Cullen, Jean Toomer, Arna Bontemps, James Weldon Johnson, Georgia Douglas Johnson and Angelina Grimké; fiction writers and dramatists Rudolph Fisher, Jean Toomer, Zora Neale Hurston, Jessie Redmon Fauset, Bruce Nugent and Eric Walrond; and woodcut prints and sketches by Aaron Douglas and Winhold Reiss. In addition, the anthology provided anthropological, sociological and art historical recovery and revaluation of African sculpture and masks, and African-American and Afro-Caribbean ways of life. These artists did not always employ the vernacular in their work; often, their ostensibly realist or mimetic forms of representation include more subtle deformations, such as the scandalous sexuality that disrupts transparent communication in favor of enigmatic statements in Nella Larsen's *Passing* or the writings of so-called second-generation Harlem Renaissance writers Wallace Thurman and Bruce Nugent. *Passing* begins with the receipt of a letter from Clare Kendry to Irene Redfield, "the long envelope of thin Italian paper with its almost illegible scrawl seemed out of place and alien" (143). The letter thematizes an unspeakable sexual and interracial desire (because Clare is passing for white) and scandalous action; it is hardly readable and foreign. Characterized by modernist inscrutability and deformation, the letter threatens to throw a wrench into the smooth, easily readable workings of Irene's life in particular, and the wider social and racial networks of American life more generally. The theme of light-skinned African-Americans who pass for whites is explored in Larsen's *Passing* (1928) and Jessie Redmon Fauset's novel *Plum Bun* (1923).

Rather than emphasizing a separate African-American culture as Baker does, we can also consider how Harlem Renaissance art and literature challenged traditions of racism in American mainstream culture. George Hutchinson attributes the success of the Harlem Renaissance to the expansion of literary and artistic markets and to the belief, held by W. E. B. Du Bois, Alain Locke and many others, that "aesthetic experience could be a powerful impetus to the destruction of social convention, the awakening of new types of consciousness, and the creation of new forms of solidarity across traditional boundaries" (13). In effect, Harlem Renaissance art and literature broke from the racist past and laid the groundwork for full integration and equality of racial minorities in the US as it raised consciousness, challenged racist conventions, and found allies across the color line. While the Crisis of the Thirties (see below) ended the fanfare of the movement, the Harlem Renaissance sparked later waves of innovative art that was connected to movements for civil rights and political freedoms (in the US, the Civil Rights Movement of the 1950s and 1960s; in Caribbean and African contexts, decolonization movements; in the UK and Commonwealth countries, pro-immigration movements). We turn next to the European Crisis in the early twentieth century that would embroil the entire world.

THE GREAT WAR (1914–18)

W. B. Yeats's famous apocalyptic poem, "The Second Coming" (1919), imagines the waning of the 2,000-year epoch of Christianity in favor of some yet-unimagined rising new order:

> Turning and turning in the widening gyre
> The falcon cannot hear the falconer;
> Things fall apart; the centre cannot hold;
> Mere anarchy is loosed upon the world,
> The blood-dimmed tide is loosed, and everywhere
> The ceremony of innocence is drowned; (#1–6).

Anarchy, violence and struggle take the place of European hegemony, or dominance, that had provided, at least for Europe, a sense of stability and "innocence." What created such a millennial, "end times" sentiment as expressed by the poet? To start, Yeats was by no means alone in thinking that the European order was doomed. For many, the Great War, or World War I, signaled nothing less than the end of humanity. Edward Grey, Foreign Secretary of Great Britain, on the eve of the war in August 1914, dramatically stated: "The lamps are going out all over Europe. We shall not see them lit again in our lifetime" (qtd. in Hobsbawm 1995: 22). As its name indicates, World War I was the first war in which the entire globe was enveloped in conflict. The historian Eric Hobsbawm maps the conflict as follows:

The First World War involved *all* major powers and indeed all European states except Spain, the Netherlands, the three Scandinavian countries and Switzerland. What is more, troops from the world overseas were, often for the first time, sent to fight and work outside their own regions. Canadians fought in France, Australians and New Zealanders forged their national consciousness on a peninsula in the Aegean – 'Gallipoli' became their national myth – and, more significantly, the United States rejected George Washington's warning against 'European entanglements' and sent its men to fight there, thus determining the shape of twentieth-century history. Indians were sent to Europe and the Middle

East, Chinese labour battalions came to the West, Africans fought in the French army.

(1995: 23)

Adding to the trauma of world conflict and the global mobilization of troops, the Great War was unsurpassed, even by World War II, in terms of tactical absurdity. The Western Front, which extended from the English Channel in Belgium to the Swiss frontier and along the entire length of eastern France, witnessed millions of men from both sides mowed down by machine gun fire and artillery bombardment, as well as the first recorded use of poison gas on troops. It is estimated that 124,000 tons of chlorine, phosgene and mustard gas were deployed over the course of the war, resulting in approximately 12,000 military and 100,000 to 260,000 civilian casualties, and tens of thousands more deaths from the delayed effects of the poison gas (Wikipedia, "Chemical Weapons in World War I"). The most horrifying aspect of this war, however, was the trench system. From the winter of 1914 until the spring of 1918, the two sides, the Allied Powers (English, French and Russian empires and, in 1917, the US) and the Central Powers (the German, Austro-Hungarian and Ottoman Empires, and Bulgaria), remained in fixed positions that usually moved only a few hundred yards and, at most, changed by a few miles.

The trenches were a series of multiple parallel dug-out lines that ran for 400 miles along the front. Historian Paul Fussell estimates that "[There were] over 12,000 miles of trenches on the Allied side alone. When we add the trenches of the Central Powers, we arrive at a figure of about 25,000 miles, equal to a trench sufficient to circle the earth" (37). The trenches were constantly filling with mud, and the men were so covered with lice that the best delousing schemes behind the lines could do nothing to combat the situation. Then, there were the rats that fed on dead soldiers and horses. One officer reported,

We are fairly plagued with rats. They have eaten nearly everything in the mess, including the table-clothe and the operations orders! We borrowed a large cat and shut it up at night to exterminate them, and found the place empty next morning. The rats must have eaten it up, bones, fur, and all, and dragged it to their holes.

(qtd. in Fussell 49)

Between the enemy lines was the infamous "No–Man's Land," a strip of land where nothing grew, pockmarked by shell craters, and strewn with barbed wire, mines and dead bodies that no one could retrieve safely. Fussell describes the scene:

> The stench of rotten flesh was over everything, hardly repressed by the chloride of lime sprinkled on particularly offensive sites. Dead horses and dead men – and parts of both – were sometimes not buried for months and often simply became an element of parapets and trench walls. You could smell the front line miles before you could see it. Lingering pockets of gas added to the unappetizing atmosphere.

(49)

Finally, as the entrenchment of the opposing armies suggests, the war quickly became a war of attrition in which each side attempted to outlast the other through sheer destruction of the other side's soldiers, weaponry and, behind the lines, their civilians and infrastructure. "Total war," defined as "a war to which all resources and the whole population are committed," became the new norm for twentieth-century wars (Saint-Amour 47). The number of casualties was astounding. "The Germans lost a million men in the first five months. France, in the 'battles of the frontiers' of August [1914] lost over 300,000 men in two weeks" (Eksteins 100). The British, in its attempt to take the Somme in July 1916, "lost 60,000 men *on the very first day* and another half million by November. . . . In the two battles of Verdun and the Somme the Germans lost about 800,000 men, slightly less than the French and the British" (Eksteins 144, emphasis added). Why the astronomical losses? In the trench system, the attackers faced a far greater risk than the defenders. As men moved forward to attack, defenders in the facing trenches could easily mow them down by means of machine guns, grenades and poison gas canisters. Meanwhile, the war spread to civilian territories. Civilians were rounded up in Belgium by the invading German army and either shot or interned in labor camps. The town of Leuven in Belgium was burnt to the ground, including the library at the University of Leuven (founded in 1426) that held over 300,000 medieval books and manuscripts (Wikipedia, "The Rape of Belgium"). On May 31, 1915, German Zeppelins, gigantic hydrogen gas-filled, cigar-shaped "ocean liners of the air," began dropping incendiary bombs and grenades on London. It is estimated that 557 persons were killed and 1,358 wounded in these bombing raids on London (Wikipedia, "German Strategic Bombing"). The Germans also bombed Paris and the Cathedral in Reims, the coronation site for twenty-five French kings and queens.

The biggest civilian catastrophe during this war, however, and one that ominously heralded even larger-scale atrocities to come in World War II, was the Armenian Genocide by the Turks. In Turkey, the Young Turks movement aimed to revitalize the weakened Otto-man Empire by creating a secular, constitutional Turkish national state. They established Turkish as the official language of government and education, and refused to assimilate ethnic and religious minori-ties, especially the Armenians. Hannah Arendt writes of the rise of totalitarian states (states like Turkey that used ideology – such as anti-Semitism or other forms of racial or ethnic intolerance – and politics to abuse their subjects) that emerged with the Great War:

> Denationalization [deporting, stripping of rights] became a powerful weapon of totalitarian politics, and the constitutional inability of Euro-pean nation-states to guarantee human rights to those who had lost nationally guaranteed rights, made it possible for the persecuting gov-ernments to impose their standard of values even upon their opponents. Those whom the persecutor had singled out as scum of the earth – Jews, Trotskyites [communist revolutionaries who followed Trotsky's exiled leadership rather than Stalin's], Armenians, etc. – actually were received as scum of the earth everywhere. [. . . Mass denationalizations] presup-posed a state structure which, if it was not yet fully totalitarian, at least would not tolerate any opposition and would rather lose its citizens than harbor people with different views.

(269–78)

During the war, the Armenians were persecuted: confined to ghettos, murdered and raped by hostile populations, and forcibly marched into the desert of northern Syria and Iraq, where they perished. It is estimated that 650,000 Armenians died from genocide, disease and military action (Sondhaus 391).

For colonial soldiers, the effects of the war were equally profound, but in a potentially positive way. In an unprecedented development, both Allied and Central Powers deployed troops from their colonies to fight their battles. While the greater share of the European Allied forces were occupied at the Western Front in France, British Indian soldiers were indispensable to the Middle East and sub-Saharan Africa campaigns. Though the Allies lost at Gallipoli (in modern-day Turkey) in 1915, they continued to fight against the crumbling Ottoman Empire in the Middle East largely by means of British colonial Indian troops. India agreed to fight in support of the British Empire in order to strengthen its hand against the British in their bid for independence after the war. (The Irish refused to fight and their armed militant resistance against the British Empire, begun with the Easter Rising in 1916, resulted in their independence, at least for the Southern Catholic half of the tiny island nation, in 1922.) The Arab national independence campaigns against the Ottoman Empire were waged during the war and cynically supported by the French and British Empires. In fact, the covert operation by "Lawrence of Arabia," the British intelligence operative, T. E. Lawrence, took credit for leading the Arabs to revolt. By defecting from the Ottoman Empire and declaring their independence (Sharif Hussein bin Ali, the Emir of Mecca, declared it officially on June 27, 1916), the Arabs achieved the turning point for the Allies in the war against the Ottoman Empire (Sondhaus 378). Tragically, the Arab freedom was short-lived. The British and French, after the war, recolonized the territories of Iraq, Palestine, Lebanon, Syria, Arabia and Egypt to ensure their own geopolitical dominance in the region. Meanwhile, in sub-Saharan Africa, the German East African *askari* (the name means "soldier" in Swahili) was recruited in a highly selective fashion and subjected to rigorous training and "paid roughly double the wages of the British King's African Rifles (KAR), raised in neighboring British colonies" (Sondhaus 114). These positions of power and prestige would influence colonial subjects' outlooks profoundly after the war. Colonial soldiers witnessed the European powers destroy each other, exposing their vulnerability and massive, destructive shortcomings. The experiences of the colonial and African-American soldiers in the Great War gave momentum to colonial independence and civil rights movements, and to the Russian Revolution of 1917 (see below).

The Great War completely altered the imperial system as the Austro-Hungarian, Ottoman and German Empires fell to the Allied powers. Likewise, the Czarist Empire of Russia collapsed during the Russian Revolution. To address this power vacuum resulting from imperial collapse, the Allies established nation-states in eastern and central Europe. Unfortunately, because of the multiethnic, multireligious and multilingual populations in these European regions, the new nations instantly created thirty million minorities, who were often persecuted and driven out of the new nations. Eastern European modernist literature (including Baltic, Polish, Czech, Slovak, Romanian and Croatian literature) often expresses the dissonance and fragmentation resulting from the clash of ethnic, imperial and national alliances, during the war and after. For example, Jaroslav Hašek's *The Fortunes of the Good Soldier Švejk During the World War* (1921) and Liviu Rebreanu's *Forest of the Hanged* (1922) are Czech accounts of the "shifting fortunes of war and the conflict of political allegiances" experienced as a result of the disintegration of the Austro-Hungarian Empire (Neubauer 177–78).

The Allies also imposed punitive war reparations on Germany that further destabilized the nation (see the rise of fascism below). Even the Allied powers were shaken. At the end of the war, in 1918, Oswald Spengler's best-selling *The Decline of the West* declared Europe's civilizational superiority outdated and false: "The Western European area is regarded as a fixed pole, a unique patch chosen on the surface of the sphere for no better reason, it seems, than because we live on it" (13). He called this **Eurocentric** view of the world the *Ptolemaic system* of history, and he argued for

The *Copernican discovery* in the historical sphere, in that it admits no sort of privileged position to the Classical or the Western Culture as against the Cultures of India, Babylon, China, Egypt, the Arabs, Mexico – separate worlds of dynamic being which in point of mass count for just as much in the general picture of history as the Classical [Greek and Roman], while frequently surpassing it in point of spiritual greatness and soaring power.
(13–14)

The precondition for the "decline of the West" came, in part, from the Great War, but it also came from the rise of Asia, especially Japan, as a world power, as we have seen above.

Experimentalism in both modernist form and content increased dramatically after the war. Artists and writers attempted to represent the unspeakable – and often unrepresentable – horrors of the Great War in their art, and they did so by cracking the representational mirror. W. B. Yeats, whose post-war poem "The Second Coming" began this section, expresses this dissolution of social and formal order: "Things fall apart; the centre cannot hold;/Mere anarchy is loosed upon the world" (#3–4). Other works that concern the horrors and loss of the war include *The Waste Land*; Erich Maria Remarque's *All Quiet on the Western Front*; Ernest Hemingway's *A Farewell to Arms*; Virginia Woolf's *Jacob's Room*, *Mrs. Dalloway* and *To the Lighthouse*; as well as works by Henri Barbusse, Ford Madox Ford, Ezra Pound, Willa Cather, May Sinclair, Rebecca West, W. Somerset Maugham, Thomas Mann, David Jones, Dorothy Sayers, Vera Brittain, David Jones, Robert Graves, John Dos Passos, Ernst Jünger and Karl Kraus. But we'll see in the next section that fragmented and innovative art forms were also a product of the profound shift in gender relations underway both before and after the war.

GENDER WARS

Not only were European powers weakened, the war overturned relations between the sexes. Virginia Woolf, looking back on the Great War in 1938 and its effect on women, wrote:

> How . . . can we explain that amazing outburst in August 1914, when the daughters of educated men . . . rushed into hospitals . . . drove lorries, worked in fields and munitions factories, and used all their immense stories of charm, of sympathy, to persuade young men that to fight was heroic . . .? So profound was her unconscious loathing for the education of the private house with its cruelty, its poverty, its hypocrisy, its immorality, its inanity that she would undertake any task however menial, exercise any fascination however fatal that enabled her to escape.
>
> (39)

By the war's end, one in four of the total male population in the UK had joined up, roughly one-half by volunteering, one-half by conscription (Wikipedia, "Recruitment to the British Army"). As a result of this mobilization, women from across classes replaced them in farms and factories. And while working-class women earned better wages than they'd ever received, middle-class women, previously confined to the private household, entered the public sphere of waged-work and travel with zeal. Sandra M. Gilbert and Susan

Gubar summarize this massive movement of women into the public workaday world: "Liberated from parlors and petticoats alike, trousered 'war girls' beam [in the Imperial War Museum photographs] as they shovel coal, shoe horses, fight fires, drive buses, chop down trees, make shells, dig graves" (271). The wartime mobilization of hundreds of thousands of women demonstrated that they could hold down first-class jobs and that they deserved top wages. This fact held, too, for African-American populations in the US, as they occupied the well-paying jobs vacated by soldiers at war.

The thrill of liberation experienced by women during the war painfully contrasted with the gloom experienced by returning veterans of the war. The veterans were often disabled, missing limbs and eyes, and beset by "shell shock" (what we now call post-traumatic stress disorder). The irony of the experience of combat for men was that, rather than the thrill of combat and the glamor of heroism, the war gave a sense of futility and unreality that lingered long after the war was over. For instance, in Virginia Woolf's novel *Mrs Dalloway*, the war veteran Septimus Smith wanders about London in full-blown shell shock before committing suicide. Even as veterans took a bitter sidelong glance at the war, women demanded the continuance of their central place in society. Alice Meynell's poem, "A Father of Women" (1917), for instance, makes this usurpation of men by women quite clear. The poem asks fathers who have lost their sons in the war to accept their daughters as substitutes. Virginia Woolf, as previously quoted, abhorred the sort of triumph Meynell expresses because of its indirect embrace of war, violence and empire. Nonetheless, Meynell's poem is instructive for how it exemplifies the emasculation and disorientation experienced by men after the war. Many post-war texts explored the altered relations between men and women as an effect of the war, including Rebecca West's *The Return of the Soldier*, Ford Maddox Ford's *The Good Soldier* and *Parade's End*, Virginia Woolf's *Mrs. Dalloway*, Ernest Hemingway's *The Sun Also Rises* and *A Farewell to Arms*, D. H. Lawrence's *Lady Chatterley's Lover* and T. S. Eliot's *The Waste Land*.

Another key component of the "sex changes," as Susan Gilbert and Susan Gubar called the altered relations between genders during this time, was the post-war emergence of the "salaried masses." The masses were a phenomenon of the "new middle class" sparked by US-style assembly-line production (Fordism) and expanded industries for

consumer goods and services. These salaried but de-skilled professionals, sometimes called petit bourgeoisie, maintained a distinction
from the working classes (because they did "clean" work in the service economy), though they accepted lower wages, less autonomy
and less security than did the traditional bourgeois (property-owning
elites who could usually live on their inheritances without working).
These urban service workers included women as well as men, due
to the unskilled or semi-skilled nature of the work and the fact that
so many men had died in the war. More fully modernized than the
gentleman squire or lawyer, these workers appeared to embrace the
anonymity and fragmentary nature of the city, just as soldiers had had
to adapt to the dehumanizing landscape of trench warfare. Intellectuals such as T. S. Eliot, Siegfried Kracauer and Georg Lukács defined
the masses' condition as "metaphysical suffering" (Kracauer 1995:
129), a "transcendental homelessness" (Lukács 41) or death-in-life:
"We who were living are now dying/With a little patience" (Eliot
16, #329–30). Exiled from a religious worldview (beyond a mere
token appreciation), local community, and authentic or unalienated
existence, the modern masses suffered from what intellectuals per-
ceived to be an existential void: a lack of higher meaning in the
world. They sought meaning, or rather distraction, in the fragmentary and fleeting pleasures of mass culture (Kracauer 1998: 7, 13).
This alienation extended to the relations between the sexes: writers
of this time period, such as T. S. Eliot and Jean Rhys, frequently
represented men and women of the salaried masses as being artificial:
men were self-satisfied fops, and women displayed "an unladylike
frankness about sexual matters" (Gilbert and Gubar 340). Despite the
frankness toward these matters, writers described their sexual relations as mechanical and abstracted.

   The tensions between the sexes, though felt more sharply after the
war, had a long history that predates the First World War. One of
the most striking and early instances of social and political change in
twentieth-century Britain, the women's campaign to win the vote,
dramatically escalated its struggle in 1905. While the women's suffrage movement had been active throughout the second half of the
nineteenth century, it had stuck to polite forms of protest: circulating
petitions and writing letters to male politicians, nicely asking them to
consider debating the women's vote in Parliament. In 1905, however,
some of the women's movement tactics changed when a splinter

group, the Women's Social and Political Union (WSPU), began adopting militant tactics to gain attention to their cause. They interrupted political meetings, heckled speakers, threw rocks wrapped with political slogans, "Deeds, not Words!" and other messages, chained themselves to government buildings, and, in one extreme case, a woman threw herself under the king's horse at a race and died. These tactics usually resulted in arrests, keeping the women's suffrage issue in the newspapers and on people's lips. In the US, the women's movement was also militant – with episodes of arrest, hunger strikes and forcible feeding, but it achieved its ends more easily. Universal suffrage was granted in 1920, (though black women (and men) continued to face widespread disenfranchisement until the passage of the Voting Rights Act in 1965) was granted in 1920.

The significance of the women's suffrage campaign cannot be overestimated. Previously confined to the home, middle-class women took to the streets and made education, career opportunities, sexual violence, contraception and divorce law into issues for all of Britain as well as for many other nations. They allied with working-class women who demanded better working conditions, higher pay, affordable housing, and an end to police brutality and enforced prostitution. All classes protested loudly and publicly to make women and family issues visible to all. Liberated women were often called "new women" and, by the 1920s, they had rejected the corset, bobbed their hair, and circulated freely in public, whether on foot, by bicycle or motorcar (whereas in Victorian England, a "proper" middle-class woman would be chaperoned). In the UK, the vote was won for propertied women over thirty in 1918, at the conclusion of the war, and universal suffrage was granted in 1928. French women did not win the vote until 1944. In post-revolutionary (1917) Russia, the Commissar of Social Welfare, Alexandra Kollontai, introduced policies that offered recognition of and support for women's reproductive labors, including pregnancy and raising children. In Germany, Rosa Luxemburg and Clara Zetkin allied the women's cause with the radical socialist labor movement during the post-World War I Weimar Republic. They helped to win the vote for women in 1918 (Gammel and Waszczuk 304).

The women's movement was not confined to Europe. Modernization movements, including women's struggles, emerged around the globe simultaneously with European women's movements in the late nineteenth and early twentieth centuries. For example, He-Yin Zhen (1884–1920) was a prominent Chinese feminist theorist and founding editor of the anarchist-leaning feminist journal *Natural Justice*, which was published by the Society for the Restoration of Women's Rights in Tokyo between 1907–08 (Liu *et al* 4–5). He-Yin Zhen not only analyzed modernity's patriarchal structures around the globe, but also critiqued progressive Chinese men's hypocrisy insofar as they promoted women's rights but still required women to be men's private property (Liu *et al* 2–3). He-Yin Zhen stressed the historical continuity between China's imperial (pre-nineteenth century) past and the early twentieth-century present, in which the world was integrated through modernity in terms of how women were subordinated. That is, He-Yin Zhen argued that the injustice of "woman" (the gendered position in society) might change its form, but the existence of this group's oppression remained constant throughout Chinese history (Liu *et al* 9–10). Rather than seeing Euro-American and Japanese feminisms as models of more liberated and advanced gender relations for the Chinese to follow, He-Yin Zhen saw them

> as representing more advanced ways in which newly emergent and now-globalizing forms of oppression – industrial waged labor, democratic politics and female suffrage, enlightenment knowledge – could attach themselves to native forms of subjection, to reconfigure and deepen these extant forms on a larger scale and in less detectable ways.
>
> (Liu *et al* 38)

In sum, He-Yin Zhen sought to enter a worldwide conversation about women's rights and emancipation rather than follow the lead of more "advanced" feminist movements.

These conversations were ongoing across the globe as "local" issues were linked to struggles elsewhere. From Adelaide Casely Hayford's "A Girl's School in West Africa" (1926) and Kikue Ide's "History and Problems of the Women's Suffrage Movement in Japan" (1928); to South Asian feminist Sarojini Naidu's "Women in National Life" (1915), Fante (from Ghana) feminist Efwa Kato's "What We Women Can Do" (1934), Attia Habibullah's "Seclusion of Women" (1936), Kamaladevi Chattopadyaya's "Future of the Indian Women's Movement" (1936) and Huda Shaarawi's "Pan-Arab Feminism" (1944), women combatted the injustices of the gendered organization of society from many angles (Moynagh). They advocated for better education, fair working conditions and pay, full citizenship and rights, as well as full equality with men.

Often, the tactics used in local women's struggles traveled to other places and issues. Elleke Boehmer documents the "cross-empire, anti-imperial cooperation" (25) between Irish and Boers (Dutch farmers in Southern Africa) against the British in the second Boer War (1899–1902). From that struggle, Boehmer traces the links between South African, Irish and Indian anticolonial political strategists in developing "self-reliance and self-development" methods of "non-violent resistance, parliamentary non-cooperation, and the cultivation of local culture and [local] language" (30). For instance, she notes Solomon T. Plaatje's "silent borrowing" of strategies of passive resistance from South Asian minorities, especially Gandhi, in South Africa (24). In *Native Life in South Africa*, Plaatje describes how black South African women used non-violent protest strategies to contest unjust legislation in the Orange Free State province of South Africa. This legislation prohibited any native woman from residing in the province without a permit showing that she is a servant of a white person (110). While this legislation was largely ignored under the Boer (Dutch) Republic, in 1910 the Act of Union joined Boer and British territories under the single nationality of South Africa. One result of Boer submission to British forces was to reanimate draconian laws such as the Pass Law. In response, Plaatje recounts,

> A crowd of six hundred women, in July 1913, marched to the municipal offices in Bloemfontein and asked to see the Mayor. [. . .] The Deputy-Mayor came out, and they deposited before him a bag containing their passes of the previous month and politely signified their intention not to buy any more passes.

> (113)

When women were arrested for not carrying their monthly passes, they were imprisoned and fined. "They all refused to pay the fines and said their little ones would be entrusted to the care of providence till their mothers and sisters have broken the shackles of oppression by means of passive resistance" (113). These non-violent tactics, of course, were not confined to the British Empire. Native Americans, African slaves, Samoans and Maori also used non-violent tactics of resistance against colonial settlers, and so, too, did many other groups in non-colonial situations.

The movements for women's emancipation frequently included sexual emancipation movements. In the late nineteenth century, Robert von Krafft-Ebing, in his canonical *Psychopathia Sexualis*, divided unruly women into four categories, or degrees of homosexual deviance. These categories were not based on women's sexual behavior, but on "their social behavior and physical appearance" (Smith-Rosenberg 269). In his scientific opinion, if a woman was unladylike, she must be a lesbian, a "degenerate" in diseased condition. Sexual emancipation movements in Europe, India, Japan and elsewhere combatted pervasive homophobia and insisted on women's sexual autonomy (i.e., that their role was more than simply to give men pleasure) as well as the legitimacy of male homosexuality. In Japan, *keishu*, or talented women writers, Higuchi Ichiyo (1872–96) and Yosano Akiko (1878–1942) wrote sympathetically about prostitution (Ichiyo) and women's sexual pleasure (Akiko). (See also Chapter 4.) Marie Stopes's wildly popular *Married Love* (1918) was, in the words of Samuel Hynes, "one of the documents that shaped [European] post-war imaginations" (qtd. in Hall 119). Stopes, a trained paleo-botanist, wrote the book after experiencing the effects of her ignorance regarding heterosexual relations – that is, when her marriage failed due to non-consummation. Combining straightforward biological information about procreation with soothing poetic idealism regarding the institution of marriage, *Married Love*, as Hall says, "genuinely changed lives, having the kind of impact on its readers and its society that few novels – perhaps *Uncle Tom's Cabin* or the works of Dickens – have ever achieved" (121). The book promoted women's sexual knowledge and pleasure within married life. In combination with Margaret Sanger's contraception movement that advocated the widespread use of contraception, women began to have more control over their sexual lives.

Homosexual emancipation movements in the early twentieth century were not usually, as they would be in the later twentieth century, organized movements marching in public. Most of their resistance occurred in literature and in semi-private salons, private homes or clandestine clubs. In India, Ismat Chughtai's short story "Lihaf" ("The Quilt"), published in 1942, escaped censorship by the British government because of its indirect evocation of a lesbian relationship.

The story concerns a homoerotic relationship between a lonely, young wife, whose husband prefers young men, and her maid, but its language evokes this sexual relationship without explicit or obscene reference. As with Rashid Jahan's one-act play, "Behind the Veil" (Parde ke Peeche), published in the Progressive Writers Association (PWA) journal *Angare* (*Burning Coals*) in India in the 1930s, both women "claimed the right to write about the female body [. . .] and its claims to pleasure and fulfillment" (Gopal 67). For these writers, women's sexual liberation is part of national liberation. They interrogated what it means for middle-class, Muslim Indian women to become modern, and how the larger structure of the nation intersected with their everyday lives.

This is not to say that resistance was limited to literary evocation. At the same time that Oscar Wilde was languishing in an English prison under sodomy charges (see Chapter 2), August Bebel, in 1898, made a speech on the steps of the German Reichstag (the lower house of parliament) in favor of homosexual emancipation. Eksteins describes the general mood of tolerance – indeed, even progress – in Germany before the Great War:

> Homosexuality in the Kaiser's [German emperor's] entourage was well known even before the journalist Maximilian Harden decided to expose it in 1906. Magnus Hirschfeld led the campaign in Germany to revise paragraph 175 of the civil code, and by 1914 his petition had 30,000 doctors, 750 university professors, and thousands of others as signatories. Berlin by 1914 had about forty homosexual bars and, according to police estimates, between one and two thousand male prostitutes.
>
> (83)

This atmosphere was reflected in the literature. Christopher Isherwood's novel *Goodbye to Berlin* (1939), structured as a series of interlinked stories, recounts the decadent gay-friendly German Weimar culture. It is set in the early 1930s, a period ominously shadowed by the rising fascist party. One of the main characters, a young cabaret singer, Sally Bowles, performs at the seedy Lady Windermere club, a reference to a play by Oscar Wilde. The novel was later adapted for the Broadway play *I am a Camera* (1951) and, later, for the musical (1966) and film (1972) *Cabaret*, both of which include risqué transgender performances.

Germany's relatively progressive movement toward legal homosexual emancipation was, in comparison to France, even a bit sluggish.
As Shari Benstock explains, France didn't need a sexual emancipation
movement because there were no legal prohibitions to begin with:

> Because the Code Napoléon [established in 1804] had made no provision
> for punishment of homosexuality, [. . .] homosexual practices were not
> banned by law and were a dominant feature of *belle époque* [the period
> of European peace and prosperity from 1871–1914] culture. Proust's writ-
> ings [especially the seven-volume novel, *In Search of Lost Time*] portray
> male homosexual practice in Paris salon culture, while by 1900 the city
> itself had an international reputation as the capital of same sex love
> among women and was designated "Paris-Lesbos."

(47)

Many famous women writers from England, the US and elsewhere
gathered in Paris, which persisted in its sexual permissiveness even after
the *belle époque*, in order to participate in semi-public queer communities. These writers included Djuna Barnes, Natalie Barney, Bryher
(the lover of poet H. D., Hilda Doolittle), Colette, Nancy Cunard,
Anais Nin, Gertrude Stein and Alice B. Toklas (Stein's "wife"). The
semi-public nature of these communities depended, however, on
maintaining a certain respect for dominant heterosexual culture. A
too-public display of same-sex desire – as with Colette and the Mar-
quise de Belbeuf, who enacted a scene of lesbian love in a pantomime
skit at the Moulin Rouge cabaret in 1907 – resulted in public outrage.
Colette's lesbian skit, for instance, created a near-riot at the theater.
The police were called in, and the play was banned (Benstock 48).
Homosexual-themed literature from expatriate communities in Paris
and from within England include Gertrude Stein's "Tender Buttons"
(1912) and *The Autobiography of Alice B. Toklas* (1933), Marcel Proust's
In Search of Lost Time (1913–27), Djuna Barnes's *Nightwood* (1936),
E. M. Forster's posthumously published *Maurice* (1971), Virginia Woolf's
Orlando (1928) and Sylvia Townsend Warner's *Lolly Willowes* (1926).

THE RUSSIAN REVOLUTION

While riots over skits, plays and films were common in the modernist
era, such riots paled in comparison with the political unrest around
the world as a result of the Russian Revolution of October 1917.

(This revolution was called the October Revolution based on the Russian Julian calendar, which was thirteen days behind the Gregorian calendar adopted throughout the Westernized world. The October Revolution actually took place on November 7 [Hobsbawm 1995: 57].) Before the revolution, Russia was a feudal state with a large rural peasant population and very little industry or modernization. It was ruled by a corrupt tsar and wearied by the Great War. The revolution began, not so dramatically, when

> a demonstration of working-class women (on the socialist movement's customary "Women's Day," March 8), combined with an industrial lockout in the notoriously militant Putilov metalworks. produced a general strike and an invasion of the centre of the capital [then called Petrograd] across the frozen river, essentially to demand bread.
>
> (Hobsbawm 1995: 60)

The tsar's rule collapsed. Four euphoric days of anarchic freedom, equality and direct democracy followed. Into this revolutionary vacuum of power emerged a powerless, unrecognized provisional government along with a multitude of grassroots, local "councils" (soviets). In the cities, workers demanded bread, better wages and shorter work hours; in the countryside, where 80% of the population lived, the peasants wanted land. Everyone wanted to end the war. By the start of the summer, Vladimir Lenin, along with other Bolshevik leaders who returned from exile, had organized and advanced the Bolshevik party with the slogan "Bread, Peace, Land." Hobsbawm notes that, contrary to Cold War mythology, Lenin was not a totalitarian dictator (though his successor, Joseph Stalin [1879–1953], was) who led a coup to gain power. Instead, he had the ability to recognize what the masses wanted and led the revolution by knowing how to follow. In fact, when the peasants expressed the desire to divide the land into family farms, he committed the Bolsheviks to this form of economic individualism (Hobsbawm 1995: 61). The support of both industrial workers and rural peasants (whose sons comprised the majority of the armed forces) allowed the unthinkable to happen: the Bolsheviks stormed the Winter Palace on November 7, 1917 (according to the Gregorian calendar), and the Provisional Government dissolved. The Bolsheviks seized power, declared worker control over existing production facilities, took over the banks, and declared peace with Germany.

Immediately, the Allied powers sent British, French, American, Japanese, Polish, Serb, Greek and Romanian troops onto Russian soil. They, along with counter-revolutionary forces within Russia (the "white" armies), intended the overthrow of the worker and peasant state, the "reds." A brutal and chaotic civil war ensued for the next three years. With the support of the peasantry as well as the military (on both sides – the soldiers and sailors on the Allied side were often mutinous, too), the Bolsheviks triumphed in 1920. Lenin's creation of the Communist Party (600,000 persons strong, strictly hierarchical and disciplined) was in large part responsible for its inexorable hold on governing power. Let us clarify the terms being used here: *socialism* is the belief in radial democracy and an equal sharing in the fruits of production; *communism* is a system of local, directly participatory democratic governance and derives from the term "communal"; the Communist Party, invented by Lenin, is a hierarchal and indirect form of leadership. Lenin coined the term "vanguard party," which refers to the elite communist leadership that directed the masses on the "proper" revolutionary path.

But the larger revolution was not yet won. The socialist revolution was supposed to spread around the world. In 1848, Marx and Engels's "Communist Manifesto" concluded with the famous slogan, "Workers of the World, unite!" For some time, it looked as though this might indeed happen. In the first few years after the Great War, insurrections swept the globe. Germany, for example, saw the abdication of the kaiser and the creation of the radical republic of Weimar, though worker revolts and communist organizers were brutally crushed, as when communist leaders Rosa Luxemburg and Karl Liebnecht were assassinated by freelance army gunmen. Hobsbawm describes the shock waves and passionate inspiration erupting immediately after the events in Russia:

> Cuban tobacco workers formed "soviets". Revolutionary student movements erupted in Peking (Bejing) in 1919 and Cordoba (Argentina) in 1918, soon to spread across Latin America and to general local revolutionary Marxist leaders and parties. The Indian nationalist militant M.N. Roy immediately fell under its spell in Mexico, where the local revolution,

> entering its most radical phase in 1917, naturally recognized its affinity
> with revolutionary Russia: Marx and Lenin became its icons, together
> with Moctezuma, Emiliano Zapata and assorted laboring Indians, and
> can still be seen on the great murals of its official artists [Diego Rivera,
> José Clemente Orozco, and David Alfaro Siquerios]. Within a few months
> Roy was in Moscow to play a major role in forming the new Commu-
> nist International's policy for colonial liberation. Partly through resident
> Dutch socialists like Henk Sneevliet, the October revolution immediately
> made its mark on the Indonesian national liberation movement's main
> mass organization, Sarekat Islam.

(1995: 65–66)

The Soviet Union offered important support for colonial liberation and anti-racist politics in the 1920s–30s and during the Cold
War. Jamaican-American poet Claude McKay, Jewish-American
poet Moishe Nadir, and African-American poet Langston Hughes
referred to their visits to the Soviet Union in the 1920s in almost
sacred terms – "magic pilgrimage" is what McKay called it – because
of its "alignment of art and revolution" (Lee 1–2). From this combination of art and radical politics "emerged many striking, eccentric
ways of expressing cultural difference [. . . and offered] visions of
world revolution in which the ethnic Other took the lead" (Lee 2).
In addition, non-Western nations saw an alternative to the capitalist organization of the world economy, and they could play the two
superpowers (the US and the Soviet Union) against one another
after World War II as they established their newly independent, non-
aligned nations.

The modernist literary movements in Russia, to some extent, mirrored those of the rest of Europe. There was a turn-of-the-century
symbolist poetry movement, followed by a cubo-futurist avant-garde
that included Velimir Khlebnikov and Vladimir Mayakovsky. The
"cubo" in the term indicates the influence that the visual art of
cubism had on these experimental writers, and the term also indicates how the Russian futurists insisted on their independence from
Italian futurism. They drew attention to their indigenous and art-
centered references, whereas Italian futurists concerned themselves
with all aspects of society. After the October Revolution, Soviet
futurists further distinguished their socialist political leanings from
Italian futurism's fascist ones (Erlich 34–38). The Russian futurist

poet Aleksandr Kurchenykh coined the term *zaum*, often translated
as "transrational," poetry in 1913 as part of an effort to develop
"universal poetic language, born organically, and not artificially like
Esperanto" (Masing-Delic 87). *Zaum* poets tried to distinguish Russia
from Europe by finding an alternative to the Indo-European lin-
guistic-based Esperanto. After the revolution, the Soviet avant-garde
carried its experimentation across all aspects of society. In 1923, it
began a journal named *LEF* ("*Left Front of the Arts*") that included
radical innovations in photography and cinematography (with con-
tributions by Alexander Rodchenko and Sergei Eisenstein). These
more easily transportable visual and verbal forms were part of an
attempt to spread the revolution around the world. The 1923 *LEF*
manifesto, published simultaneously in Russian, German and English,
called for left artists to "prepare the European Revolution. In the
USSR, strengthen it" and "Down with the boundaries of Lands and
Studios" (Kolocotroni 306).

Also spanning pre- and post-revolutionary Russia, Anna Akhmato-
va's (1889–1966) poetry deployed more conventional language
and form than did the avant-gardes. Nonetheless, she "drastically
transform[ed] poetic content, with a dynamics of implicit and tense
semantic juxtapositions" (Erlich 58). Her poetry exhibits the dissonance and displacement of fragmented form akin to *The Waste Land*, a
kind of modernist poetry that remains firmly ensconced in the poetic
tradition, but remakes the present in a manner that clearly breaks from
the recent past. Further, her poetic persona shifts from socialite, to
nun, to peasant woman, a complexity that speaks to the "unheard-
of upheavals" of "the real . . . twentieth century" as well as to the
catastrophic losses sustained in those upheavals (qtd. in Erlich 58–59).

The aesthetic doctrine of the Soviet Union shifted dramatically
in 1934 when, at the first All-Union Congress of Soviet Writers,
Andrei Zhdanov, Secretary of the Communist Party led by Joseph
Stalin, proclaimed the doctrine of **socialist realism**. Socialist realism emphasized "truth and historical concreteness of the artistic
depiction" that was combined with the task of consciousness-raising,
defined as the "ideological transformation and education of the
working people in the spirit of Socialism" (Kolocotroni 525). While
the avant-garde had sought to completely transform language, form
and media through which artists worked, socialist realist writers
concentrated on "reportage," the straightforward documentation

of social ills, with the aim of educating their audience. This form of "committed" writing and art spread around the world (as we'll explore below) as part of the general struggle against fascism and for a socialist revolution. As the term circulated, it came to be called **social realism** to denote a documentary concern with social problems without necessarily affiliating directly with the Soviet Union and its party-brand of **socialist realism**.

Other important writers of the Russian Revolution include the dramatist and novelist Maxim Gorky (1868–1936), an early proponent of socialist realism; Alexander Bogdanov (1873–1929), the science fiction writer of *Red Star* (1908) and *Engineer Memmi* (1913); Isaac Babel (1894–1940), a dramatist and short story writer; and Yevgeny Zamyatin (1884–1937), an early dissident, whose dystopian novel *We* (1921) addresses the problems of totalitarian control. This novel strongly influenced later dystopian novels that protested overly centralized social planning, including Aldous Huxley's *Brave New World* (1931) and George Orwell's *1984* (1949).

THE RISE OF FASCISM

Fascism arose after the First World War for two main purposes: first, to eliminate worker radicalism fostered by the Russian Revolution, and second, to alleviate the devastating social and economic effects of the Great War and the Great Depression (1929–39). Fascism turned against the internationalism of communism and fostered instead an organic nationalism and a rejection of Marxism, especially its emphasis on class differences and its belief that it could engineer a better society through rational means. Fascism promoted a political culture that was communal, anti-individualistic and mythic. In this regard, it rejected Enlightenment humanism (the idea that human societies can perfect themselves through reason and scientific study based on evidence). It rejected modernization insofar as modernity promoted individuality, atomization, fragmentation and displacement. Fascism rebelled against this dehumanization, but it also sought to preserve the advantages of modern technology and industrial production. It sought to fuse the relationships of individuals into an organic collectivity – the German people or the Italian people – without destroying the profit motive, private property, or the market economy. Its main concern was fighting modern values such as universalism, individualism, progress, national rights and equality (Sternhell 6–7).

In place of reason and moderation, fascism substituted mythic irrationalism, such as the idea that ties of blood and soil are stronger than reason or moderation; the cleansing qualities of violence that can destroy modern fragmentation and alienation; and masculine supremacy and female essentialism, the belief that men are supreme and women are fit only for giving birth and childrearing. We call this kind of thinking an **ideology** insofar as it promotes an idea of how society should be that is not necessarily tied to how things actually are. In this regard, socialism, communism, as well as free-market capitalism are ideologies. Fascism invented mass politics by appealing to people's emotions rather than to their reason. The fascists' anti-intellectual stance favored spectacle – great athletic and military parades – and oratory that aimed at rousing the new politicized masses into frenzies of national pride and aggression. Moreover, they developed an aestheticized politics of style: futuristic, bold, flat shapes that "invaded the cultural domain" (Carlston 24). Fascist parties made canny use of the new media for their political purposes. The German National Socialist Party (the official name of the Nazi party) produced over a thousand feature films, composed special music, flew airplanes with political banners, used cars and trucks for military parades and for the distribution of leaflets, and broadcasted speeches via loudspeakers and the wireless (Carlston 24–25).

Many European and some American writers and painters were attracted to fascist ideas as a means to restore what they viewed as an "authentic" national culture, one that maintained order and tradition. They disdained abstractions and tried to overcome the forces of "disintegration, fragmentation, romantic individualism and pluralism" in order to achieve "aesthetic integrity" as a means to the "political integrity of a people" (Carroll 105). These artistic methods varied greatly: sometimes they aestheticized violence, created new myths to purify their nation, scapegoated a minority group, or beatified virile masculinity. Adolf Hitler was very clear in terms of what fascist art was *not*. In his inaugural speech at the "Degenerate Art" Exhibition in Munich, Germany, in 1937, he characterized "Cubism, Dadaism, Futurism, Impressionism, etc. [as]

having nothing to do with our German people. For these concepts are neither old nor modern, but are only artifactitious stammerings" (Kolocotroni 561). Hitler's neologism, "artifactitious," suggests the "inner decomposition" and artificiality he perceives in avant-garde experimental art, those "worthless, integrally unskilled products" (Kolocotroni 560–62). Instead, good art, he says, should be obvious to the eye, "divinely inspired," and should participate in "an unrelenting war of purification (Kolocotroni 562–63). Artists drawn – at least partially – to these ideas include the German painter Emil Nolde; writers Ernst Jünger and Gottfried Benn; philosopher Martin Heidegger; Italian writers Curzio Malaparte, F. T. Marinetti and Gabriele D'Annunzio; French writers Ferdinand Céline, Robert Brassillach and Pierre Drieu La Rochelle; American poet Ezra Pound; Irish poet and dramatist W. B. Yeats; and Anglo-Canadian writer and painter Wyndham Lewis.

SOCIAL REALISM AND THE POPULAR FRONT

The spread of fascism was spurred on by the horrific collapse of the capitalist economy, often called the Great Depression, begun when the US stock market collapsed on October 29, 1929. While the capitalist economies appeared to "boom" in the early 1920s, this illusion of growth was based on massive loans, especially to Germany. When the Depression hit, these loans failed and US industrial production fell by 30%, and the price of exports (foodstuffs and raw materials) fell by 66%, which strongly affected non-Western areas dependent on export trade (Japanese silk, Southeast Asian rice, Brazilian coffee, West African cocoa, among many others). Unemployment reached unprecedented levels: 23% in Britain and Belgium, 24% in Sweden, 27% in the US, 29% in Austria and 44% in Germany. The Soviet Union proved immune to the capitalist crisis; rather than move backwards in terms of productivity and growth, it carried out its massive ultra-rapid industrialization under its Five Year Plans. The success of these plans spread to the capitalist world and would later launch the mid-century craze for centralized planning and development (Hobsbawm 1995: 96).

Unemployment exacerbated attraction to both communist and fascist leanings. Popular fronts, or loose coalitions of left- and centrist-leaning groups, were formed to combat fascism and unemployment in many Western countries, including the US. These fronts deployed a vital combination of politics and aesthetics. Hungarian communist philosopher Georg Lukács defined the Popular Front as

> a struggle for a genuine popular culture, a manifold relationship to every aspect of the life of one's own people as it has developed in its own individual way in the course of history. It means finding the guidelines and slogans which can emerge out of this life of the people and rouse progressive forces to new, politically effective activity.
>
> (Kolocotroni 590)

This "genuine popular culture" by necessity varied widely according to nation, language and region. In Anglophone countries, organizations such as Mass Observation in the UK; and the Federal Writers, Arts, Theater, and Music Projects in the US, documented and recorded (via the new invention of the tape recorder) the folklore and other vernacular (commonplace) cultural expressions of the working classes. In addition to oral histories, these expressions included jazz, blues and country music in the US, and folk ballads and other working-class songs in the UK. Anglo-American working-class affiliated writers came from a variety of ethnic, regional and political stripes: Zora Neale Hurston, Langston Hughes, Agnes Smedley, Meridel Le Sueur, John Dos Passos, George Orwell, Mike Gold and Christopher Isherwood, to name but a few. These writers combined modernist experimentation and realist reportage across a broad spectrum of styles that blurred the dividing line between autonomous formal experimentation and realist commitment to political struggle and raising consciousness. The combination of realism with aspects of modernist technique can be called **social realism**. This shift in modernist form and content expresses indirectly the massive historical and political crisis underway in the 1930s. We will examine some specific instances of 1930s writing in the next chapter, "Forms."

The urgency of Popular Front success increased in the second half of the 1930s as the scale of global conflict escalated: Japanese imperialist aggression in China, Italian fascist aggression in Ethiopia, and Spanish fascist aggression against its own left-leaning democratic government. The Popular Front campaigns of international solidarity, Michael Denning argues,

> transformed the ways people imagined the globe [. . .]The campaigns of solidarity for Ethiopia and the Spanish Republic depended on a larger narrative of anti-fascism and anti-imperialism that can be glimpsed in the retelling of the Haitian revolution (ranging from C. L. R. James's history *The Black Jacobins* and the novels of Arna Bontemps and Guy Endore, to Jacob Lawrence's *Toussaint L'Ouverture* paintings and the Federal Theater productions of *Black Empire, Haiti,* and the "voodoo" *Macbeth*) in the allegories of fascist invasion (from MacLeish's *Fall of the City* and Langston Hughes's *Air Raid* to Picasso's *Guernica*), and in the anti-fascist espionage thrillers.
>
> (12)

Painting, theater, poetry and novels, in addition to the emerging media of radio, film and recorded music, combined to reconfigure the prevailing world order. Denning augments this list with the genre he calls "romance of revolution," exemplified in the Soviet films of Sergei Eisenstein, the great murals of Diego Rivera and José Clemente Orozco and (not among Denning's list) W. E. B. Du Bois's novel *Dark Princess* (1928), all of which feature peoples of color and working classes in struggle with the exploitative class. These cultural productions worked to displace the governing narratives of imperialism and racial superiority. They set the stage for the civil rights struggle in the US and the decolonization of the Global South after World War II. Meanwhile, the victory of Spanish General Francisco Franco in 1939 was an ominous sign of more fascist aggression to come in Europe with the advent of World War II.

This latter conflict, the Spanish Civil War (1936–39), was a frontline contest between forces of the left and right. Most nations were neutral towards the Spanish conflict. Only the USSR and Mexico openly supported the Republican forces, while Germany and Italy gave arms and technical support to the fascist side. Thousands of unaffiliated individuals from around the world, called "The International Brigade," joined the conflict, lending moral support to the conflict, if not much in the way of military aid. George Orwell's *Homage to Catalonia* (1938) and Ernest Hemingway's *For Whom the*

Bell Tolls (1940) are the best-known Anglophone literary works to emerge from this struggle. In addition, Virginia Woolf's epistolary polemic *Three Guineas* (1938) offers an important feminist critique of the war culture of masculinity and violence. Two of the best-known Hispanophone writers of this period are poets and playwrights Miguel Hernández and Frederico García Lorca. As suggested above, however, Popular Front literature cannot be reduced to a few canonical authors. We will next turn to Chapter 4, "Forms," to look more closely at how formal experimentation and content-driven realism are part of a single spectrum of cultural production in the twentieth century, albeit one that changed drastically from decade to decade as the European world order crumbled.

SUMMARY

This chapter has covered the following topics:

• The crisis of empire and rise of imperialism;
• South Asian, Japanese, the Celtic Revival and Irish modernisms, and the Harlem Renaissance;
• World War I;
• Women's and sexual emancipation movements;
• The Russian Revolution;
• The rise of fascism, social realism and the Popular Front.

FURTHER READING

David Levering Lewis's *When Harlem Was in Vogue*, George Hutchinson's *The Harlem Renaissance in Black and White* and George Hutchinson's edited *Cambridge Companion to the Harlem Renaissance* provide excellent introductions to the Harlem Renaissance. Shari Benstock's *Women of the Left Bank: Paris, 1900–1940* and Sandra M. Gilbert and Susan Gubar's *No Man's Land: The Place of the Woman Writer in the Twentieth Century* concern the contribution of women writers in Paris and London to modernism. Maureen Moynag and Nancy Forestell's two-volume edited collection, *Documenting First Wave Feminism,* gathers statements from feminisms around the world. Paul Fussell's *The Great War and Modern Memory* is a classic account of the Great War and its effect on literature. Priyamvada Gopal's *Literary Radicalism in India: Gender,*

Nation, and the Transition to Independence surveys literature written in India during the early twentieth century. Eric Hobsbawm's *The Age of Extremes: The Short Twentieth Century, 1914–1991* is an excellent historical overview of the 20th c. and Joe Cleary's edited collection *Cambridge Companion to Irish Modernism* introduces the Celtic Revival and Irish Modernism. See Elleke Boehmer's *The Empire, the National and the Postcolonial, 1880–1920* for an introduction to how anticolonial activists affiliated with one another to overthrow colonialism. Robert J. C. Young *Postcolonialism: An Introduction* provides a world historical survey of the transition from empire to colonial independence.

WORKS CITED

Arendt, Hannah. *The Origins of Totalitarianism*. New York: Harcourt, Brace, 1976. Print.

Aydin, Cemil. "A Global Anti-Western Moment? The Russo-Japanese War, Decolonization, and Asian Modernity." In *Competing Visions of World Order: Global Moments and Movements, 1880s–1930s*. Eds. Sebastain Conrad and Dominic Sachsenmaier. New York: Palgrave, 2007. 213–36. Print.

Baker, Houston A. Jr. *Modernism and the Harlem Renaissance*. Chicago: University of Chicago Press, 1987. Print.

Benstock, Shari. *Women of the Left Bank: Paris, 1900–1940*. Austin, TX: University of Texas Press, 1986. Print.

Boehmer, Elleke. *Empire, the National, and the Postcolonial, 1890–1920*. New York: Oxford University Press, 2002. Print.

Carlston, Erin G. *Thinking Fascism: Sapphic Modernism and Fascist Modernity*. Stanford, CA: Stanford University Press, 1998. Print.

Carroll, David. *French Literary Fascism: Nationalism, Anti-Semitism, and the Ideology of Culture*. Princeton, NJ: Princeton University Press, 1995. Print.

Cleary, Joe. "Introduction." In *The Cambridge Companion to Irish Modernism*. Ed. Joe Cleary. New York: Cambridge University Press, 2014. 1–18. Print.

Deane, Seamus. *Celtic Revivals: Essays in Modern Irish Literature, 1880–1980*. Boston, MA: Faber & Faber, 1985. Print.

Denning, Michael. *The Cultural Front: The Laboring of American Culture in the Twentieth Century*. New York: Verso, 1997.

Dharwadker, Vinay. "Modernism and Its Four Phases: Literature in South Asia." In *The Modernist World*. Eds. Stephen Ross and Allana C. Lindgren. New York: Routledge, 2015. 127–35. Print.

Dube, Saurabh. "Tousled Temporalities: Modernist Practices and Intellectual-Political Currents in South Asia." In *The Modernist World*. Eds. Stephen Ross and Allana C. Lindgren. New York: Routledge, 2015. 91–99. Print.

Eksteins, Modris. *Rites of Spring: The Great War and the Birth of the Modern Age.* Boston, MA: Houghton Mifflin, 1989. Print.

Eliot, T.S. *The Waste Land.* Ed. Michael North. *Norton Critical Edition.* New York: Norton & Co., 2001. 5–26. Print.

Erlich, Victor. *Modernism and Revolution: Russian Literature in Transition.* Cambridge: Harvard University Press, 1994. Print.

Fussell, Paul. *The Great War and Modern Memory.* New York: Oxford University Press, 1975. Print.

Gammel, Irene and Cathy Waszczuk. "'A Rare Moment of Crisis': Modernist Intellectual Currents in Europe." In *The Modernist World.* Eds. Stephen Ross and Allana C. Lindgren. New York: Routledge, 2015. 301–10. Print.

Gandhi, M. K. *Hind Swaraj or Indian Home Rule.* Madras, India: G. A. Natesan & Co. 1921. Print.

Gilbert, Sandra M. and Susan Gubar. *No Man's Land: The Place of the Woman Writer in the Twentieth Century.* Vol. 2. *Sexchanges.* New Haven, CT: Yale University Press, 1989. Print.

Gopal, Priyamvada. *Literary Radicalism in India: Gender, Nation, and the Transition to Independence.* New York: Routledge, 2005. Print.

Hall, Leslie A. "Uniting Science and Sensibility: Marie Stopes and the Narratives of Marriage in the 1920s." In *Rediscovering Forgotten Radicals: British Women Writers 1889–1939.* Eds. Angela Ingram and Daphne Patai. Chapel Hill, NC: University of North Carolina Press, 1993. 118–36. Print.

Hobsbawm, Eric. *The Age of Empire, 1875–1914.* New York: Vintage, 1989. Print.

———. *The Age of Extremes: The Short Twentieth Century, 1914–1991.* London: Abacus, 1995. Print.

Hobson, J.A. *Imperialism: A Study.* London: James Nisbett & Co., 1902. Print.

Hutchinson, George. *The Harlem Renaissance in Black and White.* Cambridge: Harvard University Press, 1995. Print.

Kolocotroni, Vassiliki, Jane Goldman, and Olga Taxidou, eds. *Modernism: An Anthology of Sources and Documents.* Chicago: Chicago University Press, 1998. Print.

Kracauer, Siegfried. *The Mass Ornament: Weimar Essays.* Cambridge, MA: Harvard University Press, 1995. Print.

———. *The Salaried Masses: Duty and Distraction in Weimar Germany.* New York: Verso, 1998. Print.

Lee, Steven S. *The Ethnic Avant-Garde: Minority Cultures and World Revolution.* New York: Columbia University Press, 2015. Print.

Levitas, Ben. "Modernist Experiments in Irish Theatre." In *The Cambridge Companion to Irish Modernism.* Ed. Joe Cleary. *The Cambridge Companion to Irish Modernism.* New York: Cambridge University Press, 2014. 111–27. Print.

Lewis, David Levering. *When Harlem Was in Vogue.* New York: Penguin, 1997. Print.

Liu, Lydia H., Rebecca E. Karl, and Dorothy Ko, eds. *The Birth of Chinese Feminism: Essential Texts in Transnational Theory.* New York: Columbia University Press, 2013. Print.

Locke, Alain. "Harlem." *Survey Graphic*. 6.6 (March 1925): 629–30. Print.

Lukács, Georg. *The Theory of the Novel*. Cambridge, MA: MIT University Press, 1971. Print.

McKay, Claude. "If We Must Die." In *Anthology of Modern American Poetry*. Ed. Cary Nelson. New York: Oxford University Press, 2000. 315. Print.

Masing-Delic, Irene. *From Symbolism to Socialist Realism: A Reader*. Brighton, MA: Academic Studies Press, 2012. Print.

Mitter, Partha. *The Triumph of Modernism: Indian Artists and the Avant-Garde 1922–1947*. London: Reaktion Books, 2007. Print.

Moynagh, Maureen, with Nancy Forestell, eds. *Documenting First Wave Feminism: Vol. 1. Transnational Collaborations and Crosscurrents*. Toronto: University of Toronto Press, 2012. Print.

Neubauer, John, with Marcel Cornis-Pope, Dagmar Roberts, and Guido Snel. "1918: Overview." In *History of the Literary Cultures of East-Central Europe: Junctures and Disjunctures in the 19th and 20th Centuries*. Philadelphia: John Benjamin Publishing, 2004. 177–90. Print.

Plaatje, Sol T. *Native Life in South Africa*. Randburg, South Africa: Ravan Press, 1982. Print.

Saint-Amour, Paul K. *Tense Future: Modernism, Total War, Encyclopedic Form*. New York: Oxford University Press, 2015.

Smith-Rosenberg, Carroll. "Discourses of Sexuality and Subjectivity: The New Woman, 1870–1936." In *Hidden from History: Reclaiming the Gay and Lesbian Past*. Eds. Martin Duberman, Martha Vicinus and George Chauncey, Jr. New York: Penguin, 1989. 264–80. Print.

Sondhaus, Lawrence. *World War One: The Global Revolution*. New York: Cambridge University Press, 2011. Print.

Spengler, Oswald. *The Decline of the West*. New York: Oxford University Press, 1991. Print.

Sternhell, Zeev, with Mario Sznajder and Maia Asheri. *The Birth of Fascist Ideology*. Princeton, NJ: Princeton University Press, 1994. Print.

Wikipedia, "Chemical Weapons in World War I." http://en.wikipedia.org/wiki/Chemical_weapons_in_World_War_I (Accessed 04/02/15). Website.

Wikipedia, "German Strategic Bombing." http://en.wikipedia.org/wiki/German_strategic_bombing_during_World_War_I (Accessed 03/23/15). Website.

Wikipedia, "Great Famine Ireland." https://en.wikipedia.org/wiki/Great_Famine_(Ireland) (Accessed 12/06/16). Website.

Wikipedia, "History of Ireland." http://en.wikipedia.org/wiki/History_of_Ireland (Accessed 04/16/15). Website.

Wikipedia, "The Rape of Belgium." http://en.wikipedia.org/wiki/The_Rape_of_Belgium (Accessed 03/23/15). Website.

Wikipedia, "Recruitment to the British Army." https://en.wikipedia.org/wiki/Recruitment_to_the_British_Army_during_the_First_World_War (Acccessed 02/02/16). Website.

Williams, Raymond. *The Politics of Modernism: Against the New Conformists.* New York: Verso, 1989. Print.

Woolf, Virginia. *Three Guineas.* New York: Harcourt, Brace, 1938. Print.

Yeats, W. B. "The Second Coming." In *The Collected Poems of W. B. Yeats.* New York: Macmillan Publishing Company, 1989. 187. Print.

4

FORMS

"With the people struggling and changing reality before our eyes, we must not cling to 'tried' rules of narrative, venerable literary models, eternal aesthetic laws. We must not derive realism as such from particular existing works, but we shall use every means, old and new, tried and untried, derived from art and derived from other sources, to render reality to men [*sic*] in a form they can master."

Bertolt Brecht, "Popularity and Realism" (1938)

In Chapter 2, "Concepts," we learned that modernist writers and artists rebelled against the commercial literary and art marketplace by practicing artistic "autonomy" in which a work of art creates its own rules of practice. But not entirely. Modernist writers still needed to grapple with literary *form*, a convention that they could not jettison entirely. We define **form** as an *orientation toward representing reality*. When a writer decides to write in one of the available literary forms – fiction, poetry or drama – they accept that they will be restricted or limited "on the nature of possible aesthetic worlds" (Hayot 180). Fiction's worlds tend to be materialist, detailed, and mimetic or closely imitative of reality. Poetry inclines to more intimate registers, appealing to the reader's emotional and sensory perceptions. Drama's constraint lies with the showing of events on stage rather than the telling of them, though sometimes storytellers appear on stage. As we'll see in this chapter, each of these literary forms was fundamentally reworked by modernist writers to offer new ways of seeing and interpreting the world (Kern 2011: 2; see also Matz 2004). In effect, the massive historical, social and conceptual changes that occurred during the twentieth century were likewise felt in the transformation of literary form.

An attentive reader will notice that our three chapters – "Concepts," "Histories" and "Forms" – are really three facets of the same phenomenon of modernism. Each is necessary to the transformation of the other. Without sweeping historical changes, for instance, artistic form wouldn't feel confined and artificial. We merely separate these aspects in order to make sense of one element at a time, but we should recognize that they mutually inform one another. In the epigram above, for example, German playwright and poet Bertolt Brecht states that the representation of reality is constantly changing and that artists cannot look to "existing works," but should consider contemporary changes in philosophy, science, politics and everyday life in order to create artistic forms in which people can grasp what is occurring around them. Let's see how this urge to alter literary form shaped modernist fiction, drama and poetry.

FICTION

Fiction is a form of literature that includes the novel and the short story. While we will discuss some modernist short stories below, we will mainly focus on the novel. Unlike other literary forms such as lyric poetry and drama, the novel is primarily concerned with "particular people in particular circumstances" (Watt 15). Its characters have proper names, as if they were real individuals, and are usually ordinary people. Their lives are depicted through **realism**, a mode of representation whose aim is to present "a full and authentic report of human experiences [. . . by means of] a more largely referential use of language than is common in other literary forms" (Watt 32). By "referential use of language," Watt means a kind of lifelikeness, or verisimilitude, a close correspondence between word and thing and between language and reality. But "close correspondence" does not imply that words can ever equal reality itself. As we've discussed in Chapter 2, our experience of reality is always mediated, or shaped, through language, and therefore we can never have immediate access to reality.

What the novel conveys, more than reality itself, is a set of conventions for writing about it. These conventions include narrative, character, plot, and socially agreed upon, or normative, "reality." For instance, "the sky is blue" can be objectively or socially agreed upon. Let's begin with **narrative**. Since storytelling began, narrative structure has shaped experience by means of a beginning, middle and end, or change over time. In the novel, the narrative convention that orders action over time is called plot. **Plot** is the "organizing line, the thread of design, that makes narrative possible because finite and comprehensible" (Brooks 4). It creates interconnection and intention and strings together episodes, actions and incidents "that allow us to construct a whole" (Brooks 5). For instance, the main characters in novels often experience change over time: they undergo trials and learn how to integrate into society (commonly called a *bildungsroman* or novel of development); they decide to become an artist or writer (a *kunstelroman*); or they engage in courtship with various suitors and choose one with whom to marry (the marriage plot). These plot conventions, while always reinvented for every novel, began to break down more fundamentally at the turn of the twentieth century.

LIMITED POINT OF VIEW NARRATION

The most significant of these modernist challenges to fictional conventions is the turn to narration from the standpoint of a single, subjective consciousness. Late-eighteenth- and nineteenth-century novelists often employed a third-person omniscient narrator to present an objective, social point of view. In contrast, modernist novelists frequently prefer a first-person "I" narrator or a third-person narrator narrowly focalized (reduced to a single character's point of view) to demonstrate how an individual consciousness perceives reality. The third-person narrator, through whom we perceive the inner thoughts and feelings of the character as well as their external social observations, is also called **free indirect discourse** (as discussed in Chapter 2). Below, for example, in Henry James's novel *The Wings of the Dove* (1902), the main character, Milly Theale – a young, rich American newly arrived in Europe who secretly suffers from a fatal illness – attends a dinner party at which she meets her new best friend, Kate Croy:

> She thrilled, she consciously flushed, and all to turn pale again, with the certitude – it had never been so present – that she should find herself completely involved: the very air of the place, the pitch of the occasion, had for her both so sharp a ring and so deep an undertone. The smallest

things, the faces, the hands, the jewels of the women, the sound of
words, especially of names, across the table, the shape of the forks, the
arrangement of the flowers, the attitudes of the servants, the walls of the
room, were all touches in a picture and denotements [stage directions] in
a play; and they marked for her moreover her alertness of vision.

(149)

Milly's physical and emotional response to the party and to Kate's
presence is her *impression*: a sensory and imaginative perception of
an external event. Unlike wide, sweeping historical or social problem novels, this event is small: it is not a marriage or a momentous
discovery, merely a dinner. Most importantly, Milly's impression is
prophetic. She is certain that she will become "completely involved"
with this circle of new acquaintances. This feeling of certainty produces what she desires; it shapes her future; it renders life into a
work of art. Her intense sensory perceptiveness aestheticizes the
dinner: fleeting sounds, sumptuous details, glimpses of other people
become "touches in a picture" or "denotements in a play." Milly
transforms a scene of everyday, high-society life into a singular work
of art. We, the readers, see the scene through her youthful excitement
and likewise render it a thing of beauty. Were James to narrate this
scene through a third-person omniscient viewpoint, the dinner party
might be a tedious affair for its readers. The process of perception,
imagination and desire produces a new kind of realism, one that is
filtered through a subjective point of view that can potentially render –
and redeem – life as art. In the process of rendering life as art, the
emphasis on plot weakens and slows. For the modernist artist, perception and consciousness in the present moment are more illuminating
than action and development over time.

James discusses the relation of the modernist novel to realism in
his 1894 essay, "The Art of Fiction" when he writes, "Humanity is
immense, and reality has a myriad forms; the most one can affirm is
that some of the flowers of fiction have the odour of it, and others
have not" (148). By this, he means that *all* novels fail to capture reality,
and so the best a novelist can do is to widen the creative capacities for
rendering an *impression* of reality, one that is as ephemeral as the scent
of a flower. By impression, as mentioned above, James suggests that
only by means of aesthetic perception and imagination can a writer
have a chance of delivering a trace, or scent, of reality. Furthermore,

the injection of artistic perception into realism suggests that realism changes historically and from place to place. As modernist writers challenged the conventions of the novel, we find less a refusal to represent reality and more a transformation in *how* reality is conveyed.

Virginia Woolf also called for writers to transform how the novel represents reality in her essay "Mr. Bennett and Mrs. Brown" and elsewhere. Modern fiction, she says, is an outgrowth of the seismic shifts in modern life that can be pointed to with perhaps tongue-in-cheek precision: "On or about December 1910, human character changed" (4). This date marker distinguishes Woolf's group of Georgian writers – named after King George V, son of Queen Victoria, ascended to the throne in May 1910 – from old-fashioned Edwardian writers – named after King Edward VII, who was monarch of Great Britain and its Empire from 1901–10. In Woolf's assessment, Edwardian novelists – she singles out Arnold Bennett, H. G. Wells and Edward Galsworthy – rely on social details, legislative facts, and other externalities rather than on subjective impressions. (Bennett gets special attention, in part, because he wrote an unfavorable review of Woolf's novel *Jacob's Room*.) December 1910 also refers to the Post-Impressionist art exhibit held that month in London in which continental avant-garde art outraged the British public, *and* it refers to the growing militancy of the women's suffrage and workers' movements. Woolf declares, "All human relations have shifted – those between masters and servants, husbands and wives, parents and children" (5). The relations between the classes, genders and generations have been transformed, and so, in order to convey them, the conventions of art and literature must also shift. Like James, Woolf deploys an aestheticizing gaze that transforms a few prosaic details of the new society into a redemptive vision of modern life.

In the essay, Woolf gives only a few fragmentary details of her subject, Mrs. Brown, whom she encounters by chance in a railway carriage: "She was one of those clean, threadbare old ladies whose extreme tidiness – everything buttoned, fastened, tied together, mended and brushed up – suggests more of extreme poverty than rags and dirt," and combines these details with an indication of emotional depth: "she was crying" (98–100). We never know what happened to Mrs. Brown. There is no omniscient narrator to give us the full story. Instead, Woolf relies on her fictional impression of Mrs. Brown because she "must be rescued, expressed, and set in her high relations to the world before the train stopped and she disappeared for ever" (114). These "high relations to the world" suggest that, though the meeting is random, Mrs. Brown is part of a whole. Because of this, Woolf renders her fleeting encounter with Mrs. Brown as an authentic experience of modern life.

Woolf's description of Mrs. Brown recalibrates the perceiving subject (Woolf herself in this essay) within an increasingly fragmented and visibly class-riven society. The fact that Woolf only speculates about Mrs. Brown indicates her unwillingness to attempt to accurately represent her; instead, she relies on her imaginative capabilities and penetrating authorial gaze. But the combination is enough: Mrs. Brown's significant presence in the train (as a marker of the lived experience of working-class women) sparks Woolf's pronouncement that realist novels are "useless" and that a new novel form is in the making. She asks readers to "tolerate the spasmodic, the obscure, the fragmentary, the failure" as modern novelists search for an adequate new form of fiction that can convey the altered class, gender and generational relations of the twentieth century (24). Rather than offer new rules for art, Woolf opens the field of creative possibility so that writers might have the freedom they require to fashion their own rules in order to render the ever elusive and shifting sense of reality.

An extreme version of the inward turn that excludes most fictional conventions – including proper grammar and social censorship – is the **stream of consciousness** technique. While we discussed the concept of stream of consciousness in Chapter 2 in terms of creating a sense of continuous time that mingles past and present, stream of consciousness narrative also presents the reader with a sense of being immediately present, deep inside a character's mind, as it is bombarded with random thoughts, perceptions and sensations. This kind of narrative technique is particularly modernist in *how* it represents the subject in modern life. For instance, in 1903, social scientist Georg Simmel characterized the modern city-dweller's psychological makeup as premised upon "the intensification of emotional life due to the swift and continuous shift of external and internal stimuli" (325). Stream of consciousness narration captures the chaotic and fragmented assault on the senses that occurs in modern life. In Joyce's *Ulysses*, for example, as Leopold Bloom walks to the butchers from his home to buy a pork kidney for breakfast, we read his stream of consciousness:

> Be a warm day I fancy. Specially in these black clothes feel it more. Black conducts, reflects, (refracts it?), the heat. But I couldn't go in that light suit. Make a picnic of it. His eyelids sank quietly often as he walked in happy warmth. Boland's breadvan delivering the trays our daily but she prefers yesterday's loaves turnovers crisp crowns hot. Makes you feel young.
>
> (46–47, #78–83)

Sentences are fragmented; words are truncated. As we eavesdrop on Bloom's inner thoughts, we don't get perfectly polished sentences because we are seemingly not the intended audience. Bloom is talking to himself: a highly informal, even intimate, act. He reacts to the warm sunlight, the passing delivery van, and the thought of hot bread. The "she" in this passage is Molly, Bloom's wife, but the "you" is indeterminate, referring perhaps to the eavesdropping reader or to Bloom in dialogue with himself.

Critics distinguish between the random association of stream of consciousness (as in Bloom's thoughts above) and a kind of inward narration – called **interior monologue** – that is more deliberate and comprehensible, a step "outward" from the stream of consciousness (Matz 2004: 56). (See also Chapter 2.) In this kind of narration, it is as if we're overhearing a character having a reasoned debate with themselves. In *A Portrait of the Artist as a Young Man*, Stephen Dedalus resolves to become an artist in the following passage:

> Now, as never before, his strange name seemed to him a prophecy. So timeless seemed the grey warm air, so fluid and impersonal his own mood, that all ages were as one to him. A moment before the ghost of the ancient kingdom of the Danes had looked forth through the vesture of the hazewrapped city. Now, at the name of the fabulous artificer, he seemed to hear the noise of dim waves and to see a winged form flying above the waves and slowly climbing the air.
>
> (148)

Past and present, myth and reality merge in this passage as Stephen pledges his commitment to art. Though he is merely thinking to himself, the grandiosity of his ambitions and learning is reflected in the epic musings that merge adolescent boy with the kings and gods of old. Like the stream of consciousness technique, we enter into Stephen's inner thoughts and subjective perceptions; we cannot escape the world as Stephen perceives it in this novel, except to recognize the limits of his youthful perspective. In this regard, stream of consciousness narrations and interior monologues often reveal that modernist characters are anti-heroes: flawed, mediocre, even mad. Such outlier points of view allow modernist writers to critique normative attitudes and arrive at realizations from unexpected sources.

Unreliable narrators who give the reader false information are an extreme version of an anti-heroic character. A well-known example of this technique occurs in Ford Madox Ford's novel *The Good Solider* (1915), in which the narrator, John Dowell, relates the story of his marriage and only gradually, as the story unfolds, does the reader learn that the good solider of the title, Edward Ashburnham, has had an affair with Dowell's wife and the pair have committed suicide. Dowell relates the events as if in real time (as if the events were occurring in the present), though in actuality, all the events have already taken place. Novelist J. M. Coetzee describes Ford's novel as "a brilliantly handled conceit of ensuring that the novel's 'scheme' remains 'depend[ent] solely upon the mental tactics of the narrator'" (qtd. in D. James 102). Further, the delusion suffered by the narrator is re-experienced by the reader. And this ignorance, as the novel's title indicates, is meant as a larger indictment of the Great War underway just then. Unreliable narrators allow for a veiled, indirect mode of social critique.

Writers from around the world deployed unreliable narration to comment on their own societies, often undergoing immense change through decolonization and modernization. And the character's unreliability allows the author to avoid censorship. When the unreliable narrator is mad, for instance, the author cannot be held accountable for what he or she says. In Chinese writer Lu Xun's "Diary of a Madman" (1918), for instance, the narrator succumbs to paranoid fantasies that his fellow villagers are planning to eat him. He reads a set of "secret signals" (1240) into ordinary conversations, facial expressions and written documents. Lu Xun took the idea for the story from Russian novelist Nikolai Gogol's "Diary of a Madman" (1835), where madness served as a critique of the backwardness of Russian feudal society. Unlike Gogol, Lu Xun framed the diary as only a temporary descent into madness, leaving an opening for the character (and Chinese society) to allow the critique implicit in the mad phantasies to lead to social revolution and modernization. In another rendition of an unreliable narrator, Pakistani short-story writer Saadat Hasan Manto uses madness in "Toba Tek Singh" (1955) to critique the religious divisions driving the catastrophic Partition of India and Pakistan (1947–48). In the story, a group of Hindu and Sikh lunatics are required to move to India from an asylum in Lahore, Pakistan. The third-person narrator describes the move thus:

> It was quite a job getting the men out of the buses and handing them over to officials. Some just refused to leave. Those who were persuaded to do so began to run pell-mell in every direction. Some were stark naked.
>
> (1491)

One lunatic, Bishan Singh, decides that since his hometown, Toba Tek Singh, is in Pakistan, he will not move to India. Instead, he occupies the no-man's land between the two nations, declaring the land to be Toba Tek Singh. He stands alone on the border, muttering abuse to both nations in a mixture of Punjabi, Urdu and English. In effect, his madness serves to undermine the fiction of national purity.

Other unreliably narrated stories include German-speaking Czech writer Franz Kafka's "The Metamorphosis" (1915), in which Gregor Samsa wakes to find himself transformed into a "monstrous cockroach," an unreliable perspective, to put it mildly. Kafka's famous conceit effectively conveys his sense of extreme alienation from Czech petit-bourgeois society (1204). In William Faulkner's *The Sound and the Fury* (1929), three different unreliable narrators, one of them mentally disabled, tell three different versions of a story, and, finally, the last section relates the events from a more objective perspective. Benjy, the mentally disabled character, presents an especially compromised point of view. As his brother Quentin forces him to drink a hot drink, Benjy relates: "They held my head. It was hot inside me, and I began again. I was crying now, and something was happening inside me and I cried more" (22). In the London setting of *Mrs. Dalloway*, Virginia Woolf's shell-shocked veteran, Septimus Smith, voices the madness and trauma of the recent Great War and critiques the prevailing practices of psychiatry, something with which Woolf, who probably suffered from what we now call bipolar disorder, was quite familiar. Finally, a young girl who is innocent of sexual matters narrates Ismat Chughtai's short story, "The Quilt" (1941). This naïf relates a lesbian love affair through her innocent description of an "elephant" beneath the quilt, thereby helping Chughtai's story to evade the censor, as mentioned in Chapter 3 (12).

Non-European writers sometimes adapted limited point of view narration to represent positive elements of modernity, specifically that of personal self-actualization and collective social improvement. For example, Indian novelist Mulk Raj Anand deployed this formal technique in his first novel *Untouchable* (1935). This novel, signed by the author, "Simla – S.S. *Viceroy of* India – Bloomsbury (England)," spoke to both a British and Anglophone Indian readership as it advocated Indian self-rule and modernization to improve lives across the class and caste spectrum. The novel criticizes untouchability, part of the caste system in India where those assigned from birth to carry out the worst jobs are segregated from the rest of society because they are "unclean." Much of the novel is focalized through Bakha, a member of the non-caste of "untouchables," now called "Dalit." This focalization gives the reader a sympathetic identification with his point of view. In a marketplace scene, we are privy to Bakha's aestheticized perceptions:

> Passing through the huge brick-built gate of the town into the main street, [Bakha] was engulfed in a sea of colour. [. . .] he couldn't help being swept away by the sensations that crowded in on him from every side. [. . .] His first sensation of the bazaar was of its smell, a pleasant aroma oozing from so many unpleasant things, drains, grains, fresh and decaying vegetables, spices, men and women and asafoetida. Then it was the kaleidoscope of colours, the red, the orange, the purple of the fruit in the tiers of baskets which were arranged around the Peshawari fruit-seller.
>
> (43)

Bahka might remind us of Baudelaire's flâneur, detached yet aesthetically enjoying the multifarious sensations of modern life in a crowded urban thoroughfare (see Chapter 2). Through Bakha's autonomy and point of view, the novel makes the case that even untouchables (Dalit) are fully modern – capable of aesthetic and, implicitly, moral and rational judgment – and should be allowed full equality under the law.

AESTHETIC FORMALISM

In the section above, we've seen how some modernist fiction writers experimented with point of view in a manner that conveys a complete immersion in a particular aspect of reality, usually in order to critique society or to redeem it through aesthetic experience. Some modernists, however, attempted to eliminate realist representation entirely through **autotelic form**. The purpose of autotelic form is the aesthetic achievement of the form itself, not what it can represent. The formal experiment is to abstract the novel from reality in order to defamiliarize meaning making and to jolt the reader from their habitual perceptions and thoughts. There is a risk in this endeavor: writers who "devote themselves solely to the abstract forms of writing [. . .] risk pointlessness for the sake of art, meaninglessness for the sake of style" (Matz 2004: 76). In this fictional form, usually delivered as **free indirect discourse** (where third and first person, inner and outer perspectives merge), language becomes nearly self-enclosed within its own system of autonomous meaning. Its closest correspondence in the visual arts is **abstract art** that features only the play of shapes, colors and textures.

In literature, pure autonomy is harder to achieve because language is referential; it refers to real-world objects outside the text. However, in experimental writing by American expatriate writer Gertrude Stein and Irish expatriate writer Samuel Beckett (both lived in France), the reader becomes more enmeshed in the cadences of the prose than with the content or story being conveyed. For instance, in Stein's *Making of Americans* (1925), in which she chronicles a family over three generations, her prose takes on a life of its own:

> He was almost completely clearly feeling what he was feeling. He was extraordinarily completely clearly expressing what he was almost completely clearly feeling. He was one working in being one almost completely clearly feeling what he was feeling. He was one working, he was one needing to be clearly working, he was one needing to be completely clearly working. He was one needing to be certain that he was one being living. He was one needing to be completely clearly working to be certain that he was one being living.

(878)

The empty, formal qualities of these lines – tautology ("feeling what he was feeling"), repetitive rhythm, adverbial phrases (ending in -ly) that modify an action, consonance and assonance – mimics, as William Gass says, "the movement of life itself" (Stein x). We feel how life is lived in layers, built up over years of habit, and that in language we never get to the thing itself, but we only dance circles around it. This novel has very little plot or external causality. It makes its points indirectly through a play of language that gives us the feeling and cadences of music. The literary text is autonomous: it exists in and for itself as a work of art. This fact of autonomy, however, doesn't negate the fact that its artistic production depends on external factors. It is often remarked that Stein's literary style suggests the everyday rhythms of the body: its repetitious activities (eating, sleeping, sexual arousal, defecation and physical activity) combined with the slow forward movement of aging in which human behavior gradually ossifies into habitual and steadily narrowing patterns. Though time passes, the novel generally conveys a continuous present: it is always beginning again, and its present participles (-ing words) suggest a constant present state. We can see a similar, though more ostensibly parodied, gendered embodiment in Irish writer Samuel Beckett's novels and plays that feature outcast protagonists. In Beckett's first published novel *Murphy* (1938), Murphy stands with his eyes "closed, as for a supreme exertion, the jaw clenched, the chin jutted, the knees sagged, the hypogastrium [lower abdomen] came forward, the mouth opened, the head tilted slowly back" (14). In this scene, Murphy is meeting his fiancée Celia for the first time. His masculinity is parodied as a comic pose, and his inner thoughts are absent. Like a vaudeville slapstick comedian, gesture and body language say it all.

In other instances, autonomous language is presented as hallucinatory, a break from reality, in order to convey content that might otherwise not be written at all. At the conclusion of Jean Rhys's *Voyage in the Dark* (1934), the protagonist Anna Morgan is delirious from complications following an illegal abortion. The fever-induced hallucination takes the white Creole character back in memory to carnival celebration in the Caribbean, allowing her to acknowledge the usually repressed or disavowed Afro-Caribbean elements of her background, though such memories remain associated with the chaos of sickness. Nigerian writer Amos Tutuola's *The Palm-Wine Drinkard*

(1952), on the other hand, places hallucination on center stage, as the protagonist (another anti-hero, the palm-wine drunkard), goes into the underworld to retrieve his tapster, who has died from falling from a palm tree where he tapped his wine. The underworld closely resembles the bush, or rural undeveloped land, and develops a personality of its own. It is haunted by monsters, spirits and the "deads," and the palm-wine drunkard lurches from one surreal situation to another in an episodic, disjointed narrative often called the "picaresque." It is notable that the protagonist never seems to gain maturity or insight from his trials; rather, the bush itself becomes "an area of viable creative energy," stemming from "the chronic underdevelopment of the colonial economy" (Kalliney 175). In effect, hallucinatory prose becomes a hallmark of many colonial modernist fictions (by authors such as Wilson Harris, Bessie Head, Dambudzo Marechera and Ben Okri, to name a few) that imagine indigenous realities radically opposed to the Western novel and its accompanying mode of life.

MONTAGE

Finally, some modernist novelists, especially in the crisis era of the 1930s and the decolonizing era of the 1950s and 1960s, broke away from an emphasis on subjective perception and aesthetic form to recast the modernist novel as a spatial interweaving of images and phases that directly referenced an external world (see also social realism in Chapter 3). This kind of modernist novel is often referred to as documentary or reportage style. This externally oriented novel often looks much closer to a nineteenth-century realist novel than to a modernist one, though, upon closer examination, we can discern modernist techniques embedded within the writing style. The primary modernist technique used in reportage style was **montage**: "montage" means to juxtapose multiple perspectives of the same location in the present time. Montage is related to **collage** (to glue many fragments together), except that montage presents a single image viewed in a series of perspectives rather than a plurality of objects and materials on a single surface. In Soviet filmmaker Sergei Eisenstein's *Battleship Potemkin* (1925), called by some the best propaganda film ever made, the Odessa Steps scene jumps between inflexible details (boots, guns) of the tsar's imperial army and heart-wrenching details of the men, women and children whom the army massacres. Suspense is built as the film, using cross-cut editing (in which various scenes are spliced together to show parallel action in different locations), jumps from one scene to another in order to convey collective action, multiple perspectives, and the impending battle between the forces of repression and the people (see also Kern 1983). We are accustomed to seeing this technique in many contemporary action films, such as *The Dark Knight* (2008), *Inception* (2010) and *Interstellar* (2014), but when it was first used, and especially in conjunction with the Russian Revolution (see Chapter 3), montage technique was startling in its power to convey the complexity of mass forms of modern life.

Joyce's montage technique in the "Wandering Rocks" episode in *Ulysses* is used to represent an entire city in a single extended moment of time. The episode is comprised of nineteen segments that show the simultaneous activity of disparate characters as well as overlapping actions: Father Conmee strolls through Dublin (the unifying authority of the Catholic Church), the viceregal calvacade (the unifying authority of the British Empire) surveys the populace, and random objects take a surprising centrality. For instance, we see the same handbill three times as it floats down the river Liffey. Though there are unifying elements in this episode (the final segment shows the viceregal calvacade linking all the characters and places as it passes through the city), the montage of the city begins over and over with each segment and character. The overlap, whereby we see various characters from multiple perspectives (the central focal point, a minor focal point, and background without speaking) and who pass each other in the street, suggests simultaneous activity. The chance encounters of meeting people unexpectedly gives us the sense of "meanwhile," of simultaneous activity amongst people whom we may never meet, but who live alongside us anonymously in urban, national and global spaces.

Also using montage effect and adapting film techniques to his prose, the American novelist John Dos Passos created what he called "newsreels" in his *U.S.A.* trilogy (1930–36). These literary newsreels mimicked the first film newsreels, a precursor to television news. Early filmgoers crowded into cinemas to view film clips from around the world. These visual images made the world seem very small and familiar. Dos Passos's newsreels cross cut in a similar fashion:

OFFICIALS KNOW NOTHING OF VICE

Sanitary trustees turn water of Chicago River into drainage canal LAKE MICHIGAN SHAKES HANDS WITH THE FATHER OF THE WATERS German zuchterverein singing contest for canarybirds opens the fight for bimetallism at the ratio of 16 to 1 has not been lost says Bryan

BRITISH BEATEN AT MAFEKING
For there's many a man been murdered in Luzon

CLAIMS ISLANDS FOR ALL TIME

(2)

In this "newsreel," we are presented with headlines that juxtapose prostitution; sewage and urban engineering; music (an American classical suite, featuring "Father of the Waters" [a translation of the Native American word "Mississippi"] by Ferde Grofé); the 1896 presidential campaign by William Jennings Bryan against the gold standard; the dangers of mining for gold ("canarybirds"); the British war with the Boers in South Africa (also related to gold mines); the Spanish-American War (1898) fought partly in the Philippines (Luzon, the largest island); and reference to American Imperialism declared at the end of that war. By means of splicing together many fragments from around the world, as a newsreel might do, Dos Passos conveys the historical present of global geopolitics, a much wider setting than a traditional realist novel allows.

While US writer Dos Passos splices together fragments from around the world to critique imperialism and US nationalism from *within* its dominant location, minority and non-Western novelists often use pointed **intertextual** references in order to write *against* industrialized nations. An intertextual reference is one that is cited from another, previous source. Because it recycles sources, intertextuality disrupts linear plot lines that premise a point of origin. For example, Jamaican poet and fiction writer Claude McKay (1890–1948) deploys intertextuality in his novel *Home to Harlem* (1928) to critique race relations in the US. In this novel, the omniscient (third-person) narrator remarks, "There is no better angle from which one can look down on a motion picture than that of the nigger heaven" (315). "Nigger heaven" is the racist designation for the upper balcony of a movie theater, the only place in which black people were allowed to watch films in the US in the early twentieth century. The film in this scene features white people watching black people mimicking their white masters. McKay writes,

> It was odd that all these cinematic pictures about the blacks were a broad burlesque of their home and love life. These colored screen actors were all dressed up in expensive evening clothes, with automobiles, and menials, to imitate white society people. They laughed at themselves in such roles and the laughter was good on the screen. They pranced and grinned like good-nigger servants, who know that 'mas'r' and 'missus,' intent on being amused, are watching their antics from an upper window.
>
> (314)

But when the black characters enter a white theater and take their seats in "nigger heaven," McKay turns the tables on this "burlesque" or mocking representation of African-Americans. The upper balcony is the best location for viewing the film, McKay's narrator remarks, because the black people watch the white people watching a racist "fantasy" of black people. Aldon Nielsen glosses this intertextuality as,

> Better to *be* the amused gaze, looking down at the whites as the whites look to themselves as black [in the 1920s, it was "cool" and edgy for white people to mingle with and imitate black people in Harlem cabarets], than to feel that uneasy itch of surveillance perpetually at the back of the neck.
>
> (25)

The novel problematizes representation because, as a novel about black people, its predominant audience is white people. The novel, in this scene, asks to what extent is this novel authentic and to what extent is it a show, performed for the dominant race? By referencing two audiences watching black actors perform for whites, we see that the novel is not "reflecting" reality but crafting a knowing autonomous fiction that challenges this black–white dualism.

A later, and more biting, intertextual form, Tayeb Salih's novel *A Season of Migration to the North* (Arabic 1966, English translation 1969), both thematizes East-West cross-fertilization and conflict, and encodes it in its narrative form. It is part novel and part *hakawati*, the Arabic oral tradition invoked as it is addressed to an audience of "gentlemen" (Makdisi 814). The novel references British literature, such as Shakespeare's *Othello* and *King Lear* and Joseph Conrad's *Heart of Darkness* (1899), and is structured as a novel, but

> [it] has many of the elements of the Arabic literature technique of *mu'arada*, which literally means opposition or contradiction, and which involves at least two writers, the first of whom writes a poem that the second will undo by writing along the same lines but reversing the meaning.
>
> (Makdisi 815)

The Arabic form literally undoes the European novel as the narrative is distorted and undermined. In this case, we can say that the conflict between Arabic and European literary forms enacts the modernism of the text as it refuses to transparently mirror a story that takes place in a small village in the Sudan, and instead creates an autonomous "problem" text.

This conflict is thematized in the content as well. Both the narrator and his subject, Mustafa Sa'eed, live in the Sudan and have been educated in London. They experience the East–West conflict as an irreconcilable division in their identities. For instance, we never know the fate of the narrator; the novel ends with him calling for help in the middle of the Nile River, determined to live but threatened with drowning. The indeterminacy of the ending unravels the mimetic form of the novel, pointing instead to the reader's investment in the tale and their awareness of how the novel breaks down East/West distinctions and, above all, a European imperialist superiority that is based upon the assumption that they know and are entitled to judge the rest of the world. Instead, the novel, in modernist fashion, asks that we question our privileged but limited knowledge of the world.

DRAMA

As if answering Woolf's call above to "tolerate the spasmodic, the obscure, the fragmentary, the failure," modernist playwrights rejected traditional theatrical conventions in an effort to revolutionize the theater. These conventions are largely based on Aristotle's analysis of classic tragic drama and include:

- unity of time and place,
- empathy with the characters,
- illusionism that mimicked reality, and
- catharsis of events that purged spectators of pity and fear.

In place of traditional theatrical illusion, modernist dramatists offered many new kinds of dramas, some inspired by Japanese Noh and other Asian ceremonial theater; others by religious rituals and mythology, while still others borrowed from popular entertainments and folk customs.

SYMBOLIST THEATER

We will first examine the transformation of European theater from presenting an illusion of reality to offering the symbolism of art. The Norwegian playwright Henrik Ibsen (1828–1906) is credited with beginning the modernist transformation of theater in the West. He is known as

> the creator of the modern social drama of ideas, – [sic] a drama in prose, contemporary and realistic in scene, carefully concentrated in structure and dialogue [. . .] more philosophic [than French classical theater] in morality and more perfectly controlled by the author's thought.
>
> (Chandler xii)

Ibsen combines realistic detail with symbolic economy in a manner that stages human conflict through "the clarifying lens of art" (Chandler xiii). By "symbolic economy," we mean, for instance, how in Ibsen's play "The Master Builder" (1892), the selfish individualist who sacrifices everyone around him to his ambition succumbs to madness and falls to his death from a tower he has built. Such a climax is not realistic – how many architects fall to their deaths? – rather, the play takes a symbolic turn: it signifies something universal. The ending suggests the myth of Icarus, who flies so close to the sun that it melts his wings and he falls to his death in the sea below. Falling to one's death from a heightened position, then, is symbolic of all people who sacrifice everything to ambition and power. Ibsen's final play, *When We Dead Awaken* (1899), turned even more sharply towards symbolism and inspired "new interest in dreams, ghosts, and symbols that shaped avant-garde theater in the twentieth century, from [Swedish playwright August] Strindberg to the expressionists and absurdists" (Lewis 183).

The turn towards the symbolic was often made via intercultural borrowings. Poet and dramatist W. B. Yeats said that the influence of Japanese Noh drama on his plays was central in creating a new modernist form of drama: "With the help of Japanese plays translated by Ernest Fenollosa and edited by Ezra Pound, I have invented a new form of drama, distinguished, indirect and symbolic" (221). Yeats's symbolic drama blurred the distinction between the actors and audience – the audience needed to work at comprehending the symbolic meaning of the play, rather than be entertained by it. Audience participation broke the **fourth wall** convention in which the players on stage ignored the presence of the audience. Moreover, the invocation of ritual and magic, wearing masks and outlandish costumes, and deploying stylized movement interrupted the realistic illusion of the "well-made" play and highlighted innovative forms of art. Aesthetic appreciation rather than grasping a good story was central to modern drama.

The French surrealist Antonin Artaud (1896–1948) defines symbolism in the theater as that which exceeds language: "What the theater can still take over from speech are its possibilities for extension beyond words, for development in space, for dissociative and vibratory action upon the sensibility" (89). For Artaud, the Balinese (Indonesian) theater reveals this physical and non-verbal component of the theater that had been lost to the Western stage. So, too, as we saw in Chapter 2, Igor Stravinsky's ballet and orchestral concert *Le Sacré du Printemps* (*The Rite of Spring*) used dance, gesture, costumes and Russian "primitive" music to suggest ancient rituals and folk art that went beyond the civilized veneer of the drawing room and symbolized universal cycles of birth, death and renewal. It is this move into symbolism and ritual – into art form itself – that breaks the bond between audience and characters. No longer do dramas create empathy between the audience and the characters, nor does the audience experience a satisfying catharsis or purgation of pity and fear that stems from a satisfying or even tragic denouement of the action. Indeed, often there is no unity of time or place as the plot stalls, becomes impressionistic or symbolic, and refrains from resolving into a tidy ending. Instead, the audience experiences an aesthetic detachment from the events onstage. We go to the modernist theater to experience sensory impressions – colors, images, sounds – rather than to view snippets of a dramatized life struggle with which we can identify.

POLITICAL THEATER

This sense of aesthetic detachment is not always the case in modernist drama. Italian futurist theater provoked its audience into mayhem through the use of music hall slapstick and outright insults. Women's suffrage propaganda plays, such as Elizabeth Robins's *Votes for Women!*, sought to generate support for women's suffrage. *Votes for Women!* staged real political speeches and created sympathy for its wronged heroine and for the women's suffrage cause more generally. And theater in post-World War II Africa, according to John Conteh-Morgan, involved "the creation of new, African-based (theatrical) cultures. In other words, theirs is a political project, not the expression of existential angst" (111). In non-Western theater, especially in Africa and the Caribbean, ritual and "indigenous" performances were not used for spiritual or symbolic ends, but to generate modern cultures and societies with ties to traditional forms. Nigerian playwright, poet, novelist and Nobel Prize winner Wole Soyinka distinguishes sharply between Western modernism and dramatic innovations on the African stage:

> The difference which we are seeking to define between European and African drama [. . .] is not simply a difference of style or form, nor is it confined to drama alone. It is representative of the essential differences between two world-views, a difference between one culture whose very artifacts are evidence of a cohesive understanding of irreducible truths and another, whose creative impulses are directed by period dialectics.
>
> (38)

Soyinka characterizes the European worldview "directed by period dialectics" in terms of innovation for innovation's sake and witnessed by "fee-paying strangers" (38). By "period dialectics," he means that realism, naturalism, surrealism and absurdist theater are a string of empty European styles that produce novelty without substance. In contrast, African drama has evolved communally and is already spiritualized; it can discern the "irreducible truths" of a non–Western cosmology that is unified with the community and landscape. Ritual here solidifies African sensibilities and affirms the value and autonomy of its cultures and region.

In the Caribbean, playwright, poet and Nobel Prize winner Derek Walcott takes his theatrical cues from the self-dramatized world of poverty that he sees all around him. Ritual for him is *not* rooted in the reality of the Caribbean, a region in which Europeans massacred the indigenous and in which the current inhabitants descended from African slaves or from indentured laborers. He says,

> To set out for rehearsals in that quivering quarter-hour [twilight] is to engage conclusions, not beginnings, for one walks past the gilded hallucinations of poverty with a corrupt resignation touched by details, as if the destitute, in their orange-tinted backyards, under their dusty trees, or climbing their favelas [shantytowns], were all natural scene-designers, and poverty were not a condition but an art.

(3)

For him, reality is already hallucination and art. The dramatist need only take her/his cues from what they see around them. While Soyinka emphasizes the timelessness of communal myth, Walcott embraces the sordid present-day of Caribbean modern life. Like Soyinka, however, Walcott sees in his own people an artistic and political truth to be accepted – communally and affirmatively – unlike the Western avant-garde artist whose rebellion, by the post–World War II period, was reduced to a series of empty styles that merely repeated the earlier iconoclasm. He says of the Caribbean, "There is neither enough power nor decadence to justify experiment" (27). Rather than imitate the Western metropolitan artist, Walcott calls on dramatists and writers from the formerly colonized world to embrace their truths at hand: the truth of dispossession, poverty and resilience. Finally, many African women dramatists – such as Ama Ata Aidoo from Ghana, Werewere Living from Cameroon, and Osonye Tess Onwueme from Nigeria – have written realist plays in order to debate women's issues in modern African societies. For them, modernism lies in the content of the drama of ideas: their plays staged debates regarding the way forward for African women in modernity.

EPIC THEATER

Another important dramatic innovator, the German playwright
Bertolt Brecht (1898–1956), created epic theater, which he defined
as "interventionist" art. Its aims were to provoke spectators into a
critical awareness of their place in society as well as the constructed
nature of society (i.e., that the world can be changed). This kind of
theater rejected the **social realism** that many artists and writers
who admired or lived in the Soviet Union followed. Social realism,
as explained in Chapter 2, sought to convey documentary (mimetic)
detail in a journalistic, transparent prose style. Brecht and other modernist dramatists, such as Eugene O'Neill, Luigi Pirandello, Dada and
futurist playwrights, and Samuel Beckett, believed that social realism allowed the viewers to be too passive. They merely absorb the
realist story being told. In contrast, epic theater is instructive in a
dialectical sense. It strives to alienate or estrange the audience from
an event or character by "first of all stripping the event of its self-
evident, familiar, obvious quality and creating a sense of astonishment
and curiosity about them" (qtd. in Brooker 191). For instance, in
Brecht's play *Life of Galileo* (1939), the audience learns of the Catholic Church's enormous pressures on Galileo to recant his heliocentric
model of the universe because they feared it would adversely affect
Church doctrine. In a dialectical leap, the audience might apply this
lesson (or parable) for themselves to their contemporary situation to
understand present-day pressures to conform to particular beliefs (in
nation, capitalism, race and gender hierarchies, etc.).

Epic theater used other formal techniques to prevent the spectator
from merely absorbing the story being enacted. In order to distance
or alienate the viewer, narrative was broken – episodes were joined in
such a way that "the knots are easily noticed" (Brecht 201). In addition, stage props, set design and costumes no longer attempted to be
"realistic"; the set might be empty or wild with cubist stage sets or
futuristic outfits. The mis-en-scène (the stage setting) was static and
sculptural, rather than narrative and bourgeois (a typical bourgeois or
middle-class drama might feature the realistic interior of a well-to-do
house). Brecht may have derived this defamiliarization technique, in
part, from the acting style of Mei Lan-fang (a famous Chinese opera
artist) whom he saw perform in Moscow in 1935 (Brooker 192).
The estranging effect extended to character: actors didn't try to fully
inhabit their role. They might switch roles with one another, recite

stage directions along with their lines, or read in the third person (Brooker 196). They might look directly at the audience or even bring the play into the audience, a move that breaks the **fourth wall** convention. Finally, we see background and foreground merging, as with modernist painting, to eliminate Renaissance perspective (see Chapter 1). Brecht recounts:

> Not only did the background adopt an attitude to the events on the stage – by big screens recalling other simultaneous events elsewhere, by projecting documents which confirmed or contracted what the characters said, by concrete and intelligible figures to accompany abstract conversations.
>
> (71)

Epic theater was a multimedia affair. It was also pedagogical: spectators learned about events all over the world; they received statistics, and listened to debates on such pressing issues as "oil, inflation, social struggles, the family, religion, the meat market" (71). Such denaturalizing effects allowed for the audience's critical self-reflection. They could examine their expectations and interrupt their easy acceptance of what is told to them.

POETRY

We began this book with a close reading of a section of T. S. Eliot's *The Waste Land*. In part, we did this to introduce the reader to the concept of modernist **difficulty** that is most apparent in the cryptic lines of modernist poetic form. With its seemingly random jottings and scrapbook **montage** form, modernist poetry initially repulses the novice reader. With this in mind, it is worth returning to another example of modernist poetic fireworks to see how and why modernists wrote like this.

PARIS: A POEM

We turn next to *Paris: A Poem* by Hope Mirrlees (1887–1978), published in 1920 by the Hogarth Press (an independent press owned and operated by Leonard and Virginia Woolf). Mirrlees was the heiress to the Scottish Mirrlees-Tongaat Company, based in Natal, South Africa, a lucrative South African sugar manufacturer (Parmar xii). Mirrlees herself spent much of her time in South Africa and France, in exile from the UK. She could well afford to publish only 175 copies of her poem with the Hogarth Press and later, when asked in 1946 by Leonard Woolf to republish the poem, to refuse to have it reissued. She deliberately refrained from promoting the book, and it soon vanished from literary history in favor of T. S. Eliot, James Joyce and Ezra Pound's self-advertising prominence in the modernist canon, as discussed in Chapter 1. Only recently has Mirrlees's work begun to receive the critical attention it deserves. *Paris* is remarkable: the cover presents a bright geometric pattern and, inside, the reader is confronted with:

I want a holophrase

NORD-SUD
ZIG-ZAG
LION NOIR
CACAO BLOOKER

Black-figured vases in Etruscan tombs

RUE DE BAC (DUBONNET)
SOLFERINO (DUBONNET)
CHAMBRE DES DEPUTES

Brekekekek coax coax we are passing under the Seine

DUBONNET

The Scarlet Woman shouting BYRRH and deafening
St John at Patmos.

(Mirrlees 1–2, #1–13)

While Baudelaire's poetry is, to some extent, experimental and modernist in its self-consciousness, it still obeys most conventions of poetic form, as discussed in Chapter 2. By contrast, *Paris* looks and sounds utterly different: words in capitals, single-word lines (and, elsewhere in the poem, "There is no lily of the valley" is written vertically as a single letter per line), bars of music, phrases in italics, song lyrics, and odd spaces scatter across the eighteen-page poem. It is written in three languages (English, French and classical Greek, as "brekekekek" is a quotation from Aristophanes' ancient Greek comedy *The Frogs*). Next to this classical reference sit contemporary advertisements for Blooker's cocoa, Lion Noir black shoe-polish,

French liqueurs (Dubonnet), Zig-zag cigarette papers; and even the scarlet woman (a prostitute) from the biblical Book of Revelations, written by St. John of Patmos, is advertising "Byrrh," a French aperitif made by mixing red wine with tonic water.

What is going on? At first glance, the poem appears to be a mishmash of unrelated phrases, a schizophrenic madness where one random snippet of text is arbitrarily placed next to another and where high learning is juxtaposed with popular songs, ads and ordinary speech. Most reviews of the poem concurred. The literature feature of a mainstream British newspaper, *The Times Literary Supplement*, had the following to say about *Paris*:

> This little effusion looks at the first blush like an experiment in Dadaism; but there is method in the madness which peppers the pages with spluttering and incoherent statement displayed with various tricks of type. It seems meant by a sort of futurist trick to give an ensemble of the sensations offered by a pilgrim through Paris. But it is certainly not a "Poem," though we follow the author's guidance in classing it as such. To print the words "there is no lily of the valley" in a vertical column of single letters must be part of a nursery game. It does not belong to the art of poetry.
>
> (qtd. in Parmar xxxix)

The review compares Mirrlees's poem to continental futurist and Dadaist poetic experiments, and rightly so: there is a method to the madness. "Nord-Sud," French for North-South, refers to the name of a painting by futurist Gino Severini, an acquaintance of Mirrlees's in Paris. Similar to cubist painting discussed in Chapter 1, the futurist painting eliminates foreground and background, removing the "realist" perspective that provides a vanishing point for the viewer's sightlines (the illusion of three dimensions, where background provides depth). In Severini's painting, because there is no vanishing point, the viewer is disoriented by being refused perspectival distance. Hence, the title "Nord-Sud" is ironic because direction and spatial orientation are lacking in this painting. In fact, Severini's aim, as stated in "The Exhibitors to the Public 1912" manifesto, was that the spectator "must in future be placed in the centre of the picture" (Apollonio 48). Signs and posters crowd one's field of vision and give the viewer a sense of immersion and simultaneity because everything seems to happen at once (Howarth 5–6). In Mirrlees's poem, the immersive effect is achieved through the elimination of syntactical subordination: we experience in reading the poem an onslaught of random advertisements combined with snippets of remembered quotations from classical Greek that are loosely associated, presumably by the speaker, with the images of the modern city. There seems to be no cause and effect, no before and after, past or present. Modern-day Paris and classical Greece merge into what Gertrude Stein called a "continuous present" by which memory is triggered by random sensory data (qtd. in Howarth 9).

In addition to the "futurist trick" of random, fragmentary and often nonsensical word associations, what the futurist leader F. T. Marinetti called "words-in-freedom" (Apollonio 95–106), Mirrlees's poem also invokes a "primitivist" function of language. The poem begins with the statement "I want a holophrase." This term refers to what Mirrlees's partner, Jane Ellen Harrison, the first woman classical scholar at Cambridge, defined as "a primitive stage of language in which long words expressed complex relationships more fully and less analytically than in more developed languages" (Briggs 85). Readers may be more familiar with the term "holograph" in which an image is projected in three dimensions; it appears almost solid or lifelike. Similarly, a holophrase attempts to bypass mimetic reflection and abstract analysis, and to merge with the world in all of its complex relationality. This modernist idealization of an imagined primitive wholeness, in which language and the world were one, was a way of rejecting the rationality of contemporary science and bureaucracy. The appeal of primitivism served as a modern form of mythmaking and irrationality that would, in the hands of political leaders, result in the appeal of fascism (see Chapter 3). In this poem, however, mythical plenitude is lacking as indicated by the statement "I want a holophrase." The speaker wants, but does not have, a way of directly conveying the advertisements, buildings and people she sees on the streets and subway of Paris.

But the lack of direct relation does not mean that there is no relation at all. Rather than read the poem as "sputtering" and "incoherent" as the reviewer above does, we can read the fragments as related in indirect ways:

> Without syntax to restrict the fragment's meaning to their immediate context [. . .], they can now connect to each other in multiple and unexpected

> ways: not only through the theme of undergrounds and underworlds [. . .] but [also] in the covert links of empire that bind lions, cocoa, the Algerian soldier whose face advertised Zig-Zag, and the tyrannical empire St John saw personified in the Scarlet Woman.
>
> (Howarth 6–7)

The poem has no narrative or formal connection from one image to another except in the loose sense of a "pilgrimage" referred above in the review. "NORD-SUD," besides referring to a painting by Severini, is also a reference to the Paris métro line that runs north and south through Paris. It describes the speaker's travels, a female descendent of Baudelaire's flâneur, from the south, "Rue de Bac" on the Left Bank, underneath the Seine river, to the Place de la "Concord." This name also alludes to the Peace Conference that was held at Versailles to reach an agreement, or concord, amongst the two sides of the First World War. The Versailles Peace Treaty imposed draconian war reparations on Germany that set the stage for the further destabilization of Europe and the eventual onset of the Second World War (Briggs 85). As the speaker descends into the underground subway system, the poem conflates that dark depth with Greek mythology's Hades, the land of the dead. In this regard, the poem maintains a classical epic structure in which the hero must, as in Homer's *Odyssey* and Dante's *Inferno*, descend into the underworld. Adding a modernist twist to this classical reference, *Paris* integrates modern subjective consciousness with this external Hell.

As a "psycho-geography," the poem combines both the mental and physical traumas of the Great War. Inner, subjective consciousness is conflated with the external, objective world. The inhabitants of Paris are haunted by the mass graves of soldiers slaughtered in combat; the impoverished veterans, permanently disabled by combat; and displaced peasants fleeing the rural conflict for the city. The speaker refers to a "trance" (3, #20), and "haschich" (4, #45), to create a sense of drug-induced hallucination expressive of the unreality of war and its aftermath. She hears the plaintive cries, "*messieursetdames*," of war widows begging for alms, and while "petites bourgeoises with tight lips and strident voices" give money, "their hearts are the ruined province of Picardie" (9, #190–94). The poem layers the war-torn fields of Picardy onto French citizen's hearts, destroying rural province and fellow feeling of urban community alike.

"Nord–sud" also refers to the colonization of the south (Algeria) by the north (France). The "black–figured vases in Etruscan tombs" refers not only to literal vases used in ancient burial rites, but to the black soldiers, now also in tombs, who fought for France in the war. The head of a Zouave, an Algerian soldier, advertises a colonial product, tobacco, while Blooker's cocoa refers to a Dutch colonial product. Finally, St John of Patmos prophesized death and destruction for a tyrannical empire symbolized by the monstrous, Scarlet Woman. The prophesy dovetails with the general gloom of Europe regarding its empires after the war. Finally, the fragments express isolation and dissolve center/margin distinctions between Paris and its colonial outposts. The effect of this dissolution is to challenge the normative exclusions of gender, sexual, racial or national difference (Howarth 7). For instance, if Algierians were central to the war effort, international trade, consumption and even drug use (elsewhere in the poem, poet Paul Verlain smokes "Algerian tobacco"), then their exclusion from what counts as French is a myth (a false belief). This myth of Algerian inferiority is what created the French superior identity in the first place.

Last, *The Times Literary Supplement* reviewer objected to "there is no lily of the valley" printed in single letters vertically arranged on the page. Was Mirrlees playing a nursery game, as the reviewer suggests? Of course not. Mirrlees had learned from the *fin de siècle* French poet Stéphane Mallarmé, whose meditation on art, *Un coup de dés* (*A throw of the dice*), explains how the page itself becomes a unit of meaning by spreading out the reading process, while "the white spaces acquire a special significance, and are immediately striking. They were always needed for poetry, creating a surrounding silence" (qtd. in Briggs 84). Like constellations scattered across the sky, the reader absorbs the relation of silence and emptiness that negatively, or indirectly, connect the fragments. The poet who served as an early spokesperson for cubism, Guillaume Apollinaire, took the spatial arrangement on the page pioneered by Mallarmé a step further in *Calligrammes* (1918). There, he arranged the letters on the page to create pictorial shapes – the Eiffel Tower, birds, a water fountain, flowers and geometrical figures – in a form of concrete or visual poetry. Mirrlees followed his example, prefacing her single column of letters with the phrase "The first of May" (10, line 235). May Day, or International Workers' Day, was typically celebrated in Paris with lilies of the valley. In 1919, however, this holiday was disrupted by a general strike that made the flowers unavailable. Given this historical context, the image of the single-file letters might suggest the picket line or even the stem of a flower.

Paris: A Poem is exemplary of modernist poetic form in several ways. First, it immerses the reader in an onslaught of sensory experience. It is as if we, too, ride the métro and, later in the poem, stroll through Paris. The speed and intensity of the posters whizzing past us, the overheard fragments of voices and songs, the various shapes of buildings, and the topology of the city that includes a descent into the underground are disorienting and overwhelming. And yet, despite the fragmentary nature of the poem, we can discern the wholeness or unity of the modern metropolis. Though at first the poem doesn't seem to be about anything at all, on second glance, it is filled with politics, culture and history. Second, the experimental style and wild mixing of languages and discursive registers ("low" or popular songs, conversations, advertisements as well as "high" or elite classical and literary references) signal a rejection of traditional poetic forms and literary institutions. Modernist poetry eschews the literary establishment and the commercial marketplace, and is rewarded by negative reviews and a very small circle of readers. It rejects middle-class respectability and class divisions, bringing in sexuality (in *Paris* there are references to lesbian relationships and the female body) and taking its cue from the lower-middle and working classes. Many other poets, including Eliot, as we have seen in Chapter 1, deployed cut-up phrases, lack of syntax, unclear references, and quick cuts between ancient and modern worlds and random details of contemporary culture (Howarth 3). Their aim, like Mirrlees's, was to "immerse [their] reader in a kind of unity unavailable to detached thought, and recreate lost forms of collective being" (Howarth 31). As we'll next see, in other locations around the world, modernist poetic forms are different because their "collective being" has been formed through different histories.

VERNACULAR POETRY

When modernist poets write poetry in non-European locations, they frequently assume different aims and shapes than do their European counterparts. One primary aim – not unlike that of non-Western modernist dramatists and fiction writers – was to represent

non-European communities as modern by incorporating local traditions and culture into modernist poetic form. The St. Louis-born
American poet and critic T. S. Eliot articulated the quintessential
formula of this cross-cultural modernism in his essay "Tradition and
the Individual Talent" (1919). There, he argued for a way of recali-
brating tradition so as to renovate it. He salvages the past, borrowing
and hence rewriting literary tradition:

> The poet's mind is in fact a receptacle for seizing and storing up number-
> less feelings, phrases, images, which remain there until all the particles
> which can unite to form a new compound are present together.
>
> (1964: 41)

His insights are significant for understanding the development of
vernacular modernism around the globe. By "vernacular modernism," I draw from what Matthew Hart calls the "synthetic vernacular,"
a mixture of official colonizing languages (English, French, Spanish,
German and others) and a textual representation of those who are
excluded from the culture of power, conveyed in "broken English,"
creole, or dialect (7).

Prior to Eliot's intervention, dialect was simply a marker of inferiority.
Barbadian poet Edward Kamau Brathwaite (b. 1930) reminds us that

> the word "dialect" has been bandied about for a long time, and it carries
> very pejorative overtones. Dialect is thought of as "bad English." Dialect
> is "inferior English". Dialect is the language used when you want to make
> fun of someone.
>
> (1984: 13)

Michael North notes that dialect was used in nineteenth-century
minstrel shows in which white actors "blacked up" in order to stereotype and mock African-Americans (7). By contrast, in "Tradition
and the Individual Talent," Eliot reconceives of tradition in order to
revitalize European culture, but also, as Marc Manganaro argues, to
expand "what could count as aesthetic, as Culture with a capital C.
Poems, great poems, could now contain footnotes, could point fin-
gers at readers in foreign tongues, could have sex, and sex changes"
(53). And, as Brathwaite tells us, Eliot "introduce[d] the notion of the
speaking voice, the conversational tone" (1984: 30). Eliot incorporated

dialect or informal spoken language as part of "high" literary culture. As an American living in London, Eliot was very much the outsider, and his reformulation of the "great" European and classical literary tradition allowed him to infuse this tradition with the creole culture of St. Louis where he grew up to produce his modernist poetry. **Creole** refers to the mixture of African, sometimes Asian or Amerindian, and European cultures found in the New World and beyond.

Instead of bemoaning the passing of high European traditions, T. S. Eliot turned the demise of European cultural dominance into a positive one for poetry, and modernist art more generally, when he grafted new voices, social formations, technologies and media onto the European tradition. What Eliot calls tradition is the historical sense of the "whole of the literature of Europe from Homer" as it is experienced in the present (1964: 38). The two elements – past and present – exist in a mutually transformative fashion. He expands on this notion:

> This historical sense, which is a sense of the timeless as well as of the temporal and of the timeless and temporal together, is what makes a writer traditional. And it is at the same time what makes a writer most acutely conscious of his place in time, of his own contemporaneity.
>
> (1964: 38)

Tradition weighs upon a writer or painter, but

> for order to persist after the supervention of novelty, the *whole* existing order must be, if ever so slightly, altered; and so the relations, proportions, values of each work of art toward the whole are readjusted; and this is conformity between the old and the new.
>
> (1964: 38–39)

What Eliot shows in *The Waste Land* is that tradition is not so much dead, inert matter, but instead, when recombined with other traditions and contemporary references, articulates a vital new art form for post-war Europe. In that sense, Eliot was an early DJ "sampler": he takes old tunes and remixes them in a new way.

In salvaging the past to articulate a sense of fragmentation in the present, Eliot, as well as other artists from around the world, interrupted an understanding of history as progressive unfolding and development, and instead offered a bricolage of past and present. The term **bricolage** comes from the French term for "bricklaying" and refers to the practice of taking random blocks of material and juxtaposing them in a heterogeneous and simultaneous fashion to form something new. This "sampling" approach to the past, in effect, created an entry for people all over the world to produce modernist art and literature and a means by which all sorts of traditions (oral, ancient, Western and Eastern, popular and elite) could be compared and referenced. Eliot did not invent vernacular modernisms, which were practiced in South and East Asia as well as in Latin America prior to him, but for now, it's important to note that literary history was being recalibrated. Rather than advocate a poetic tradition that strictly marches through history in a linear, developmental fashion, Eliot and other modernists emphasize a simultaneous regard for both past tradition and present poetic creation. In effect, they accord themselves the ability to revise the inherited European tradition.

Importantly, Eliot emphasizes that it is his labor rather than his inherited authority that can effect a reconstruction of the "Great Tradition." And, as mentioned above, *The Waste Land* breaks new ground for what could be considered poetic. Listen for the rhythmic syncopation that breaks up the standard iambic pentameter (a five-unit short–long syllabic meter): "O O O O that Shakespeherian Rag – /It's so elegant/So intelligent" (1963: 57, #128–30). Shakespeare is "jazzed" by means of a black rhythmic vernacular, a spoken cadence that breaks free from standard poetic meter. Eliot roams historically through multiple classical traditions – Renaissance England, classical Greek and Latin, and Sanskrit – and geographically through Asia, North Africa, Europe and the New World, and he includes popular cultural references to African-American and British working classes. The romance quest myth (the barren waste land is regenerated by rain) gives a cyclical order to the fragments. The Fisher King persona in *The Waste Land* says as much: "These fragments I have shored against my ruins" (1963: 69, #432). In this sense, Eliot reaffirms the Euro-modernist hierarchies by using vernacular culture to "shore" up what remains of European high culture. We will see below that other non-European writers employ vernacular modernisms to vastly different ends.

As we turn next to non-European poetry, we can compare vernacular poetic form to the intervention in modern art made by Wilfredo Lam in *La Jungla* discussed in Chapter 1. In that painting, the hierarchies between civilized Europe and primitive Africa are dismantled in favor of a cross-section of Cuban life that includes nature, men and women, workers, religion, and ideas from Europe and Africa that are amalgamated in the crucible of the Caribbean plantation.

In effect, the Afro–Cuban elements of that painting serve to dismantle the cultural hierarchies between Europe and Africa. In a like manner, Barbadian poet Kamau Brathwaite defines **creolization** as the confrontation between the colonizing (European) culture in power and the subordinated, but still influential, colonized culture. **Vernacular** modernism, with its emphasis on the written text, represents this creole mixture in literature. For instance, Caribbean poet Louise Bennett, "Miss Lou" (1919–2006), suffuses English poetic meter and rhyme with what Brathwaite calls the submerged "riddims" of black diasporic speech in her poem "Pedestrian crosses":

> If a cross yuh dah-cross
> Beg yuh cross mek me pass.
> Dem yah crossin' is crosses yuh know!
> Koo de line! Yah noh se
> Cyar an truck backa me?
> Hear dah hoganeer one deh dah-blow!

> (qtd. in Brathwaite 1984: 29)

A translation of this stanza into standard English is as follows:

> If you're crossing,
> Please cross and let me pass.
> These crossings are really a cross, you know!
> Just look at the line! Don't you see
> All the cars and trucks behind me?
> And just listen to that hoggish one blowing the horn!

> (Cooper 6)

The play between "crossing" and "passing" depends on destabilizing what Cooper calls "somewhat convergent meanings of passing and crossing – to cross is to pass in opposite directions" (7). As the poem makes visible the different meanings of "cross" and "pass," the reader discerns that there exists a deeper conflict between pedestrians and motorists, one that is a class conflict over the right to use the streets. The poem, as a vernacular poetic form, clearly sides with those who have no other mode of transportation than their feet. "Pedestrian crosses" draws our attention to social and political struggle waged at the level of language: a cacophony of voices. Creolized language and form asserts the performative nature of this conflict; it appropriates language to wrest small victories from more powerful opponents. "Pedestrian crosses" demonstrates how non-European cultures transform **Eurocentric** modernism for their own ends.

In other non-European locations with a long literary tradition, the engagement with tradition assumes a different form altogether. Japanese poet Yosano Akiko (1878–1942) wrote in the long-standing tradition of *keishu*, or "talented woman," who were expected to write solely about the domestic landscape (Yamauchi 1). She used this expectation of *keishu* to draw attention to wider gender iniquities and the treatment of "fallen" women. Akiko's small volume of 400 *tanka* poems, *Midaregami or Tangled Hair* (1901), centers on the female body and her desire. She tried to "establish a literary lineage of women writers in the recent past, building a bridge between the widely heralded, but distant, literary achievements of classical antiquity and the contemporary world where female authors were rare" (qtd. in Yamauchi 37–38). Akiko also links her contemporary poetry "with classical forms and genres to literally recreate her idea of the feminine: based on tradition, reshaped for modernity, and tinged with Western thought" (Yamauchi 48). For example, in classical Japanese poetry, the "morning-after" poem is melancholic, as the man departs and the woman is sorrowful. Akiko's morning-after poem presents the same moment from the woman's perspective:

> Land of spring
> Country of love
> In the half-light of dawn
> That clarity – is it hair?
> Oil of the flowering plum

> (Beichman 200 #105)

Instead of sadness, the dawn brings clarity. She does not miss her lover. We only identify this poem as a morning-after poem because of the similarity of imagery, "spring," "country of love," the coming dawn. Her lover seems almost unnecessary. The woman finds satisfaction through her body and sensuality (Yamauchi 49). The rewriting of traditional form creates new modern meanings.

Sometimes tradition takes the form of the unwritten history of a people. Poetry from non-dominant locations often carries the buried history of colonization, especially because colonizers deny this version of history. Here, in Brathwaite's *The Arrivants: A New World Trilogy*, the poem "Limbo" evokes the rhythm of the limbo sticks that also convey the non-representational quality of the middle passage from Africa into New World slavery:

> And limbo stick is the silence in front of me
> *limbo*
>
> *limbo*
> *limbo like me*
> *limbo*
> *limbo like me*
>
> long dark night is the silence in front of me
> *limbo*
> *limbo like me*
>
> stick hit sound
> and the ship like it ready
>
> stick hit sound
> and the dark still steady
>
> *limbo*
> *limbo like me*
>
> long dark deck and the water surrounding me
> long dark deck and the silence is over me [. . .]
>
> *limbo*
> *limbo like me*
>
> sun coming up
> and the drummers are praising me
>
> out of the dark
> and the dumb gods are raising me
>
> up
> up
> up
>
> and the music is saving me
>
> hot
> slow
> step
>
> on the burning ground.

(194–95 #1–17; 40–51)

The poetic persona in this poem is Caliban, the slave in Shakespeare's *The Tempest*. The repetition in this poem induces a trance-like state in Caliban, the limbo dancer, as he recreates the suppressed historical memory of the maritime passage into slavery. Layered onto this memory is the present-day folk ritual of spirit possession. The "silence" and "darkness" of slavery figures the violence – beyond language – by which the transported Africans were dispossessed of their language, culture and lands. Rather than offer a reflection of colonial reality, Brathwaite's poem figures a negatively inflected inner state of being. Instead of representing redemption positively, as a thing, it is invoked through silence, darkness, rhythm and movement. We can imagine the sticks clapping together and Caliban's body dropping and then rising. The poem evokes a mesmeric quality for the reader as well as the dancer and his circle. We sense the reclamation of Afro-Caribbean experience from its suppression under slavery that occurs at the level of the body and spirit.

While this reading may sound mystical, it is important to consider the colonial violence of naming and of external reference (for the colonizer, black skin stands for evil, childishness, savagery) that Brathwaite is rejecting. By turning within and invoking rhythm, silence and darkness, Brathwaite shares the strategy of modernist form – but to vastly different ends – with other modernists such as Beckett and Stein. The darkness creates a mood or atmosphere that envelops the dancer and the reader. This heady, suffocating atmosphere joins Africa to the New World, here and there, into a single diasporic collectivity, that is felt rather than coherently articulated as a thing. To corroborate this point, Kalliney suggests that the repetitions in Brathwaite's poetry "have the effect of deferring any directly instrumental or political applications of his poetry by depicting the poet [here in this poem the persona Caliban] as a hesitant, stuttering, and frequently incapacitated figure" (104). Rather than use words instrumentally to effect direct action and to name an experience within the colonizer's language and literary forms, Brathwaite's poetry circles around words and points to what they cannot convey, a modernism from below. Brathwaite famously pronounced, "unity is submarine" (1974: 64). In indirectly exposing the submerged history of the African diaspora, Brathwaite's poetry confronts the violence and repressions of modernity and forges a community that shares this unspoken experience.

OBJECTIVIST POETRY

Objectivist poetry is largely a misnomer, as this type of modernist poetry attempts to convey though "flexible, jagged resort [. . .]

the virtual impossibility of lifting to the imagination those things which lie under the direct scrutiny of the senses" (qtd in Howarth 111, Williams 1954: 5). That is, objectivist poetry is more concerned with the relationship between human observers and the observed object. But, as we discussed in Chapter 2, we can never directly perceive the object world. Instead, in the quotation above, poet William Carlos Williams says that modernist poetry, with its formal innovations of "flexible, jagged resort," can point to realities that language cannot grasp directly. Because poetry can gesture toward silence, empty space, and indirect, oblique ways of knowing and being, it comes closest to imagining objects as they really are. American poets, such as Williams, Marianne Moore and Wallace Stevens, are often grouped under this heading, though many other poets (such as H. D. and Elizabeth Bishop) were also concerned with the ordinary, objective descriptions of small scenes. Like the earlier group, the imagists (discussed in Chapter 2), these poets strip away extraneous details, sentiment and morality, and attempt to present the thing itself, rendered as objectively as possible. In Williams's poetry, as with Walcott's drama above, a democratic ethos prevails – a desire to create art out of the ordinary. He states, "the question of FORM is so important because it is the very matter itself of a culture" (qtd. in Howarth 116). Howarth explains that Williams published *Spring and All* (1923) in order to demonstrate how innovative poetic form can renovate culture: "Its furious sequence of mixed-up chapter headings, angry replies to his critics, semi-automatic writings on art, and luminous spaced-out poems remains one of the most radical volumes of modernist poetry ever published" (116). Let's examine his most famous poem, "The Red Wheelbarrow," from this collection:

> so much depends
> upon
> a red wheel
> barrow
> glazed with rain
> water
> beside the white
> chickens.

(1985: 56 #1–6)

Unlike the abstract nature of symbolist poetry and drama, Williams attempts to be as concrete and particular as possible. The simplicity of his diction rejects traditional poetic form: there's no metaphor or symbol here. Howarth underscores the tension between "so much depends" and the simple barrow. The extremely short lines and breaks further emphasize the object itself. The poem never says quite *what* depends upon the wheelbarrow. Rather, it's that unnamed pressure between simple object and the whole that gestures toward the thing in-itself – what the object would be without an observing human subject, its thingness. The poem also suggests the Japanese *haiku* poetic form, a form that inspired the imagists as well (as discussed in Chapter 2). Its stillness and simplicity emphasizes the present moment rather than change and transformation.

We conclude this section with a rejoinder by W. B. Yeats on the frequent poetic allusions to the exotic and static East. In his 1938 poem, "Lapis Lazuli," Yeats contrasts the war-torn West with the peaceful contemplation of an eighteenth-century Chinese carving on a piece of lapis lazuli:

> Two Chinamen, behind them a third,
> Are carved in Lapis Lazuli,
> Over them flies a long-legged bird
> A symbol of longevity;
> The third, doubtless a serving-man,
> Carries a musical instrument.

(295, #37–42)

The symbol of longevity and the static nature of the carving, at first glance, projects an image of the exotic, timeless East in contradistinction with the constant change and strife of the modern West. However, critic Jehan Ramazani points out that the next two lines begin to collapse this East-West binary, "as time and ruin invade the scene" (111):

> Every discoloration of the stone,
> Every accidental crack or dent,

(295, #43–44)

The Chinese sculpture shifts, too, with time. Indeed, Yeats imagines that the figures look upon a tragic scene with gay, glittering eyes, delighting to play "mournful melodies" (295, #53). Poets from cultures that have been held by the West to be "outside time" (Ireland, too, had been viewed this way) are entirely suspicious of representations that seem to stand outside history, so they instead assert their dynamic natures.

SUMMARY

This chapter discussed:

- How literary form is an orientation toward representing reality. We then examined how modernist literary forms (novel, drama and poetry) allowed new aspects of reality to be represented.
- We examined literary impressionism in the novel, limited point of view narration, autotelic form (in which aesthetic experimentation is more important than telling a good story) and montage form (showing many different perspectives at once).
- We explored symbolist theater (Ibsen, Yeats, Artaud), political theater (futurist, women's suffrage, Nigerian, Caribbean), and Bertolt Brecht's epic theater to see how each formal innovation challenges the classical demands of illusion on the stage.
- We analyzed the first stanza of the experimental, post-World War I poem, *Paris: A Poem* by Hope Mirrlees, to understand why fragmented form, mythic allusions and polyglot language attempted to capture modern life.
- We considered the transformation of tradition called for by T. S. Eliot, the use of vernacular in modernist poetry, and how silence, blank space and indirection in modernist poetry might capture aspects of the past that remain unspeakable.
- Finally, we discussed objectivist poetry and why non-Western poets might be resistant to this form of poetic innovation.

FURTHER READING

For form in the modern novel, see Jesse Matz, *Literary Impressionism and Modernist Aesthetics*. For explorations of form in modernist Caribbean literature, see Simon Gikandi, *Writing in Limbo: Modernism and Caribbean Literature*; Charles W. Pollard, *New World Modernisms: T. S. Eliot, Derek Walcott, and Kamau Brathwaite*; and Peter Kalliney, *Commonwealth of Letters: British Literary Culture and the Emergence of Postcolonial.* For further treatment of modernist poetry, see Peter Howarth, *The Cambridge Introduction to Modernist Poetry*, and Jehan Ramazani, *A Transnational Poetics.* For more on modernist drama, see Brecht, *Brecht on Theatre: The Development of an Aesthetic;* "Modernism in Drama" by Christopher Innes; and *The Cambridge Companion to Modernism,* ed. Michael Levenson.

WORKS CITED

Anand, Mulk Raj. *Untouchable.* New York: Penguin, 1940. Print.

Apollonio, Umbro, ed. *Futurist Manifestoes.* Boston, MA: MFA Press, 2001. Print.

Artaud, Antonin. *The Theater and its Double.* New York: Grove Press, 1958. Print.

Beckett, Samuel. *Murphy.* New York: Grove Press, 1957. Print.

Beichman, Janine. *Embracing the Firebird: Yosano Akiko and the Birth of the Female Voice in Modern Japanese Poetry.* U of Hawaʻii P, 2002.

Brathwaite, Edward Kamau. *The Arrivants: A New World Trilogy.* New York: Oxford University Press, 1973. Print.

———. *Contradictory Omens: Cultural Diversity and Integration in the Caribbean.* Mona, Jamaica: Savacou Publications, 1974. Print.

———. *History of the Voice.* London: New Beacon Books, 1984. Print.

Brecht, Bertolt. *Brecht on Theatre: The Development of an Aesthetic.* Ed. John Willett. New York: Hill and Wang, 1964. Print.

Briggs, Julia. "'Modernism's Lost Hope': Virginia Woolf, Hope Mirrlees and the Printing of Paris." Chapter 5 in *Reading Virginia Woolf.* Edinburgh: Edinburgh University Press, 2006. 80–95. Print.

Brooker, Peter. "Key Words in Brecht's Theory and Practice of Theatre." In *The Cambridge Companion to Brecht.* Eds. Peter Thomson and Glendyr Sacks. New York: Cambridge University Press, 1994. 185–200. Print.

Brooks, Peter. *Reading for the Plot: Design and Intention in Narrative.* New York: Vintage, 1985. Print.

Chandler, Frank Wadleigh. "Introduction." In *Ibsen's Plays.* New York: Macmillan, 1927. vii–xxvi. Print.

Chughtai, Ismat. *The Quilt and Other Stories.* New York: Sheep Meadow Press, 1994. Print.

Conteh-Morgan, John. "The Other Avant-Garde: The Theater of Radical Aesthetics and the Poetics and Politics of Performance in Contemporary Africa." In *Not the Other Avant-Garde: Transnational Foundations of Avant-Garde Performance.* Eds. James M. Harding and John Rouse. Ann Arbor, MI: University of Michigan Press, 2006. 92–124. Print.

Cooper, Carolyn. "'Pedestrian crosses': Sites of Dislocation in 'Post-Colonial' Jamaica." *Inter-Asia Cultural Studies.* 10.1 (2009): 3–11. Print.

Dos Passos, John. *The 42nd Parallel.* New York: Mariner Books, 2000. Print.

Eliot, T. S. *Collected Poems 1909–1962*. New York: Harcourt, 1963. Print.

———. *Selected Prose of T.S. Eliot*. New York: Harcourt, 1964. Print.

Faulkner, William. *The Sound and the Fury*. New York: Vintage, 1984. Print.

Gikandi, Simon. *Writing in Limbo: Modernism and Caribbean Literature*. Ithaca, NY: Cornell University Press, 1992. Print.

Hart, Matthew. *Nations of Nothing but Poetry: Modernism, Transnationalism, and Synthetic Vernacular Writing*. New York: Oxford University Press, 2010. Print.

Hayot, Eric. *On Literary Worlds*. New York: Oxford, 2012. Print.

Howarth, Peter. *The Cambridge Introduction to Modernist Poetry*. New York: Cambridge University Press, 2012. Print.

James, David. *Modernist Futures: Innovation and Inheritance in the Contemporary Novel*. New York: Cambridge University Press, 2012. Print.

James, Henry. "The Art of Fiction." In *Modernism: An Anthology of Sources and Documents*. Eds. Vassiliki Kolocotroni, Jane Goldman, and Olga Taxidou. Chicago: Chicago University Press, 1998. 147–9. Print.

———. *The Wings of the Dove*. New York: Penguin, 1986. Print.

Joyce, James. *A Portrait of the Artist as a Young Man*. Ed. John Paul Riquelme. New York: Norton, 2007. Print.

———. *Ulysses*. New York: Random House, 1986. Print.

Kafka, Franz. "The Metamorphosis." In *The Norton Anthology of World Literature*. Vol. 2. Ed. Martin Puchner, Suzanne Akbari, Wiebke Denecke, Vinay Dharwadker, Barbara Fuchs, Caroline Levine, Pericles Lewis and Emily Wilson. New York: Norton, 2013. 1204–35. Print.

Kalliney, Peter. *Commonwealth of Letters: British Literary Culture and the Emergence of Postcolonial Aesthetics*. New York: Oxford University Press, 2013. Print.

Kern, Stephen. *The Culture of Time and Space, 1880–1918*. Cambridge, MA: Harvard University Press, 1983. Print.

———. *The Modernist Novel: A Critical Introduction*. New York: Cambridge University Press, 2011. Print.

Lewis, Pericles. *The Cambridge Introduction to Modernism*. New York: Cambridge University Press, 2007. Print.

Makdisi, Saree S. "The Empire Renarrated: Season of Migration to the North and the Reinvention of the Present." *Critical Inquiry*. 18 (Summer 1992): 804–20. Print.

Manganaro, Marc. *Culture, 1922: The Emergence of a Concept*. Princeton, NJ: Princeton University Press, 2002. Print.

Manto, Saadat Hasan. "Toba Tek Singh." In *The Norton Anthology of World Literature*. Vol. 2. Eds. Martin Puchner, Suzanne Akbari, Wiebke Denecke, Vinay Dharwadker, Barbara Fuchs, Caroline Levine, Pericles Lewis and Emily Wilson. New York: Norton, 2013. 1487–92. Print.

McKay, Claude. *Home to Harlem*. Boston, MA: Northeastern University Press, 1987. Print.

Matz, Jesse. *Literary Impressionism and Modernist Aesthetics*. New York: Cambridge University Press, 2001. Print.

———. *The Modern Novel: A Short Introduction*. Malden, MA: Blackwell, 2004. Print.

Mirrlees, Hope. "Paris: A Poem." In *Collected Poems*. Ed. Sandeep Parmar. Manchester: Carcanet Press, 2011. 1–18. Print.

Nielsen, Aldon Lynn. "The Future of an Allusion: The Color of Modernity." In *Geomodernisms: Race, Modernism, Modernity*. Eds. Laura Doyle and Laura Winkiel. Bloomington: Indiana University Press, 2005. 17–30. Print.

North, Michael. *The Dialect of Modernism: Race, Language and Twentieth-Century Literature*. New York: Oxford University Press, 1994. Print.

Parmar, Sandeep. "Introduction." In *Collected Poems. Hope Mirrlees*. Ed. Sandeep Parmar. Manchester: Fyfieldbooks, 2011. ix–xlviii. Print.

Pollard, Charles W. *New World Modernisms: T. S. Eliot, Derek Walcott, and Kamau Brathwaite*. Charlottesville, VA: University of Virginia Press, 2004. Print.

Ramazani, Jehan. *A Transnational Poetics*. Chicago: University of Chicago Press, 2009. Print.

Simmel, Georg. "The Metropolis and Mental Life." In *On Individuality and Forms*. Ed. George Levine. Chicago: Chicago University Press, 1971. 324–39. Print.

Soyinka, Wole. *Myth, Literature and the African World*. New York: Cambridge University Press, 1976. Print.

Stein, Gertrude. *The Making of Americans*. (1925) New York: Dalkey Archive Press, 1995. Print.

Walcott, Derek. *Dream on Monkey Mountain and Other Plays*. New York: Farrar, Strauss, 1970. Print.

Watt, Ian. *The Rise of the Novel: Studies in Defoe, Richardson, and Fielding*. London: Chatto & Windus, 1957. Print.

Williams, Carlos William. *Selected Essays of William Carlos Williams*. New York: Random House, 1954. Print.

———. *Selected Poems*. Ed. Charles Tomlinson. New York: New Directions, 1985. Print.

Woolf, Virginia. "Mr. Bennett and Mrs. Brown." In *The Captain's Death Bed and Other Essays*. Ed. Leonard Woolf. New York: Harcourt, Brace, 1950. 94–119. Print.

Xun, Lu. "Diary of a Mad Man." In *The Norton Anthology of World Literature*. Vol. 2. Eds. Martin Puchner, Suzanne Akbari, Wiebke Denecke, Vinay Dharwadker, Barbara Fuchs, Caroline Levine, Pericles Lewis and Emily Wilson. New York: Norton, 2013. 1238–46. Print.

Yamauchi, Devon. "*Keishu* Writers and the Discourse on Women in Meiji Japan: Huguchi Ichiyo and Yosano Akiko." Senior Honors Thesis, Department of English, University of Colorado, Boulder, March 22, 2012. Print.

Yeats, W. B. *The Collected Poems of Y. B. Yeats*. Ed. Richard J. Finneran. New York: Macmillan, 1989. Print.

———. *Essays and Introductions*. London: Macmillan, 1961. Print.

AFTERWORD
MODERNISM TODAY

> Historical understanding is understanding of the past as a shaping force upon the present. Insofar as that shaping force is tangibly felt upon our lives, historical understanding is part of the present. Our historical being is part of our present.
>
> J. M. Coetzee, *Stranger Shores* (2001)

Now that you've read these chapters, let us return to our opening question: what is modernism? In answering this question, it is helpful to remember the main points that we've made thus far:

- In Chapter 1, we introduced modernism as a mode of writing and painting that involved dissonance and displacement (abrupt jumps to different times and places), fragmented form, irony, allusiveness, indirection and compression. Just before and in the decades following World War II, critics, editors, scholars and writers considered this highly experimental form to be a strictly Western invention and canonized a select number of mostly male, European and American authors in anthologies, university curricula, scholarly books and articles. Modernism, in this guise, is the pinnacle of European sophistication, universalism (something that is true for all people), and the last gasp of civilizational triumph before Europe's fall from prominence in World War II.

• Then, we showed how canonized modernists – chiefly, T. S. Eliot and Pablo Picasso – used language and objects from other parts of the world to reshape how artists could represent reality. Picasso's African masks and Eliot's colloquial and jazzed speech broke from the standard ways in which Western artists represented the world. This fact suggests strongly that modernism is fundamentally beholden to non-European cultures that shaped their experimental aesthetics in the first place.

   Simon Gikandi contends that without African masks, there would be no modernism. Cubism's encounter with African art, he writes, is "dynamical, dialectical, and constitutive of the field of European and American culture" (2006: 421). By dialectical, he means that the object of history – African culture as written about by Europeans – becomes its subject, infusing new life and iconoclastic energy into European representations and transforming both. The African masks interrupt the continuity of European space and time, and the banal repetitions of everyday life. The masks are abstract forms that bring viewers up short – in shocked surprise, perhaps – and make them question their assumptions and beliefs, including the belief that the West stands alone at the pinnacle of civilization, in a continuous history of progress. *Les Demoiselles* demonstrates that European art is only one among many other realities and art styles that exist in the world. This encounter with, and recognition of, other cultures produced an international and cosmopolitan way of imagining the world. Modernism attempts to get us to think, read, and look at the world differently, more complexly, and certainly in wider terms.

• This bigger picture – Western and non-Western cultures in dialogue with one another – led us to ask: how is modernism related to modernity? We answered that modernism is a critical engagement with modernity, defined as a world-historical force of borrowing, interchange, contestation and transformation amongst different peoples. Modernity has many meanings that are perpetually contested: it signifies the great aspirations of liberalism and cosmopolitanism (freedom, equality, protection from harm), along with Enlightenment principles of reason and evidence that gave rise to scientific and technological advancements, but it also carries with it histories of violence, exclusion, dispossession, forced migrations and instrumentalism of the worst sort. We discussed this with reference to Marx and Engels's "The Communist Manifesto" and to histories of colonialism and imperialism around the world.

Further exploring the effects of modernity on modernism, in Chapters 1–3, we examined many crucial world historical events and transformations during the early twentieth century: the crisis of empire in which the European colonial system collapsed; the two world wars; the Great Depression; the Russian Revolution; women's, minority and workers' movements; the emergence of new media, new technologies and other forms of modernization; revolutions in philosophy, science, linguistics and psychology; and movements for national independence around the world. Modernism, as we defined it, is a crisis in the ability of the arts to represent the world when it was changing so drastically.

- Given that the world changes differently in different places, we saw in Chapter 4 that modernism assumes a variety of forms depending on the location in which it is created. Modernism, like modernity, then, "is a *shifter*, whose meaning derives from the context of its use" (Comaroff and Comaroff 10, emphasis added). Modernism marks the *now* by breaking from previous ways of representing reality, whether that means new formal ways of representing, new content to represent, or (most likely) a combination of both. By combining historically and culturally specific content with modernist techniques, this mode of representation can make visible experiences that had previously not been available to those from outside that location. For instance, modernist fiction, with its stream of consciousness technique, its free indirect discourse and intensity of sensory perception (how we see, feel and sense the onrush of modern life), brings "to light a peripheral insidedness that [. . .] 'remains systematically invisible at the center'" (Young 614). No matter where modernist artistic practice occurs, its aesthetic nature conveys what it feels like to inhabit that place, under those particular conditions of modernity, whether in Africa, the Caribbean, Asia, the Middle East, or in an immigrant or minority enclave in the first world "center." At the same time, modernism's critical edge – its dissonance, its obscurity, its polylingualism, its silences – allows artists and writers to resist a complete capitulation to modernity. This expanded notion of

modernism is decidedly *not* about exporting a single brand of
modernism around the world or about co-opting the specificity
of particular cultural practices in order to make another culture
look and sound *like* the West.

Indeed, as we have shown, the flow of modernist innovation is
not unidirectional. We've seen how the Japanese haiku poetry and
Noh drama, Chinese ideographs, Hindu Upanishads, and African
masks inform European modernism. Conversely, in the case of Mulk
Raj Anand, Kamau Brathwaite, Wilfredo Lam and others, European
modernism directly shapes their non-European writing and painting. Often, however, these lines of transmission cannot be traced
so directly. For example, a general sense of melancholy suffuses the
poetic meditations on modernity in Yosano Akiko's morning-after
poem and in Derek Walcott's ruminations on the petty dramas of
poverty in "What the Twilight Says," both discussed in Chapter 4.
These writings might come after Baudelaire's dark thoughts concerning the Paris underworld, but they have more to do with an
engagement with modernity in Japan and Trinidad, respectively,
than with the reworking of European modernism. The modernism
crafted by these writers articulates an encounter with a gendered or
class-based otherness produced within their own historical settings.
   We can now answer a question posed in Chapter 1: is global modernism simply an imitative absorption of a European trend? It can be,
but this would make for very poor art. The best modernist writing
and art must "make it new" again and again, each time encountering
and reanimating the traditions of the past and combining them with
content emerging in the present. So while *modernism* traditionally
refers to experimental art produced in the West during the early
twentieth century, its critical and aesthetic aims – "its unfinished
project" (James "Introduction" 6) – extend into the twenty-first
century in the works of poets, novelists, painters and other artists
that engage with modernity as it manifests itself in distinctive ways
depending upon its location around the world.
   Joe Cleary summarizes this widening of what counts as modernism in literary terms as follows:

Modernism might today be described less as the antithesis of realism
than as a term for a wide variety of literary experiments [. . .] that sought

to bring into being either radical new types of literature or radical new roles for literature.

(261)

Nothing is less modernist than to repeat what has come before, as Derek Attridge has noted (5). Cleary draws our attention to how modernism no longer means, or looks, one particular way. It combines with realist representation to produce something new or to create a new relation with its audience – more participatory, as we've seen with modernist drama, or channeled through new media to attract a wider audience who reads, listens and views art differently than those trained in elite institutions might. To conclude, we will discuss how modernism can be defined in relation to two other contemporary terms: postmodernism and postcolonialism.

POSTMODERNISM

In architecture, postmodernism is often quite clearly defined against modernism. According to postmodernist critics of architecture, modernism is pure, autonomous, authoritarian, as rendered in modernist skyscrapers designed by Mies van der Rohe, Le Corbusier, Gropius, Louis Kahn and others in the manner of post-war International Style. Stripped of ornamentation or historical reference, these buildings repel the crowds below them and rise sublimely – monumentally – to the sky. They appear to transcend history and fragmentation and, in the case of government buildings in decolonizing nations such as Brazil and Bangladesh, gesture toward a utopian world in which chaos recedes and rationality prevails. In reality, these buildings, especially when funded by emerging multinational corporations, are self-involved and technocratic, and they assert "the great divide" between modernist elites and the vulgar masses. This architectural style was often accompanied by notorious urban renewal schemes that bulldozed vibrant working-class and immigrant communities and displaced them into mass public housing complexes, often at a distance from city centers and other valuable real estate locations. By contrast, postmodern architecture is vernacular, colorful, inviting to the public, and heterogeneous as it references many artistic styles.

Unlike the clarity of the architectural division between modernism and postmodernism, **postmodernism**, like the term modernism, when referencing literature, can mean many different things. In fiction, postmodernism is often defined as a move *away* from narrative and realist representation. Postmodern literature, in this case, is a turn toward self-reflexiveness, in what is often called "metafiction," and practiced by writers such as Samuel Beckett, Vladimir Nabokov, John Barth and Donald Barthelme. Self-reflexiveness, or metafiction, rejects mimesis, the claim that language can adequately represent reality. Self-reflexive fictions "conceive of themselves as sheer text, as a process of production of representations that have no truth content, are, in this sense, sheer surface or superficiality" (Jameson 75). But, the reader might ask, isn't that also what formally innovative kinds of modernist texts do? Readers will remember that we've already discussed Samuel Beckett as a modernist, but here, he is claimed as a postmodernist. So, too, James Joyce's *Finnegans Wake* (1939) has been claimed as both a modernist and postmodernist work of literature. If we assume a New Critical definition of modernism (that modernism is elite and difficult writing that distinguishes itself from the vulgar masses), then postmodernism breaks from this authoritarian stance. Postmodern literature is playful and eclectic, and more willingly embraces popular culture. Nabokov's *Lolita* (1955) is an early and notorious instance of this new trend. In it, the refined European aesthete Humbert Humbert, a boarder in a small New England town, falls in love with and kidnaps Dolores Haze (Lolita), who is not quite thirteen years old. Escaping on a desperate and doomed road trip, they tour kitsch-America with its cheap diners, gas stations and seedy motels. Its language playfully (and also cynically) constructs a world of illicit desire and schlock consumerism that refuses to puncture its veneer of cheap pleasure in order to confront the depraved morality driving both consumerism and pedophilia.

Peter Howarth, in his excellent introduction to modernist poetry, notes that many of the most famous modernist long poems – Basil Bunting's *Briggflatts* (1966), Ezra Pound's *The Cantos* (nearly complete version, 1970), William Carlos Williams's *Paterson* (1963), and Louis Zukofsky's "A" (1978) are clearly latecomers to modernism, defined in the strict period terms of the first half of the twentieth century. More than merely excluding these Western poets, limiting modernism to the first half of the twentieth century also assumes that modernity unfolds uniformly across the world. Even a cursory glance at the dates of national independence, especially in Africa, the Caribbean and Asia, suggests different kinds of encounters with modernity occurring simultaneously, whether at the birth of a new nation or the waning of the European empires. Susan Stanford Friedman cogently states, "A full spatialization of modernism changes the map, the canon, and the periodization of modernism dramatically" (426). Every location has a different history and, given that postmodernism disavows an explicit engagement with history (including narratives of liberation), then modernism might better define the attempts by writers to engage with questions of national destiny and autonomy from the West.

Decades ago, Raymond Williams, in *The Politics of Modernism*, set the terms for revisions of modernism still underway today:

> If we are to break out of the non-historical fixity of post-modernism [its eclectic, self-reflexive references that refuse historical narrative], then we must search out and counterpose an alternative tradition taken from the neglected works left in the wide margin of the century, a tradition which may address itself not to this by now exploitable because quite inhuman rewriting of the past but, for all our sakes, to a modern future in which community may be imagined again.

(35)

What Williams is saying here is that we need to distinguish between modernism as it was institutionally canonized (through New Criticism) and modernism as "the scene of an unfinished argument about [its] critical and formal potentiality" (James *Modernist Futures* 3). What possibilities – of belonging together, of artistic expression, of freedom – did other modernist writers and painters express that we have not yet fully recognized?

POSTCOLONIALISM

For colonized peoples and peoples of the African and Asian diaspora (those Africans and Asians forcibly brought to the New World to work as slaves or indentured servants on plantations and elsewhere), modernity is experienced more along the lines of catastrophe than as anything to be celebrated. Hence, for its writers and artists, it might be tempting to avoid European influences altogether and focus instead on pre-colonial or pre-diasporic cultures and languages. However, such an emphasis on the distant past does not serve present-day needs. Colonization and slavery have irrevocably altered these societies. According to the colonizer, indigenous cultures had no value and, therefore, colonizers felt no need to preserve them. Understandably, then, writers and artists from non-European locations were reluctant to call themselves modernists, if by modernism what is meant is an erasure of indigenous history and cultures in the name of modernity. This is so especially when modernism is understood as a predominantly white, European, middle-class phenomenon that is hierarchical.

Indeed, many writers and artists from the formerly colonized territories of Europe have explicitly condemned modernism. Michael Thelwell, an important Jamaican novelist and critic, targets modernism's autonomy of art and calls it "the excuse and justification for a general retreat from [a] wide-ranging engagement with social and moral questions" (qtd. in Gikandi 1992: 3). For colonial and minority artists and writers, it was vitally important to engage with suppressed colonial and non-Western history and with the West's hierarchical representations of other peoples and women. But they also share with European modernists the need to critique modernity as it exists in its current form. Remember from Chapter 1 that modernity demands constant development, usually at the expense of those territories and peoples most peripheral and vulnerable to those in charge of never-ending growth. Therefore, modernism from the colonies and other non-Western locations takes different forms from that of European modernism. Gikandi describes how Caribbean modernism engages in different questions from those addressed by Europe:

> Caribbean writers cannot adopt the history and culture of European modernism, especially as defined by the colonizing structures, but neither can they escape from it because it has overdetermined Caribbean cultures in many ways. Moreover, for peoples of African and Asian descent, the central categories of European modernity – history, national language, subjectivity – have value only when they are fertilized by figures of 'other' imagination which colonialism sought to repress. In this sense, Caribbean modernism is highly revisionary.
>
> (1992: 3–4)

Colonized and diasporic writers (writers who were forced to migrate), as Gikandi puts it, simultaneously affirm the horrors of colonial history and acknowledge their unofficial (unwritten and unrecognized by the colonizer) indigenous and creole past and present.

How can we consider art that is engaged with social, political and historical content still practicing modernism? To answer this question, we need to understand autonomous or experimental art as always being related and dependent upon that which it represses. These repressed forces often return to haunt the modernist work of art. Repression does not mean the elimination of something; rather, it suggests not wanting to acknowledge something that still exists. At the same time, peripheral as well as women and working-class writers and artists have a fierce need to acknowledge the repressed elements of modern life as they tend to be identified with those elements. Hence, their art openly acknowledges all sorts of disavowed history. In this model, cultural hierarchies are frequently dismantled in favor of social relations that displace, contradict, reverse, multiply and open.

Postcolonial writers have often borrowed European modernist techniques and themes, but they have made much different use of them. Neil Lazarus explains how modernism in decolonizing settings – for instance, in the work of Brathwaite, Bennett and Salih, discussed in Chapter 4 – was instrumental in creating an autonomous national identity. These writers did this by criticizing **Eurocentric** assumptions and asserting their own language, history and style. Lazarus writes,

> Nationalism has become a dirty word in some circles [because it can become, as in Nazism, an extreme form of intolerant communal behavior], but for the colonized it was a redemptive project that needed an aesthetic dimension in order to fulfill its mandate.

(28–29)

Moreover, Lazarus reminds us of the critical function of "modernist writing after the canonization of modernism [. . . It] says, 'no'; refuses integration, resolution, consolation, comfort; [it] protests and criticizes" (31). As Lazarus's comments suggest, the assumption that modernism ignores or disavows colonialism and imperialism is changing. New readings of Mohsin Hamid's *The Reluctant Fundamentalist* (2007), Abdelrahman Munif's *Cities of Salt* (1988), Arundhati Roy's *The God of Small Things* (1997) as well as poetry by Agha Shahid Ali, Lorna Goodison, Derek Walcott and Christopher Okigbo, among others, have recontextualized modernism to account for its translation into other histories and traditions. (See Rubenstein, Mattar, Friedman and Ramazani.) Postcolonial texts incorporate aspects of modernist technical innovation in order to update *and* criticize modernist texts and histories of the early twentieth century.

In sum, when we track how modernism travels, we need to ask the following questions:

- How has modernism been translated? How do we move beyond thinking about the English language, or Anglophone modernism, "as starting point, endpoint, or center of gravity for studies of translation in global modernisms?" (Rogers 249). How do non-Western modernists (for instance, from South and East Asia, Latin America and Africa), or those who write in minor European languages (Spanish and Portuguese) exchange work among themselves without referring to English-speaking modernism? For example, Spanish-language poet Juan Ramón Jiménez translated the poetry of Bengali-speaking Rabindranath Tagore between 1913–22. He used English as a common language (Tagore translated his own poetry into English; Jiménez translated the English version of Tagore's poetry into Spanish), but only insofar as it served as a medium for connecting the two peripheral modernisms (Rogers 248–62).
- How does modernism say no? Refuse capitalist modernity? Refuse racism and sexism? Give voice to grief, loss and violence that is, as Walter Mignolo puts it, the dark underside of modernity? Recent work by Ewa Ziarek and Madelyn Detloff examine modernist women's melancholic writing. For Detloff, the linkage between modernist melancholia and twenty-first century violence is not one of direct lineage or remote correspondence, but rather, modernist melancholia is a "patched" or grafted component of the present that can teach us something about how to understand contemporary trauma, militarized violence and imperial loss in writings by Pat Barker, Hanif Kureishi and Susan Sontag.
- How have contemporary novelists reinvented modernist techniques? David James (*Modernist Futures*) argues for the renewed pertinence of modernism in writers as disparate as Milan Kundera (from Czechoslovakia), Philip Roth (Jewish-American), Michael Ondaatje (from Sri Lanka and Canada), J. M. Coetzee (South

African) and Toni Morrison (African-American). Rebecca L. Walkowitz has argued for the reinvention of a modernist ethics of cosmopolitan style in contemporary novelists Salman Rushdie, Kazuo Ishiguro and W. G. Sebald.

In short, I hope that *Modernism: The Basics* has given you, the reader, a taste of the density and complexity, but also of the excitement and possibility, of modernism. It was born in a world that was increasingly interrelated and one that experienced great stirrings of liberation, discovery and transformation in the sciences, philosophy, technology and the social sciences. And while modernism as a historical period may have ended, the formal elements that slow us down, make us think, and certainly make us see the world in a different way, continue to offer new ways of engaging with the pitfalls and promises of modernity.

FURTHER READING

The following books explore afterlives of modernism in contemporary literature: Rebecca L. Walkowitz *Cosmopolitan Style: Modernism Beyond the Nation*; David James *Modernist Futures: Innovation and Inheritance in the Contemporary Novel*; Neil Lazarus *The Postcolonial Unconscious* and Madelyn Detloff *The Persistence of Modernism: Loss and Mourning in the Twentieth Century*.

WORKS CITED

Attridge, Derek. *J. M. Coetzee and the Ethics of Reading: Literature and the Event*. Chicago: Chicago University Press, 2004. Print.

Cleary, Joe. "Realism after Modernism and the Literary World-System." *Modern Language Quarterly*. 73.3 (September 2012): 255–68. Print.

Comaroff, Jean and John L. Comaroff. *Theory from the South or, How Euro-America Is Evolving toward Africa*. Boulder, CO: Paradigm Press, 2012. Print.

Detloff, Madelyn. *The Persistence of Modernism: Loss and Mourning in the Twentieth Century*. New York: Cambridge University Press, 2009. Print.

Eliot. T. S. *The Waste Land*. Ed. Michael North. *Norton Critical Edition*. New York: Norton & Co., 2001. 5–26. Print.

Friedman, Susan Stanford. "Periodizing Modernism: Postcolonial Modernities and the Space/Time Borders of Modernist Studies." *Modernism/Modernity*. 13.3 (September 2006): 425–43. Print.

Gikandi, Simon. *Writing in Limbo: Modernism and Caribbean Literature*. Ithaca, NY: Cornell University Press, 1992. Print.

———. "Preface: Modernism in the World." *Modernism/Modernity*. 13.3 (September 2006): 419–24. Print.

Howath, Peter. *The Cambridge Introduction to Modernist Poetry*. New York: Cambridge University Press, 2012. Print.

James, David. "Introduction: Mapping Modernist Continuities." In *The Legacies of Modernism: Historicizing Postwar and Contemporary Fiction*. Ed. David James. New York: Cambridge University Press, 2012. 1–19. Print.

———. *Modernist Futures: Innovation and Inheritance in the Contemporary Novel*. New York: Cambridge University Press, 2012. Print.

Jameson, Fredric. *Signatures of the Visible*. New York: Routledge, 1992. Print.

Lazarus, Neil. *The Postcolonial Unconscious*. New York: Cambridge University Press, 2011. Print.

Mattar, Karim. "The *Shabbah* of World Literature: Bedouin Cartographies in Abdulrahman Munif's *Cities of Salt*." *English Language Notes*. 52.2 (Fall/Winter 2014): 35–52. Print.

Ramazani, Jahan. *A Transnational Poetics*. Chicago: University of Chicago Press, 2009. Print.

Rogers, Gayle. "Translation." In *Global Modernism: Towards a New Lexicon*. Eds. Eric Hayot and Rebecca L. Walkowitz. New York: Columbia University Press, 2016. 248–62. Print.

Rubenstein, Michael. "Environment, Economentality, and the Water-Energy Nexus: Mohsin Hamid's Geomodernism." Paper presented at the "Locating Geomodernisms: Ten Years Later" seminar, Modernist Studies Association Conference, Pittsburgh, 2014. Print.

Walkowitz, Rebecca L. *Cosmopolitan Style: Modernism beyond the Nation*. New York: Columbia University Press, 2006. Print.

Williams, Raymond. *The Politics of Modernism: Against the New Conformists*. New York: Verso Press, 1989. Print.

Young, Paul. "Peripheralizing Modernity: Global Modernism and Uneven Development." *Literature Compass*. 9.9 (2012): 611–16. http://onlinelibrary.wiley.com.colorado.idm.oclc.org/doi/10.1111/lic3.12005/epdf (Accessed 09/15/16).

Ziarek, Ewa Plonowska. *Feminist Aesthetics and the Politics of Modernism*. New York: Columbia University Press, 2012. Print.

GLOSSARY

Abstract Art Art that breaks from representation, for example, in the form of patterns, lines, shapes and colors that do not refer directly to anything outside the canvas.

Aestheticism A late-nineteenth-century school of art and writing that held that art had no inherent moral values and that the artist and writer should pursue the ideal of beauty solely for its own sake.

Autonomous Art/Autonomy The idea that a work of art creates its own rules by which it can be interpreted and understood, independent of conventional expectations.

Autotelic Form The goal is the achievement of the form itself, not what it can represent. It is characterized by attention to form itself, a new aesthetic style.

Avant-Garde A style of art and writing that attempts to integrate art with everyday life by rejecting artistic conventions.

Bricolage Artwork that juxtaposes diverse, random materials to make something new. The term is a French word that refers to "bricklaying."

Close Reading The critical practice of carefully analyzing a text in terms of its content, language, style and form. When reading closely, the reader is not to generalize or paraphrase from the text, but to focus on the elements in the text that are difficult, ambiguous or paradoxical.

Collage From the French verb, "to glue." This technique combines heterogeneous artistic or textual fragments on a single visual plane or narrative. It differs from **montage** in that it has multiple objects, rather than, as in **montage,** multiple perspectives of a single object.

Colonialism A process of geographic expansion achieved by the political and economic suppression of other territories and often forcible displacement of peoples by the invading powers.

Condensation Freud's theory that dreams, like language, have multiple meanings and therefore present several seemingly unrelated elements or themes at once.

Contexts The circumstances that impact the relevance of what is written or painted. Circumstances can include prevailing attitudes, conditions, settings and intercultural exchanges that indirectly inform works of art.

Creolization/Creole The mixture of a colonizing culture and the subordinated culture, usually African, Asian and/or Amerindian.

Crisis of Reason A resistance to rationality and the acknowledgement of hidden truths; in art, it involves an emphasis on irrationality and blind impulses.

Crisis of Representation An awareness of the limitations of language, specifically how language and visual signs can never fully capture the meaning of the objective world.

Dandy Like the **flâneur**, but also eccentric and frivolous, often wearing feminine or outrageous outfits designed to startle the public.

Decolonization/Decolonize The cultural, social and political transformation of a territory from being colonized to becoming a sovereign (independent) state.

Difficulty According to T. S. Eliot in "The Metaphysical Poets," modern art must be difficult because the contemporary world is so complex and various, so art must reflect this situation. It does this by spanning a wider geographical and temporal range, alluding to other works of art and culture and becoming more indirect or mediated in how it represents the world.

Displacement Freud's theory that dreams are empty of historical or logical connection and therefore contain arbitrary fragments put together in ways that defy causality and continuity.

Dissonance The discordant or jarring juxtaposition of unlike shapes, references or sounds; the opposite of harmonious.

Eurocentric The universalization of a European perspective and history according to the belief that the rest of the world should imitate Europe.

Flâneur A man (usually) who leisurely strolls through the streets of an urban environment and who gazes at people and goods on display.

Form (literary) Restrictions or limitations on how one can represent an aesthetic or imagined world, i.e., fiction, poetry, drama; an orientation toward representing reality.

Fourth Wall A convention in drama that separates the audience from the events on stage by rendering them invisible and immaterial to the action.

Free Indirect Discourse In prose, when a narrator paraphrases a character's thoughts instead of presenting them in quotations, therefore blurring the distinction between narrator and character points of view.

Free Verse In poetry, the rejection of conventional rhyme, meter and stanza form.

Ideology A kind of thinking that promotes an idea of how society should be that serves as the basis for policy and theory.

Imperialism The rule over large territories by means of colonization, military force or other forms of domination. The idea of superiority justifies the extension of authority and control over another people.

Interior Monologue A form of first-person narration in which a character thinks to him/her self in a manner that is more coherent and comprehensible than a **stream of consciousness** narration.

Intertextuality/intertextual References within a text, often implicit rather than explicit, to related ideas, themes, characters or events in other texts.

Irony/Ironic In literature, a technique of indicating an intention or attitude opposite to that which is actually stated.

Language Game Language that does not reflect the "real" world outside of itself, but rather creates its own cultural context.

Manifesto A document distributed by a group of artists or writers that posits a break from previous ways of art or writing and outlines a new program of art or politics.

Mémoire Involuntaire A French term meaning "involuntary memory," the belief that the past is stored in the body – in this case, in sensory data of taste and smell – and can be triggered by a similar prompt in the present.

Mimesis The representation of the real world in art and literature.

Modern A term that means "now" as opposed to the past of tradition. It is a narrative category, a story one tells about a way of life: we used to do things in a traditional manner; now we do them differently.

Modernism A historical period of intensive innovation in the arts as well as a more broadly defined movement in the arts that both represents aspects of modernity and criticizes them.

Modernity The social, political, economic and philosophical conditions that produce the "new" and characterize tradition in self-conscious ways. Modernity is a worldwide process characterized by exciting growth and transformation as well as displacement and destruction of peoples and lands.

Modernization The socioeconomic transformation of feudal and tribal societies into modern ones, organized by market exchanges, wage labor and urbanization.

Montage An art, film and literary technique that juxtaposes multiple perspectives of the same location in the present time. (See also **collage**.)

Narrative A way of ordering experience by means of a beginning, middle and end, or change over time.

Naturalism A nineteenth-century school of realist drama and novels that conveyed in great detail the sordid side of society, especially the underworld of crime, addiction and prostitution.

Omniscient Narrator In prose, a narrative point of view with access to characters' inner thoughts as well as outer actions, usually presenting normative viewpoints of society.

Plot The organizing line or the thread of design of a story. It creates interconnection and intention and strings together episodes, actions and incidents into a finite whole.

Portmanteau The French word for "suitcase." It refers to a technique in which two separate words are joined into one to create multiple meanings: brunch, cockapoo, jazzercise, mockumentary, frappucino and paralympics are examples of portmanteau words.

Postcolonial The historical condition of having been colonized and the ongoing critique of the continuation of colonial values, knowledge and ways of being.

Postmodernism An art movement that generally comes after and is critical of modernism. It is self-reflexive or critical of mimetic representation, playful, eclectic and embraces popular culture more openly than modernism.

Primitivism The belief that non-Western peoples are less civilized than Europeans and, therefore, are in closer touch with their instinctual impulses than are Europeans.

Realism/Realist A style of art and literature that attempts to present society from an objective point of view and describe it in empirical or readily observable terms.

Signifier/Signified The signifier is the "sound-image" (what we hear or picture) and the signified is the concept. For example, the signifier "cup" in English refers to the concept of a vessel that holds liquids.

Simultaneity An artistic style in which multiple perspectives are presented at once, suggesting a sense of movement around a single object or compression of space and time.

Social Realism A style of writing and painting that aimed to convey concrete, realistic detail about social problems without affiliating with the Communist Party and its ideologies.

Socialist Realism A style of realism developed in the Soviet Union that sought to convey documentary detail in a journalistic, transparent prose style. It also aimed to educate its readership about social problems.

Spatial Form As developed by Joseph Frank, spatial form is a static method of reading. There is no narrative causation or subordination, only "the interplay of relationships" between fragments "within an immobilized time-area."

Stream of Consciousness A prose technique aimed at presenting the associational quality of a character's inner thoughts without conventional ordering techniques such as standard grammar, syntax and logical subordination.

Symbolism Evoking, alluding to or suggesting indirectly some sort of ideal truth in literature or art.

Technique [in modernism] Experimentation with literary and visual representation. These experiments defamiliarize, or make strange, conventional life and ideas.

Unreliable Narrator In literature, a narrator with a subjective point of view that gives the reader distorted information.

Vernacular The representation of "broken English," creole or dialect, languages excluded from dominant culture in literary and visual art forms.

MODERNIST TIME LINE

If entry is unmarked, the work of literature or artwork is a work of fiction.

Date	Historical Events	Literature and Artwork
1848	Revolutions begin in Sicily and spread to France, Germany, Denmark, Austria, Hungary and elsewhere.	
1856		Gustave Flaubert (France), *Madame Bovary*
1857		Charles Baudelaire (France), *The Flowers of Evil* (poetry)
1874	First Impressionist Exhibition	
1876	Queen Victoria named Empress of India	
1882		Bankim Chandra Chatterjee (Bengal), *Ananda-matha (The Sacred Brotherhood)*
1884		Joris-Karl Huysmans (France), *À Rebours (Against Nature)*
1888		Ruben Dario (Nicaragua), *Azul* (literary journal)

Date	Historical Events	Literature and Artwork
1889		W. B. Yeats (Ireland), *The Wanderings of Oisin and Other Poems*
1891		Oscar Wilde (Ireland), *The Picture of Dorian Gray*
1894–99	The Dreyfus Affair	
1895	Trial of Oscar Wilde	Higuchi Ichiyo (Japan), *Nigorie (Troubled Waters)*
1899	Henrik Ibsen, *A Doll's House* performed in London	Joseph Conrad (UK), *Heart of Darkness*
1899–1902	Second Anglo-Boer War (South Africa)	
1901		Yosano Akiko (Japan), *Midaregami (Tangled Hair)*
1902		J. A. Hobson (UK), *Imperialism: A Study* (nf)
1903		W. E. B. Du Bois (USA), *The Souls of Black Folk* (nf)
1905	Russo–Japanese War First Russian Revolution	
1906	Militant Women's Suffrage Movement in England begins	
1907		Pablo Picasso (Spain), *Les Demoiselles d'Avignon* (painting) J. M. Synge (Ireland), *The Playboy of the Western World* (drama)
1908		Rabindranath Tagore (India), *At Home in the World*
1909	F. T. Marinetti publishes "Futurist Manifesto" in leading newspaper in France NAACP founded in the USA	Mohandas Gandhi (India), *Hind Swaraj* (nf)
1910	First post-impressionist exhibition in London	Marcel Proust (France), *Swann's Way* (first volume of *In Search of Lost Time*)
1913	Igor Stravinsky's *The Rite of Spring* ballet performed in Paris	

(Continued)

Date	Historical Events	Literature and Artwork
	Rabindranath Tagore awarded Nobel Prize for Literature	Blaise Cendrars and Sonia Delaunay-Terk (France), *La Prose du*
		Transsiberien et de la Petite Jehanne de France (mixed media)
		Ezra Pound (USA), "In a Station of the Metro" (poem)
1914–1918	World War I	
1915	Armenian Genocide	H. D. (USA), *Oread* (poems)
1916		James Joyce (Ireland), *A Portrait of the Artist as a Young Man*
		Y. B. Yeats, (Ireland) "Easter, 1916" (poem)
1917	Second Russian Revolution	V. I. Lenin (Soviet Union), *Imperialism: The Highest Stage of Capitalism* (nf)
		Marcel Duchamp (France), *Fountain* (sculpture)
1918		Lu Xun (China), "A Madman's Diary"
		Oswald Spengler (Germany), *The Decline of the West*
1919		Claude McKay (Jamaica), "If We Must Die" (poem)
		Hope Mirrlees (UK), *Paris: A Poem*
1920		Langston Hughes (USA), "A Negro Speaks of Rivers" (poem)
1922	Irish Republic declared	James Joyce (Ireland), *Ulysses*
	Benito Mussolini's March on Rome and seizure of power to begin Fascist rule of Italy	T. S. Eliot (USA), *The Waste Land* (poem)
		Ezra Pound (USA), *The Cantos* (begun) (poem)
1923	W. B. Yeats awarded the Nobel Prize for Literature	
1924		E. M. Forster (UK), *A Passage to India*
1925	George Bernard Shaw awarded the Nobel Prize for Literature	Virginia Woolf (UK), *Mrs. Dalloway*

Date	Historical Events	Literature and Artwork
		Gertrude Stein (USA), *The Making of Americans*
1928		Oswald de Andrade (Brazil), *Manifesto Antropófago*
1929	Stock market collapse; Great Depression begins	
	Museum of Modern Art founded in New York	
1930		Solomon T. Plaatje (South Africa), *Mhudi*
1933	Adolf Hitler elected Chancellor of Germany	Mulk Raj Anand (India), *Untouchable*
1934		George Orwell (UK), *Burmese Days*
1935	Italian invasion of Ethiopia	Jorge Luis Borges (Argentina), *A Universal History of Infamy*
1936–39	Spanish Civil War	
1937		Wyndham Lewis (Canada), *Blasting and Bombadiering* (autobiography)
		W. H. Auden (UK, USA) "Spain, 1937" (poem)
1938		Raja Rao (India), *Kanthapura*
		Samuel Beckett *Murphy*
		C. L. R. James (Trinidad), *The Black Jacobins* (nf)
1939	Germany invades Poland; World War II begins	Aimé Césaire (Martinique), *A Notebook of a Return to My Native Land* (poem)
		James Joyce (Ireland), *Finnegans Wake*
1940		Richard Wright *Native Son*
1944		Ismat Chughtai (India), *The Quilt and Other Stories*
		Wilfredo Lam (Cuba), *La Jungla* (painting)
1946		Peter Abrahams (South Africa), *Mine Boy*

Date	Historical Events	Literature and Artwork
1947	India and Pakistan declare independence from the British Empire	Jacques Roumain (Haiti), *Masters of the Dew*
	Partition of India/Pakistan	
1948		G. V Desani (India), *All About H. Hatterr*
		Saadat Hasan Manto (Pakistan), "Toba Tek Singh"
1949	China becomes a Communist state	Alejo Carpentier (Cuba), *The Kingdom of this World*
1950	Start of the USA-Korean War	Pramoedya Ananta Toer (Indonesia), *Perburuan (The Fugitive)*
1951	Independence for Libya	
1952		Amos Tutuola (Nigeria), *The Palm-Wine Drinkard*
		Frantz Fanon (Martinique), *Black Skin, White Masks* (nf)
1953		George Lamming (Barbados), *In the Castle of My Skin*
		Samuel Beckett (Ireland), *Waiting for Godot* (play)
1954	Algerian War of Independence; end of French-Vietnam war	
1955	Bandung Conference (Indonesia)	Aimé Césaire (Martinique), *Discourse on Colonialism* (nf)
1957	National Independence, Ghana	
1958	Formation of the West Indies Federation	Chinua Achebe (Nigeria), *Things Fall Apart*
1959	Cuban Revolution	Frantz Fanon (Martinique), *A Dying Colonialism* (nf)
1960	Independence for the French colonies in Africa	George Lamming (Barbados), *The Pleasures of Exile* (nf)
1962	Independence for Algeria; Cuban Missile Crisis	Carlos Fuentes (Mexico), *The Death of Artemio Cruz*
1963	Independence for Kenya	Mario Vargas Llosa (Peru), *The Time of the Hero*

(Continued)

Date	Historical Events	Literature and Artwork
1964	Nelson Mandela (South Africa) sentenced to life imprisonment	Christopher Okigbo (Nigeria), *Lament of the Masks* (poems)
		Ngugi wa Thiong'o (Kenya), *Weep Not, Child*
		Wole Soyinka (Nigeria), *The Interpreters*
1965	Independence for Rhodesia (now Zimbabwe) from Britain	Kwame Nkrumah (Ghana), *Neo-Colonialism: The Last Stage of Imperialism* (nf)
1966	Independence for Barbados, Botswana, Guyana, Lesotho	Louise Bennett (Jamaica), "Pedestrian crosses" (poem)
		Jean Rhys (Dominica), *Wide Sargasso Sea*
1967	Nigerian Civil War	Gabriel García Marquez (Colombia), *One Hundred Years of Solitude*
	Six Day Arab-Israeli war	Ngugi wa Thiong'o (Kenya), *A Grain of Wheat*
		V. S. Naipaul (Trinidad), *The Mimic Men*
1968	Czechoslovakia "Prague Spring"	Ayi Kwei Armah (Ghana), *The Beautyful Ones are Not Yet Born*
	Martin Luther King, Jr. assassinated (USA)	Ahmadou Kourouma (Ivory Coast), *The Suns of Independence*
1971	East Pakistan becomes Bangladesh	Roberto Fernández Retamar (Cuba), "Caliban: *Notes Toward a Definition of Culture in Our America*" (nf)
1973	OPEC Oil Crisis; Salvador Allende (Chile) assassinated	Kamau Brathwaite (Barbados), *The Arrivants* (poems)
1974	Independence for Guinea-Bissau and Grenada	Bessie Head (Botswana/South Africa), *A Question of Power*
1976	Soweto student uprising (South Africa)	Wole Soyinka (Nigeria), *Myth, Literature and the African World* (nf)
1980	Independence for Zimbabwe	J. M. Coetzee (South Africa), *Waiting for the Barbarians*

(Continued)

Date	Historical Events	Literature and Artwork
		Salman Rushdie (India), *Midnight's Children*
		Michael Thelwell (Jamaica), *The Harder They Come*
1986	Haitian dictatorship of Jean-Claude Duvalier overthrown	Nuruddin Farah (Somalia), *Maps*
		Hanif Kureishi (UK), *My Beautiful Laundrette*
1987	First Intifada (insurrection) (Palestine)	Toni Morrison (USA), *Beloved*
		Agha Shahid Ali (India), *The Half-Inch Himalayas* (poems)
1989	Fall of the Berlin Wall; collapse of the Soviet Union	Kazuo Ishiguro (UK), *The Remains of the Day*
1990	Nelson Mandela released from prison	Derek Walcott (Saint Lucia), *Omeros* (poems)
1991	First USA invasion of Kuwait, war against Iraq	Ben Okri (Nigeria), *The Famished Road*
		Michael Ondaatje (Sri Lanka/ Canada), *The English Patient*
		Patrick Chamoiseau (Martinique), *Texaco*
1997	Mobuto's dictatorship ousted in a coup (Democratic Republic of Congo)	Arundhati Roy (India), *The God of Small Things*

INDEX

Italic page references indicate photographs.